MW00851474

Project Management with Dynamic Scheduling

Mario Vanhoucke

Project Management with Dynamic Scheduling

Baseline Scheduling, Risk Analysis and Project Control

Second Edition

 Springer

Mario Vanhoucke
Ghent University
Fac. Economics and Business Administration
Ghent
Belgium

ISBN 978-3-642-40437-5   ISBN 978-3-642-40438-2 (eBook)
DOI 10.1007/978-3-642-40438-2
Springer Heidelberg New York Dordrecht London

Library of Congress Control Number: 2013956213

Printed on acid-free paper

Springer is part of Springer Science+Business Media (www.springer.com)

Preface

Project scheduling began as a research track within the mathematical field of Operations Research in order to determine start and finish times of project activities subject to precedence and resource constraints while optimizing a certain project objective (such as lead-time minimization, cash-flow optimization, etc.). The initial research done in the late 1950s mainly focused on network based techniques such as CPM (Critical Path Method) and PERT (Program Evaluation and Review Technique), which are still widely recognized as important project management tools and techniques.

From this moment on, a substantial amount of research has been carried out covering various areas of project scheduling (e.g. time scheduling, resource scheduling, cost scheduling). Today, project scheduling research continues to grow in the variety of its theoretical models, in its magnitude and in its applications. While the focus of decennia of research was mainly on the static development of algorithms to deal with the complex scheduling problems, the recent research activities gradually started to focus on the development of dynamic scheduling tools that are able to respond to a higher uncertainty during the project's progress.

The topic of this book is known as *dynamic scheduling* and is used to refer to three dimensions of project management and scheduling: the construction of a *baseline schedule* and the analysis of a project *schedule's risk* as preparation for the *project control* phase during the progress of the project. This dynamic scheduling point of view implicitly assumes that the usability of a project's baseline schedule is rather limited and only acts as a point of reference in the project life cycle. Consequently, a project schedule should especially be considered as nothing more than a predictive model that can be used for resource efficiency calculations, time and cost risk analyses, project control and performance measurement. In all upcoming chapters, the project control phase will also be called project *tracking* or project *monitoring*.

In this book, the three dimensions of dynamic scheduling are highlighted in detail and are based on and inspired by a combination of academic research studies at Ghent University (www.ugent.be), in-company trainings at Vlerick Business School (www.vlerick.com) and consultancy projects at OR-AS (www.or-as.be).

First, the construction of a project baseline schedule is a central theme throughout the various chapters of the book. This theme is discussed from a complexity point of view with and without the presence of project resources. Second, the creation of an awareness of the weak parts in a baseline schedule is highlighted, known as schedule risk analysis techniques that can be applied on top of the baseline schedule. Third, the baseline schedule and its risk analyses can be used as guidelines during the project control step where actual deviations can be corrected within the margins of the project's time and cost reserves.

Scope

The goal of this book is not to compete with excellent handbooks on general project management principles nor to give an extensive overview of all project management aspects that might contribute to the overall success of a project. Instead, the aim is to bring a clear and strong focus on the preparatory phases, the project baseline scheduling and the schedule risk analysis phases, to support the project control phase where project performance measurement is a key issue for a project's success. The intention is to hold the middle between a research handbook and a practical guide for project schedulers or project management software users. To that purpose, the content of this book is brought in such a way that it is able to inform a wide audience about the current state-of-the-art principles in dynamic project scheduling. The target audience can consist of undergraduate or MBA students following a project management course, participants of company trainings with a focus on scheduling or software users who search for added value when using software tools.

Book Overview

Chapter 1 gives a short introduction to the central theme of the book and highlights the three components of dynamic project scheduling: project scheduling, risk analysis and project control. The chapter gives a brief overview of the project life cycle and makes a distinction between project complexity and uncertainty using a *project mapping* matrix. The *complexity* dimension is related to the absence or presence of project resources under limited availability, as discussed in Parts I (low complexity) and II (high complexity) of the book. The *uncertainty* dimension is related to the need of a project's schedule risk analysis and is discussed in individual Chaps. 5 and 10 of both parts. Example files and more information can be downloaded from www.or-as.be/books.

Part I. Scheduling Without Resources

Part I is devoted to dynamic scheduling principles for projects without resources. It is assumed that project resources are not limited in availability, which leads to simple and straightforward scheduling tools and techniques that can be considered as basic techniques for the more complex resource-constrained scheduling methods of Part II.

Chapter 2 gives an overview of the basic scheduling principles without using resources and thereby lays the foundation for all future chapters to predict the timing and cost outline of a project. The basic critical path calculations of project scheduling are highlighted and the fundamental concept of an activity network is presented. Moreover, the Program Evaluation and Review Technique (PERT) is discussed as an easy yet effective scheduling tool for projects with (low) variability in the activity duration estimates.

Chapter 3 presents an interactive game that acts as a training tool to help practitioners and project management students to gain insight in the basic project scheduling techniques. The game involves the iterative re-scheduling of a project within the presence of uncertainty. Each project activity can be executed under different duration and cost combinations, which is known as the critical path method (CPM). The game is set up to highlight the importance of a thorough knowledge of baseline scheduling techniques and to create an awareness of the need for schedule risk analyses (discussed in Chap. 5).

Chapter 4 serves as an illustrative chapter based on a case study of a capacity expansion project at a water production center in the northern part of Belgium. It shows that the clever use of basic critical path scheduling algorithms can lead to a realistic baseline schedule once the scheduling objective is clearly defined. It will be shown that scheduling the project with certain techniques will improve the financial status of the project, as measured by its net present value.

Chapter 5 highlights the importance of a schedule risk analysis (SRA) once the baseline schedule has been constructed. This second dimension of dynamic scheduling connects the risk information of project activities to the baseline schedule and provides sensitivity information of individual project activities as a way to assess the potential impact of uncertainty on the final project duration and cost. When management has a certain feeling of the relative sensitivity of the project activities on the project objective, a better management focus and a more accurate response during project control should positively contribute to the overall performance of the project.

Chapter 6 describes the first part of a series of three case exercises (Parts II and III can be found in Chaps. 11 and 14). Each case description is an integrated exercise to get acquainted with the scheduling principles discussed in the previous chapters. The case of Chap. 6 assumes the construction of a baseline schedule and knowledge of basic critical path scheduling principles and allows the extension to basic calculations of risk in order to take protective actions. The solution and the educational approach depend on the wishes and needs of the students who solve the case and the teacher who can act as the moderator during the case teaching session. A teaching session should allow enough freedom to extend the original topic to various other dynamic scheduling related issues.

Part II. Scheduling with Resources

Part II extends the previously discussed dynamic scheduling principles to projects with resources that have a limited availability. In these complex scheduling settings, activities are executed by resources that are restricted in availability over time. This resource restriction leads to an increase in scheduling complexity, as will be shown in the various chapters of this part.

Chapter 7 gives an extensive overview of tools and techniques for resource-constrained project scheduling. It is shown that the introduction of resources in project scheduling leads to an increase in scheduling complexity. The importance of the choice of a scheduling objective is highlighted in detail by showing various resource-constrained scheduling models. The ability to assess the quality of the resource feasible schedule as well as a basic knowledge about scheduling software functionalities are discussed throughout the sections of this chapter.

Chapter 8 further elaborates on the resource-constrained project scheduling topics of the previous chapter and presents some advanced results obtained by various research projects. This chapter extends the resource models to other scheduling objectives, studies the effect of activity splitting and setup times and introduces learning effects in a resource-constrained project environment. These topics are brought together in a separate chapter such that the reader can skip these advanced topics without losing overview of the general dynamic scheduling theme.

Chapter 9 presents, similar to Chap. 4, an illustrative case study of a practical project scheduling study. The project to construct a tunnel to connect the two sides of the Westerschelde in the Netherlands is used to illustrate the importance of the scheduling objective as discussed intensively in the previous chapters. More precisely, it will be shown that the minimization of a bottleneck resource's idle time during the scheduling phase can lead to important cost savings.

Chapter 10 elaborates on the construction of a resource feasible project schedule as discussed in the previous chapter, but extends this scheduling approach to a more flexible baseline schedule protected against unexpected events. The Critical Chain/Buffer Management (CC/BM) approach incorporates a certain degree of flexibility in the activity start times in order to easily monitor schedule deviations and quickly respond by taking corrective actions to keep the whole project on schedule. The technique is initiated by E. M. Goldratt in his groundbreaking book "Critical Chain" as a practical translation of the so-called *Theory of Constraints* in a project scheduling environment.

Chapter 11 presents the second part of a fictitious case exercise introduced in Chap. 6 that aims at the construction of a resource feasible project schedule using project scheduling software tools. The goal of the student is to go further than submitting software print-outs to the project team. Instead, the purpose is the integration of the resource-constrained scheduling principles of the previous chapters within the features of a project scheduling tool in order to provide an easy and understandable information sheet on the predicted project execution to the various members of a project team. It allows the integration of CC/BM techniques of the previous chapter to highlight the advantages and potential weaknesses.

Part III. Project Control

Part III uses the schedules constructed in the previous chapters as inputs for the project execution phase where project's progress needs to be measured and monitored in order to take corrective actions when the project runs into trouble. This third dimension of dynamic scheduling completely relies on the quality of the two other dimensions (baseline scheduling and risk analysis) discussed in the previous chapters. The construction of a baseline schedule based on a sound methodology as well as the knowledge of the sensitivity of each project activity on the project's time and cost dimensions act as inputs during the project control step to better support corrective actions in case the project is in danger.

Chapter 12 gives an overview of the Earned Value Management (EVM) method to measure a project's time and cost performance. It gives an overview of all EVM metrics and performance measures to monitor the time and cost dimension of a project's current progress to date. Moreover, it also illustrates how this performance information can be used to predict the expected remaining time and cost to finalize the project that serve as triggers to take corrective actions to bring the project back on track, when needed.

Chapter 13 is a summary chapter of a large simulation study to predict the final duration of a project in progress using EVM forecasting methods. The chapter briefly discusses results that give an idea of the accuracy of different EVM forecasting methods along the life cycle of the project. It also presents an extension to the classical use of EVM to measure the adherence of a project in progress to the original baseline schedule. The main results of this chapter have been awarded by the International Project Management Association (www.ipma.ch) with the IPMA 2008 Research Award.

Chapter 14 is a third fictitious case exercise that allows the integration of EVM reports in the project control phase in order to get acquainted with the terminology and characteristics of EVM. It assumes a dynamic multi-project setting where three projects are executed in parallel. The purpose is the clever use of EVM methods and metrics and the critical review of these methods as a dynamic time/cost performance measurement system.

Part IV. Scheduling with Software

Part IV presents the main features of a software tool that integrates the three dynamic scheduling dimensions (scheduling, risk analysis and control) discussed in the previous sections.

Chapter 15 gives a brief overview of the main features of the software tool ProTrack (acronym for *Project Track*ing). Although ProTrack is a commercial software tool and is therefore not free of charge, a student friendly version with time-limited functionalities can be freely downloaded from www.protrack.be such that the main dynamic scheduling principles discussed in this book can be easily tested in a fictitious project environment.

Part V. Conclusions

Part V contains Chap. 16 and provides overall conclusions on dynamic scheduling. It provides an overall summary of all chapters and gives directions for practical use of software tools and suggestions for further actions on research and practical applications.

Acknowledgements

This book is the result of several research projects, consultancy tasks and fruitful discussions with both academics and practitioners. I am therefore indebted to many people who have helped me in writing this book.

I would like to thank my father, Robert Vanhoucke, for the fruitful discussions while writing Chap. 4 during the final stages of my PhD period. He helped me with the technical details of the project at a water production center (Vlaamse Maatschappij voor Watervoorziening) and provided me with useful information about it. I am also grateful to Dr. Stan Beernaert, chief executive at the Vlaamse Maatschappij voor Watervoorziening at the time of the project scheduling phase, for giving me the permission to use the data of the project. Last but not least, I would like to thank ir. Paul Suenens, project leader for the project, for providing me with a detailed description of the project by means of a Microsoft Project file.

I would like to thank Iris Vodderie for drawing my attention to the construction project in the Netherlands as described in Chap. 9. I am also grateful to Karel De Bel, Senior consultant Plancon and Theun Steinfort, projectmanager "Ontwerp en Voorbereiding", for giving me the permission to use the data of the project and for providing me with a detailed description of the project. I want to especially thank Koen Van Osselaer for the nice and pleasant collaboration during this project.

I am also thankful to Prof. Dr. Bert De Reyck from London Business School (UK) and University College London (UK) who allowed me to use the project description that was used during the writing of the Chaps. 6, 11 and 14. Although the case exercises of these chapters go far beyond the original purpose of his bridge project example, the general project characteristics of this bridge example were used as the foundation to describe the three case exercises.

I also would like to thank Prof. Dr. Roel Leus from the Katholieke Universiteit Leuven (Belgium) for the co-writing of parts of Chap. 10 as a foundation article used in the Project Management course at Ghent University.

I am obviously very much indebted to Tom Van Acker, partner at OR-AS, for the co-development of our software tool ProTrack as described in Chap. 15. Obviously, without his help, this book was not what it is now. The close relation between the various chapters of the book and the features and characteristics of the software tool is the results of years of work, both at the programming side of our software tool as at the consultancy side when dealing with real project schedules and all corresponding difficulties related to that. Both the software and the book is therefore the result of joint efforts of all OR-AS customers, a team of volunteers (both researchers as people from practice) and PhD students in project scheduling who all contributed in one way or another. A special thank you goes to Stephan Vandevoorde, who always supported and motivated the OR-AS team when our activities progressed slower than expected. A special word of thank goes to Sylvain Beernaert, Vincent Van Peteghem, Broos Maenhout, Veronique Sels, Thomas De Jonghe, Jeroen Colin, Christophe Van Huele and Mathieu Wauters for their careful attention during proofreading the final manuscripts. Thank you, all.

I acknowledge the support by the Research collaboration fund of PMI Belgium received in Brussels in 2007 at the Belgian Chapter meeting, the support for a research project funding by the Flemish Government (2008), Belgium, the research support of the National Bank of Belgium (NBB) as well as the support given by the "Fonds voor Wetenschappelijk Onderzoek (FWO), Vlaanderen, Belgium" and the "Bijzonder Onderzoeksfonds (BOF)"at Ghent University. Parts of the research topics in this book have been awarded by the IPMA Research award in 2008 during the 22nd world congress in Rome (Italy) with the study "Measuring Time – An Earned Value Simulation Study". Thanks to this support and these financial sources, I was able to write parts of Chap. 12 based on data from various real-life consultancy projects.

It goes without saying that all of this took a lot of time, both during the weeks and the weekend. I am therefore especially thankful to Gaëtane for the many hours of proofreading and editing and the kids, Joyce and Thierry, for their never-ending patience when I was working on the software tool often 7 days a week.

London, UK   *Mario Vanhoucke*
Ghent, Belgium

Contents

Part IV   Scheduling with Software

Part V   Conclusions

Chapter 1
Introduction

Abstract This chapter gives a short introduction to the central theme of the book and highlights the three components of dynamic project scheduling: the construction of a project baseline schedule, a risk analysis of this schedule and the project's performance measurement and control component. The chapter also gives a short introduction to the *project life cycle* to provide a guidance to the various chapters of the book. A simple and intuitive project mapping approach is briefly described and will be used to put all techniques discussed throughout the various chapters into perspective.

1.1 Introduction

Project management is the discipline of planning, organizing and managing resources to bring about the successful completion of specific project goals and objectives. The project management discipline can be highlighted from various angles and sub-disciplines and contains important issues such as project objective and scope management, human resource management and setting the roles and responsibilities of all participants and stakeholders of a project, planning principles and resource allocation models, etc. The current book does not aim at providing a general overview on project management, but instead has a clear focus on the planning aspect of projects. The topic of the book could be best described as *dynamic project scheduling* to illustrate that project scheduling is a dynamic process that involves a continuous stream of changes and that it is a never ending process to support decisions that need to be made along the life of the project. The focus of the book lies on three crucial dimensions of dynamic scheduling, which can be briefly summarized along the following lines:

- Scheduling: Construct a timetable to provide a start and end date for each project activity, taking activity relations, resource constraints and other project characteristics into account and aiming at reaching a certain scheduling objective.

M. Vanhoucke, *Project Management with Dynamic Scheduling*,
DOI 10.1007/978-3-642-40438-2_1, © Springer-Verlag Berlin Heidelberg 2013

Fig. 1.1 The three
components of dynamic
project scheduling

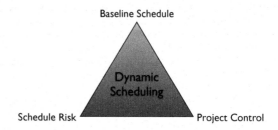

- Risk Analysis: Analyze the strengths and weaknesses of the project schedule
  in order to obtain information about the schedule sensitivity and the impact
  of unexpected changes that undoubtedly occur during project progress on the
  project objective.
- Control: Measure the (time and cost) performance of a project during its progress
  and use the information obtained during the scheduling and risk analysis steps to
  monitor and update the project and to take corrective actions in case of problems.

The scope and purpose of the book is to bring a mixed message trying to combine
theoretical principles from literature with practical examples and case exercises. To
that purpose, the reader should take a step back from the buttons and looks of the
project management software tools and/or the daily practice of project management
to see what the dynamic scheduling principles have to offer. Rather than solely
focusing on the latest state-of-the-art scheduling techniques from the academic
literature, the reader will be drowned into a wide variety of scheduling and control
principles and an often pragmatic project scheduling and monitoring approach, each
time illustrated by means of short examples, practical case examples or fictitious
integrated exercises. Figure 1.1 highlights the three basic components of dynamic
scheduling.

Each of these three dimensions of dynamic scheduling plays an important role
in the project life of a project. In the next section, the so-called project life cycle
is briefly discussed from different angles and the link with dynamic scheduling is
shown.

1.2   The Project Life Cycle (PLC)

Typically, a project goes through a number of different phases, which is often
referred to as the project life cycle. In this book "Managing high-technology
programs and projects", Archibald (1976) describes the project life cycle as follows:

> The project life cycle has identifiable start and end points, which can be associated with
> a time scale. A project passes through several distinct phases as it matures. The life cycle
> includes all phases from point of inception to final termination of the project. The interfaces
> between phases are rarely clearly separated, except in cases where proposal acceptance of
> formal authorization to proceed separates the two phases.

Consequently, the PLC is defined by the time window between the initial start of the project and the final termination and consists of a number of phases, separated by major milestones. The number of phases and their corresponding titles differ from industry to industry and from project to project. The next two subsections elaborate on the project life cycle with a number of examples, without having the intention to provide a full literature review.

1.2.1 Project Phases

A project consists of sequential phases. These phases are extremely useful in planning a project since they provide a framework for budgeting, manpower and resource allocation and for scheduling project milestones and project reviews. The method of dividing a project into phases may differ somewhat from industry to industry and from product to product and it can be summarized as follows:

- Concept (initiation, identification, selection).
- Definition (feasibility, development, demonstration, design prototype).
- Execution (implementation, production, design/construct/commission, install and test).
- Closeout (termination and post completion evaluation).

Archibald (1976) argues that the number of phases and the titles are so generic that they are of little value in describing the project life cycle process. Although the construction and presentation of a generic project life cycle seems to be difficult, if not impossible, each PLC shares a number of common characteristics.

- The major milestones between the phases represent high-level decision points.
- The phases may, and frequently will, overlap.

Between the various phases are decision points, at which an explicit decision is made concerning whether the next phase should be undertaken. A major review of the entire project occurs at the end of each phase, resulting in authorization to proceed with the next phase, cancellation of the project, or repetition of a previous phase.

1.2.2 The PLC in PMBOK

In the first edition of PMBOK,[1] the project life cycle concept was not mentioned at all. In the later editions, PMI realized the importance of the "divide and conquer"

---

[1]The Project Management Body of Knowledge, published by the Project Management Institute (PMI) – www.pmi.org.

Fig. 1.2 Accomplishment
of a project through the
integration of five project
management processes
(PMBOK)

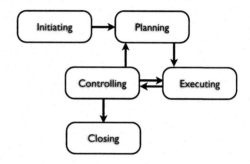

principle as the complexity and the size of the project increase and included the
PLC concept in the book. More precisely, PMBOK describes the project life cycle
as follows:

> Because projects are unique undertakings, they involve a degree of uncertainty. Organiza-
> tions performing projects will usually divide each into several project phases to improve
> management control and provide for links to the ongoing operations of the performing
> organization. Collectively, the project phases are known as the project life cycle.

Each project is marked by the completion of one or more deliverables, such as a
feasibility study or a detail design. These deliverables, and hence the phases, are part
of a generally sequential logic designed to ensure proper definition of the project.
The conclusion of each phase is generally marked by a review. These reviews, often
called milestones, phase exits, stage gates or kill points, are necessary to:

- Determine if the project should continue to the next phase.
- Detect and correct errors cost effectively.

Although PMBOK presents a sample generic life cycle as shown in Fig. 1.2,
they argue that many project life cycles have similar phase names with similar
deliverables required but few are identical. The next section presents a similar
generic project life cycle that will be used throughout all chapters of this book.

1.2.3   The PLC Used in This Book

Figure 1.3 shows an illustrative project life cycle that will be used throughout
the remaining chapters of this book. This generic project life cycle was initially
constructed and used for a consultancy study summarized in Chap. 4 and serves as
an ideal tool to illustrate the dynamic scheduling approach taken in this book.

This generic project life cycle is based on a life cycle description by Klein (2000)
and consists of a project conception phase, a project definition phase, a phase in
which the project has to be scheduled, the execution of the project, the project
control phase and the termination of the project.

At the beginning, in the so-called conceptual phase, an organization identifies the
need for a project or receives a request from a customer.

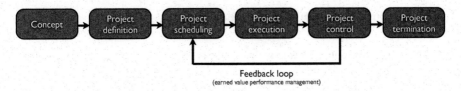

Fig. 1.3 An illustrative Project Life Cycle (PLC)

In the definition phase, the organization defines the project objectives, the project specifications and requirements and the organization of the whole project. The project objectives need to be refined and translated into a list of activities, a set of technological precedence relations and the resource availabilities and requirements. In doing so, the organization decides in detail on how it is going to achieve these objectives. The refinement of these project objectives into a final activity network containing activities and precedence relations is the subject of Chap. 2. The extension to resource availabilities and requirements is discussed from Chap. 7 onwards.

The next phase, the scheduling phase, aims at the construction of a timetable for the project activities. The construction of a precedence and/or resource feasible schedule determines a start and finish time for each activity, and hence, relies on the information obtained by the previous phase. In the following chapters of Parts I and II, a detailed overview of the scheduling principles using different techniques and aiming at reaching different targets is discussed.

During the execution and project control phases, the project has to be monitored and controlled to see whether it is performed according to the existing schedule. If deviations occur, corrective actions have to be taken. This control mechanism has been incorporated in the project life cycle by means of the feedback loop between the control phase and the scheduling phase of Fig. 1.3. This topic is the subject of Part III of this book. An update of a schedule can be done in two basic ways:

1. Reactive scheduling: This principle aims at the construction of a deterministic schedule, without taking possible risk factors or uncertainty events into account. During project execution, the project progress needs to be monitored using the information of the schedule and adaptations to the schedule need to be made when the deviations become too large. A reactive scheduling approach is the subject of Chap. 3.
2. Proactive scheduling: The uncertainty is embedded in the schedule to construct a buffered schedule. This schedule is robust and protected against possible uncertain events. In doing so, the feedback loop can be avoided within certain ranges. A proactive scheduling approach is presented in Chap. 10 of this book.

The termination phase involves the completion and a critical evaluation of the project. This information can then be used during the project life cycle of future, similar projects since the specifications of a project, the estimates of the durations, costs and resource requirements are often determined based on averages of past performance.

1.3   Dynamic Scheduling Methodology

In this section, a simple yet effective guidance is presented to classify projects along two dimensions: complexity and uncertainty. This project mapping approach will be used throughout all chapters of this book during the detailed explanation of the three dimensions of dynamic project scheduling.

1.3.1   Project Mapping

Although project scheduling is often considered to be an art more than a science, a thorough knowledge of the tools and techniques available is necessary to create a realistic project schedule. Obviously, the selection of the right tool and technique depends on the characteristics of the project and the background and knowledge of the project manager.

The approach taken along the various chapters in the book is a very pragmatic and nonscientific way of mapping projects along two dimensions as shown in Fig. 1.4: complexity and uncertainty. The advantage of this simple yet intuitive mapping approach lies in its ability to classify most project planning and scheduling techniques in one of the four quadrants. Although it is recognized that project management is more than a simple reduction to a set of scheduling tools and planning techniques, it creates awareness that techniques need to be put into perspective and need to be used only if the underlying assumptions and corresponding advantages/disadvantages are thoroughly known and understood.

The classification of scheduling techniques along the dimensions of complexity and uncertainty makes sense since dynamic scheduling is, in a way, a careful balance between dealing with complexity (mostly with the help of a commercial software tool to construct a (resource-constrained) project baseline schedule) and coping

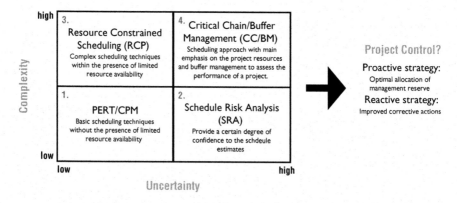

Fig. 1.4 Project mapping approach used throughout the chapters of this book

with uncertainty (realizing that a schedule obtained by a software tool will be subject to changes during the project's progress). This careful balance needs to be made by the project manager/planner and constitutes the basic starting point of this book. The ultimate goal of measuring and coping with complexity and uncertainty is to provide a basic tool to the project manager to monitor the performance of his/her project during progress. Consequently, Fig. 1.4 shows the three dimensions of dynamic scheduling: project scheduling (complexity), risk analysis (uncertainty) and project control. The complexity/uncertainty dimensions as well as their impact on the project control phase are briefly outlined in the following three subsections.

1.3.2 Complexity

The complexity dimension of Fig. 1.4 is completely related to the first dimension of dynamic scheduling: the construction of a project's baseline schedule. More precisely, it is related to the absence or presence of resources during the construction of a schedule and is used to distinguish between Parts I and II of this book.

The basic project scheduling techniques, often known under the general PERT/CPM abbreviation, assume that projects need to be done within the presence of an infinite resource capacity. Despite their simplicity, they still are considered as the basic scheduling techniques, and their principles are applicable to more advanced techniques. Due to this simplicity, their use is obviously restricted to simple and straightforward projects where resources are not assumed to be relatively highly constrained and are ignored during the scheduling process (quadrants 1 and 2 of Fig. 1.4). These resource-unconstrained project scheduling techniques are discussed in Part I of this book in Chaps. 2–6.

However, it is generally accepted that the presence of resources under limited availability is a matter of degree in practical business projects, which results in a dramatic increase in problem complexity when constructing a project baseline schedule (quadrants 3 and 4). Therefore, Part II of this book reviews the resource-constrained project scheduling techniques. The academic literature on resource-constrained project scheduling (RCP) is rich and has a main focus on the development of algorithms and procedures to solve often very complex project models. Although it is not the intention of this book to give a summary of these algorithms, it illustrates that the presence of limited resources in projects leads to an increasing complexity. The topics are discussed in Part II in Chaps. 7–10 of this book.

1.3.3 Uncertainty

When the level of uncertainty is assumed to be high, the schedule of a project becomes more and more subject to unexpected changes during project progress, and a certain knowledge of risk is therefore often indispensable. This second dimension of dynamic scheduling, project risk analysis, is shown by the uncertainty dimension of Fig. 1.4.

Schedule Risk Analysis (SRA) stems from the recognition that the construction of a project schedule is an uncertain art of estimating the set of activities, their network logic and their times and costs. Consequently, in order to provide a certain degree of confidence within each schedule estimate, SRA assigns distributions on top of the schedule to calculate a probability of meeting the scheduled end dates and cost targets (quadrant 2).

The Critical Chain/Buffer Management (CC/BM) approach can be seen as an extended view on schedule risk analysis, since it integrates the uncertainty of schedule estimates within the complexity view of resource scheduling principles (quadrant 4). This integrated view on resource complexity and schedule estimate uncertainty has led to a new scheduling framework that contains valuable principles applicable to practical project settings.

1.3.4   Control

It has been mentioned earlier that the project progress has to be monitored and controlled to measure whether the project is performed according to the original baseline schedule. Both a reactive and a proactive scheduling approach can be mapped into the quadrants of the project mapping approach, in order to allow taking timely corrective actions when the project is in trouble. This third dimension of dynamic scheduling, project control, is extensively discussed in Part III of this book.

1.4   Conclusions

This chapter gave a short and basic introduction to the principle of dynamic scheduling as the main topic of this book. This dynamic scheduling perspective consists of three connected sub-topics, i.e. the art and science of project scheduling, the analysis of risk and sensitivity of a project schedule's estimates and the project monitoring and control during the progress of the project. It has been shown that these three dynamic scheduling dimensions completely fit into the project life cycle concept presented in various sources in the literature.

A simple and straightforward project mapping framework has been presented as a general guidance for the various dynamic scheduling methods and techniques discussed in this book. This complexity/uncertainty framework will be used throughout the chapters of Parts I and II and aims at the construction of a feasible project schedule, which serves as a baseline point of reference for the project monitoring and control chapters discussed in Part III.

Part I
Scheduling Without Resources

Chapter 2
The PERT/CPM Technique

Abstract Completing a project on time and within budget is not an easy task. The project scheduling phase plays a central role in predicting both the time and cost aspects of a project. More precisely, it determines a timetable in order to be able to predict the expected time and cost of each individual activity.

In this chapter, the basic critical path calculations of a project schedule are highlighted and the fundamental concept of an activity network is presented. Throughout all chapters of Part I, it is assumed that a project is not subject to a limited amount of resources. The project is structured in a network to model the precedences between the various project activities. The basic concepts of project network analysis are outlined and the Program Evaluation and Review Technique (PERT) is discussed as an easy yet effective scheduling tool for projects with variability in the activity duration estimates.

2.1 Introduction

In this chapter, the basic concepts of the definition phase (Sect. 2.2) and the scheduling phase (Sect. 2.3) of the project life cycle are discussed. It is assumed that projects belong to the first quadrant of the project mapping matrix of Fig. 1.4 and hence are assumed to have no resource limits and a low level of uncertainty.

The chapter aims to give answers to fundamental questions, such as:

- What is the expected project finish date?
- How can precedence relations between activities be modeled in a network?
- What are the expected activity start and finish times?
- What is the effect of variability in activity time estimates on the project duration?

2.2   Project Definition Phase

In the definition phase of a project's life cycle, the organization defines the project objectives, the project specifications and requirements and the organization of the entire project. In doing so, the organization decides on how it is going to achieve all project objectives.

The Work Breakdown Structure (WBS) is a fundamental concept of the definition phase that, along with the Organizational Breakdown Structure (OBS), identifies the set of activities needed to achieve the project goal as well as the responsibilities of the project team for the various subparts of the project.

This information needs to be transformed into a network diagram that identifies a list of project activities and the technological links with the other activities. This project network is an easy and accessible tool for the critical path calculations to determine the earliest and latest activity start times of the scheduling phase.

2.2.1   WBS and OBS

The preparation of a Work Breakdown Structure (WBS) is an important step in managing and mastering the inherent complexity of the project. It involves the decomposition of major project deliverables into smaller, more manageable components until the deliverables are defined in sufficient detail to support development of project activities (PMBOK 2004). The WBS is a tool that defines the project and groups the project's discrete work elements to help organize and define the total work scope of the project. It provides the necessary framework for detailed cost estimation and control along with providing guidance for schedule development and control. Each descending level of the WBS represents an increased level of detailed definition of the project work.

The WBS is often displayed graphically as a hierarchical tree. It has multiple levels of detail, as displayed in Fig. 2.1.

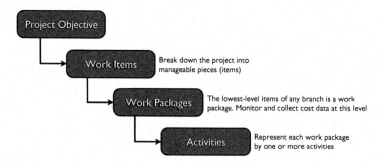

Fig. 2.1 Four levels of a Work Breakdown Structure

- Project objective: The project objective consists of a short description of the scope of the project. A careful scope definition is of crucial importance in project management.
- Work item: The project is broken down into manageable pieces (items) to be able to cope with the project complexity.
- Work package: The monitoring and collection of cost data often occurs at this level.
- Activity: The lowest level of the WBS, where the accuracy of cost, duration and resource estimates can be improved, and where the precedence relations can be incorporated.

The WBS is often used in conjunction with the Organizational Breakdown Structure (OBS). The OBS indicates the organizational relationships and is used as the framework for assigning work responsibilities. The WBS and the OBS are merged to create a Responsibility Assignment Matrix (RAM) for the project manager. The RAM displays the lower levels of both the WBS and the OBS and identifies specific responsibilities for specific project tasks. It is at this point that the project manager develops control accounts or work packages.

Figure 2.2 shows a graphical picture of a WBS/OBS conjunction and shows the RAM for a fictitious project. In the figure, the RAM uses the lowest level of the

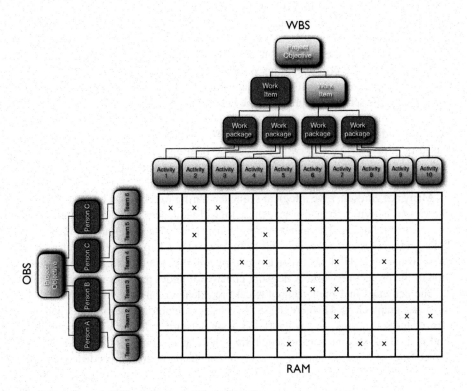

Fig. 2.2 A Responsibility Assignment Matrix (RAM)

WBS (activity level) and OBS and defines the specific person/department from the OBS assigned to be responsible for completing the activity from the WBS (indicated by an 'x'). Obviously, in practice, the responsibilities are often assigned to higher WBS levels (work package or work item level).

An illustration of a WBS is given in Chap. 4 of this book. The assignments and scheduling of resources from the OBS to the project activities is extensively discussed in the resource-constrained scheduling techniques of Chaps. 7 and 8.

2.2.2   Network Analysis

In order to construct a complete and detailed WBS, the work packages of a WBS need to be further subdivided into activities. In doing so, it might improve the level of detail and accuracy of cost, duration and resource estimates which serve as inputs for the construction of a project network and scheduling phase. Note that a clear distinction between the project definition phase and the project scheduling phase will be made throughout this chapter. The definition phase, which determines the list of activities, the precedence relations, possible resource requirements and the major milestones of the project, is different from the scheduling phase in the level of detail and the timing of project activities. Indeed, the scheduling phase aims at the determination of start and finish times of each activity of the project, and consequently, determines the milestones in detail. This can only be done after the construction of the network in the definition phase. Therefore, the activity description with the corresponding WBS-code and the estimates for its duration, cost and resource requirement are the main outputs of the definition phase and serve as inputs for the scheduling phase. In the latter phase, the earliest and latest possible start (and finish) time will be determined, given the technological precedence relations and limited resource constraints. The construction of a project schedule based on a project network with precedence relations is discussed in Sect. 2.3 of this chapter, while the introduction of resources in a project network is the topic of Part II of this book.

Many activities involve a logical sequence during execution. The links between the various activities to incorporate these logical sequences are called technological precedence relations. The annex *technological* is used to distinguish with the so-called *resource* relations, which will be introduced in Chaps. 7 and 8. Incorporating these technological links between any pair of activities is a first step in the construction of the project network. A network consists of nodes and arcs and incorporates all the activities and their technological precedence relations. A network can be seen as a graph $G(N, A)$ where the set N is used to denote the set of nodes and A to denote the set of arcs. The network has a single start node and a single end node and is used as an input for the scheduling phase as discussed in Sect. 2.3. The set of activities of a project and their corresponding technological precedence relations can be displayed as a network using two formats: an activity-on-the-node (AoN) and an activity-on-the-arc (AoA) representation. In the next subsections, these two formats are discussed in more detail.

Activity-on-the-Arc (AoA)

In an AoA format, activities are displayed by means of arcs in the network. The nodes are events (or milestones) denoting the start and/or finish of a set of activities of the project. The technological link between activity i and activity j can be displayed as in Fig. 2.3. Since activities can be labeled with their corresponding start and end node event, it is said that activity (2,3) is a successor of activity (1,2) and activity (1,2) is a predecessor of activity (2,3).

Moder et al. (1983) have suggested six rules to construct AoA networks, as follows:

1. Before any activity may begin, all activities preceding it must be completed.
2. Arrows imply logical precedence only. Neither the length nor its "compass" direction have any difference.
3. Event numbers must not be duplicated in a network.
4. Any two events may be directly connected by no more than one activity.
5. Networks may have only one initial event (with no predecessor) and only one terminal event (with no successor).
6. The introduction of dummy activities is often necessary to model all precedence relations.

Dummies are introduced for the unique identification of activities and/or for displaying certain precedence relations. These activities are represented by dashed arrows in the network and do not consume time nor resources.

Figure 2.4 displays an example project with a dummy arc to identify all activities in a unique way. The network contains two activities that can be performed in parallel (i.e. there is no technological precedence relation between the two activities). Rule 4 states that two events may not be connected by more than one activity to ensure the unique identification of each activity (both activities i and j can be labeled as activity (1,2)). Therefore, an extra dummy activity needs to be embedded in the project network, represented by the dashed arcs. In doing so, the network starts and ends with a single event node (rule 5) and each activity has been defined by a unique start/end event combination (rule 4).

Table 2.1 displays a list of project activities with each their immediate predecessors to illustrate the necessity of dummy arcs to incorporate all precedence relations. In Fig. 2.5, this activity information has been translated into an AoA network in

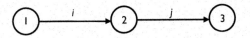

Fig. 2.3 The AoA representation of the technological link between activities i and j

two ways. Figure 2.5a has three dummies (D-E, G-J and I-J) while Fig. 2.5b only has one dummy activity (D-E). This single dummy activity is necessary to incorporate the precedence relation between activity 4 and its successor activity 8. However, the incorporation of dummy activities implies different possible alternative translations of the project data into a network and hence the project network is not unique.

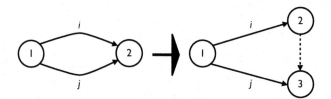

Fig. 2.4 Dummy arc for the unique identification of activities *i* and *j*

Table 2.1 List of activities with their immediate predecessors

Activity	Predecessors
1	—
2	1
3	1
4	2
5	2
6	3
7	4
8	4, 5
9	6
10	8
11	7, 9, 10

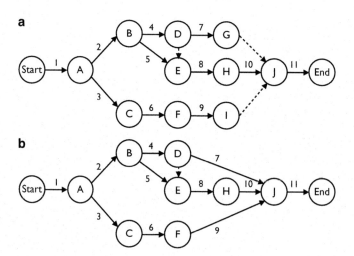

Fig. 2.5 Two AoA networks for the example project of Table 2.1

The introduction of dummy activities, which leads to different network represen-tations of the same project, unnecessarily increases the project network complexity. Many researchers have focused on the development of (complex) algorithms to minimize the number of dummy activities in an AoA network. These algorithms are, due to their inherent complexity, outside the scope of this book. However, Wiest and Levy (1977) have presented some guidelines for reducing the number of dummy activities. Although these guidelines do not aim at minimizing the number of dummy activities in an AoA network, they can be very helpful in reducing superfluous dummy activities and hence, the project network complexity. The rules are as follows:

1. If a dummy node is the only activity emanating from its initial node, it can be removed.
2. If a dummy activity is the only activity going into its final node, it also can be removed.
3. If two (or more) activities have identical sets of predecessors (successors) then the two jobs should emanate from a single node connected to their predecessors (successors) by dummy activities.
4. Dummy jobs that show predecessor relations already implied by other activities may be removed as redundant.

As an example, the first rule was used to reduce the number of dummy activities from 3 to 1 in Fig. 2.5.

Activity-on-the-Node (AoN)

An AoN network displays the activities by nodes and precedence relations by arcs. Most commercial software tools rely on the activity-on-the-node format. The construction of an AoN network is very simple and is, in contrast to an AoA network, not subject to a set of rules. Dummy activities are not necessary, apart from a single initial start and a single end activity, which makes an AoN network always unique. The AoN representation of the technological link between activity i and activity j can be displayed as in Fig. 2.6.

The AoN network for the project of Table 2.1 is given in Fig. 2.7. The three steps to follow in order to construct an AoN network are:

1. Draw a node for each network activity.
2. Draw an arc for each immediate precedence relation between two activities.
3. Possibly add a dummy start and dummy end node to force that the network begins with a single start activity and finishes with a single end activity.

Fig. 2.6 The AoN representation of the technological link between activities i and j

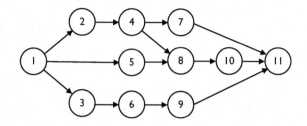

Fig. 2.7 The AoN network
for the example project of
Table 2.1

Although both formats are only alternative ways to represent a project network, there might be reasons to have a preference towards one of the formats. Probably, many project managers will rely on the activity-on-the-node format, since this allows for the incorporation of generalized precedence relations (see Sect. 2.2.3), and is embedded in most resource allocation models of commercial software tools. However, some people might feel a preference for the activity-on-the-arc format, since the first scheduling principles (e.g. PERT (discussed at the end of this chapter) and CPM (Chap. 3)) have originally been developed for AoA networks. In the remainder of this book, we rely on the AoN format to represent project networks. More precisely, it is always assumed that a project is represented by an activity-on-the-node network where the set of nodes, N, represents activities and the set of arcs, A, represents the precedence constraints. The activities are numbered from 1 to n (i.e. $|N| = n$), where node 1 and node n are used to denote the dummy start and dummy end activity, respectively. The dummy start activity is a predecessor for all activities in the network and is used to denote the start of the project. In a similar way, the dummy end activity n denotes the finish of the project and is a successor for all activities of the project. No further dummies are used in the AoN format.

2.2.3 Generalized Precedence Relations

In the previous subsections, technological precedence relations between project activities were implicitly assumed to be of the "Finish-Start" type. This section shows that these technological precedence relations can be extended to other types in three ways:

- Time-lag of precedence relations: zero or nonzero.
- Type of precedence relation: finish-start, finish-finish, start-start and start-finish.
- Time-lag requirement of a precedence relation: minimal or maximal.

In what follows, the three extensions are described in detail. Note that these precedence relations do not specify when activities have to start and end, but only describe possible relations between them. The former will be determined in the scheduling phase, while the latter is still subject to the definition phase. Indeed, while the definition phase determines *what* needs to be done in order to achieve the project goals, the scheduling phase determines *when* all these necessary steps need to be performed.

Time-Lag

A finish-start relation with a zero time-lag can be represented as follows:

$$FS_{ij}$$

Activity j can only start after the finish of activity i

A zero time-lag implies that the second activity j can start immediately after the finish of the first activity i, or later. It does not force the immediate start after the finish of the first activity, since the definition phase only describes the technological requirements and limitations and does not aim at the construction of a timetable.

A finish-start relation with a nonzero time-lag can be represented as follows:

$$FS_{ij} = n$$

Activity j can only start n time periods after the finish of activity i

Type

The default precedence relation, finish-start, can be extended to other types of precedence relations, and can be used in combination with both zero and nonzero time-lags. The extensions are as follows:

$$SS_{ij} = n$$

Activity j can only start n time periods after the start of activity i

$$FF_{ij} = n$$

Activity j can only finish n time periods after the finish of activity i

$$SF_{ij} = n$$

Activity j can only finish n time periods after the start of activity i

Figure 2.8 graphically displays the four types of precedence relations between activities i and j.

Fig. 2.8 Four types of
precedence relations between
activities i and j

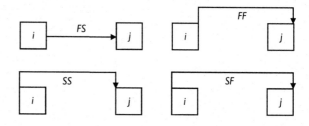

Minimal/Maximal

In the previous sections, precedence relations were assumed to be minimal requirements between two activities. These technological requirements can be easily
extended to maximal requirements.

A finish-start relation with a minimal time-lag of n can be represented as follows:

$$FS_{ij}^{min} = n$$

Activity j can only start n or more time periods after the finish of activity i

A finish-start relation with a maximal time-lag of n can be represented as follows:

$$FS_{ij}^{max} = n$$

Activity j can only start n or less time periods after the finish of activity i

Logically, the extension from a minimal to a maximal time-lag also holds
for start-start, finish-finish and start-finish precedence relations. The precedence
relations can, and often will be used in combination, as shown in an illustrative
project network of Fig. 2.9. The numbers above each node denote the activity
durations and the labels associated with the arcs refer to the generalized precedence
relations.

Note that a maximal time-lag can be represented by a negative minimal time-
lag in the opposite direction. Consequently, project networks with generalized
precedence relations can be represented by cyclic networks. Figure 2.10 shows such
a transformation from a $FS_{ij}^{max} = 3$ to a $SF_{ij}^{min} = -3$ relation. Activity j has to
start maximum 3 time periods after the finish of activity i, which is exactly the same
as specifying that activity i can only finish minimum -3 time periods after the start
of activity j.

The various time lags can be represented in a standardized form by transforming
them to, for example, minimal start-start precedence relations l_{ij}, using the following transformation rules (Bartusch et al. 1988):

$$s_i + SS_{ij}^{min} \leq s_j \qquad \rightarrow \quad s_i + l_{ij} \leq s_j \quad \text{with} \quad l_{ij} = SS_{ij}^{min}$$
$$s_i + SS_{ij}^{max} \geq s_j \qquad \rightarrow \quad s_j + l_{ji} \leq s_i \quad \text{with} \quad l_{ji} = -SS_{ij}^{max}$$
$$s_i + SF_{ij}^{min} \leq s_j + d_j \qquad \rightarrow \quad s_i + l_{ij} \leq s_j \quad \text{with} \quad l_{ij} = SF_{ij}^{min} - d_j$$

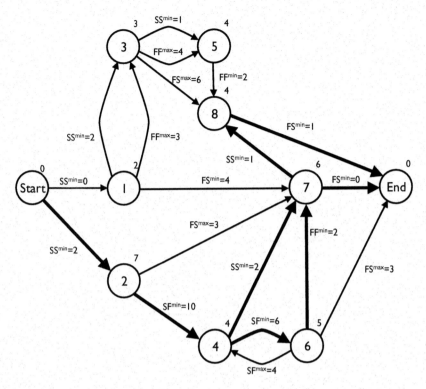

Fig. 2.9 An activity network with generalized precedence relations (Source: De Reyck 1998)

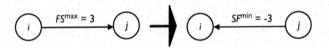

Fig. 2.10 The equivalence of minimal and maximal time lags

$$s_i + SF_{ij}^{max} \geq s_j + d_j \qquad \rightarrow \quad s_j + l_{ji} \leq s_i \quad \text{with} \quad l_{ji} = d_j - SF_{ij}^{max}$$
$$s_i + d_i + FS_{ij}^{min} \leq s_j \qquad \rightarrow \quad s_i + l_{ij} \leq s_j \quad \text{with} \quad l_{ij} = d_i + FS_{ij}^{min}$$
$$s_i + d_i + FS_{ij}^{max} \geq s_j \qquad \rightarrow \quad s_j + l_{ji} \leq s_i \quad \text{with} \quad l_{ji} = -d_i - FS_{ij}^{max}$$
$$s_i + d_i + FF_{ij}^{min} \leq s_j + d_j \qquad \rightarrow \quad s_i + l_{ij} \leq s_j \quad \text{with} \quad l_{ij} = d_i - d_j + FF_{ij}^{min}$$
$$s_i + d_i + FF_{ij}^{max} \geq s_j + d_j \qquad \rightarrow \quad s_j + l_{ji} \leq s_i \quad \text{with} \quad l_{ji} = d_j - d_i - FF_{ij}^{max}$$

with s_i the start time and d_i the estimated duration of activity i. If there is more than one time lag l_{ij} between two activities i and j, only the maximum time lag is retained. Figure 2.11 shows the project network of Fig. 2.9 after applying the transformation rules. The bold arcs in these two figures are used to display the so-called critical path, which will be explained in Sect. 2.3.2.

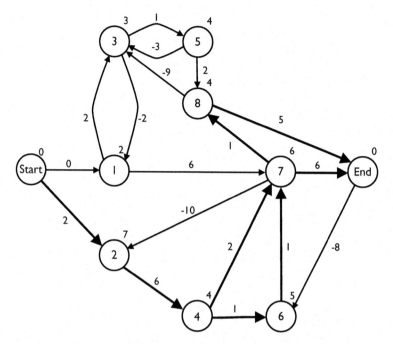

Fig. 2.11 The activity network of Fig. 2.9 with only minimal time lags

2.2.4   Other Constraint Types

The previous sections described the way how the technological relations between project activities can be incorporated in the project network. However, other project-specific requirements might show up in practice. A number of frequently occurring constraint types are:

- *Ready dates* imply earliest start or finish times on activities and hence force the activity to start or finish no earlier than the defined time instance. These constraints are known as ready start times (RST) or ready finish times (RFT).
- *Due dates* imply latest start or finish times on activities and force activities to start or finish no later than a predefined time instance. These constraints are referred to as due start times (DST) or due finish times (DFT).
- *Locked dates* imply a fixed time instance and force the activity to start or finish on a predefined time instance, known as locked start times (LST) or locked finish times (LFT).
- *And/Or* constraints allow activities to start when a predefined subset of predecessor activities has been finished.
- *Time-switch* constraints imply a project calendar to the activities to define shift workload patterns.

This nonexhaustive list can be easily extended, depending on the specific needs and requirements of the project. Many of these constraint types can be incorporated in an AoN project network by adding extra arcs in the network. Ready times, for example, can be incorporated in the network by adding an arc (dummy start, i) of type $SS_{1,i}^{min} = r_i$ with r_i the ready time of activity i. In doing so, activity i can not start earlier than time instance r_i. A natural generalization of ordinary precedence constraints are so-called *and/or* precedence constraints. In the default *and* constraint, an activity must wait for all its predecessors while in an *or* constraint, an activity has to wait for at least one of its predecessors. A complete description of all possible constraint types is outside the scope of this chapter.

Time-switch constraints have been introduced as a logical extension to the traditional models in which it is assumed that an activity can start at any time after the finish of all its predecessors. To that purpose, two improvements over the traditional activity networks have been introduced by including two types of time constraints. *Time-window* constraints assume that an activity can only start within a specified time interval. *Time-schedule* constraints assume that an activity can only begin at one of an ordered schedule of beginning times. Moreover, these time constraints can be extended by treating time as a repeating cycle where each cycle consists of two categories: (1) some pairs of rest and work windows and (2) a leading number specifying the maximal number of times each pair should iterate. By incorporating these so-called time-switch constraints, activities are forced to start in a specific time interval and to be down in some specified rest interval. A typical example of a time-switch constraint is a regular working day: work intervals are time intervals between 9 and 12 a.m. and 1 and 5 p.m. while all the time outside these two intervals is denoted as rest intervals (Vanhoucke et al. 2002; Vanhoucke 2005).

A shift-pattern is very widely used by many companies and can be considered as a special type of time-switch constraints that force activities to start in a specific time period and which impose three different work/rest patterns:

- day-pattern: an activity can only be executed during day time, from Monday till Friday. This pattern may be imposed when many persons are involved in executing the activity.
- d&n-pattern: an activity can be executed during the day or night, from Monday till Friday. This pattern may be followed in situations where activities require only one person who has to control the execution of the activity once in a while.
- dnw-pattern: an activity can be in execution every day or night and also during the weekend. This may be the case for activities that do not require human intermission.

2.3 Project Scheduling Phase

The project network diagram and the activity time estimates made by the project manager during the definition phase will be used as inputs for the scheduling phase. The scheduling phase aims at the construction of a timetable to determine the activity start and finish times and to determine a realistic total project duration within the limitations of the precedence relations and other constraint types. Although the minimization of the project lead time is often the most important objective during the scheduling phase, other scheduling objective are often crucial from a practical point of view. In this chapter, only a time objective is taken into account. The extension to other scheduling objectives is the topic of Chaps. 7 and 8.

2.3.1   Introduction to Scheduling

Scheduling is an inexact process that tries to predict the future. More precisely, it aims at the construction of a timetable for the project where start and finish times are assigned to the individual project activities. Since activities are subject to several (precedence and resource-related) constraints, the construction of a schedule can be enormously complex. Indeed, project activities are precedence related and their execution may require the use of different types of resources (money, crew, equipment, ...). The scheduling objectives (often referred to as a measure of performance) may take many forms (minimizing project duration, minimizing project costs, maximizing project revenues, optimizing due date performance, ...).

The early endeavors of project management and scheduling date back to the development of the Gantt chart by Henry Gantt (1861–1919). This charting system for production scheduling formed the basis for two scheduling techniques, which were developed to assist in planning, managing and controlling complex organizations: the Critical path Method (CPM) and Program Evaluation and Review Technique (PERT). The Gantt chart is a horizontal-bar schedule showing activity start, duration, and completion.

The Critical Path Method was the discovery of M. R. Walker of E. I. Du Pont de Nemours and Co. and J. E. Kelly of Remington Rand, circa 1957. The first test was made in 1958, when CPM was applied to the construction of a new chemical plant. In March 1959, the method was applied to a maintenance shut-down at the Du Pont works in Louisville, Kentucky. The Program Evaluation and Review Technique was devised in 1958 for the POLARIS missile program by the program evaluation branch of the special projects office of the U.S. Navy. Due to the similarities of both techniques, they are often referred to as the PERT/CPM technique.

Thanks to the development of the personal computer, project scheduling algorithms started to shift to resource allocation models and the development of software with resource-constrained scheduling features (see Chaps. 7 and 8). From the 1990s on, numerous extensions of resource allocations and the development of tools (e.g. the CC/BM approach of Chap. 10) allowed the project manager to deal with both complexity and uncertainty at the same time (see the project mapping picture of Fig. 1.4).

In this chapter, the basic critical path calculations are discussed where it is assumed that projects are not subject to limited availability of resources and the scheduler follows a time-perspective scheduling objective. In Sect. 2.4, the Program

Evaluation and Review Technique is discussed, which extends the time objective of a schedule to probability calculations. In Part II of this book, the scheduling principles will be extended to projects with limited resource availabilities and scheduling objectives different from time minimization will be discussed.

2.3.2   Critical Path Calculations

Consider the data of Table 2.2 for a fictitious project with 12 nondummy activities (and a dummy start (1) and end (14) activity). The sets P_i and S_i are used to refer to the direct predecessors and successors of an activity i. Note that precedence relations will be of the $FS_{ij}^{min} = 0$ type, unless indicated otherwise. All models and principles discussed throughout the chapters can be extended to generalized precedence relations between project activities, resulting in an increase in complexity but not in a fundamental difference in scheduling approach. Figure 2.12 displays the AoN network of Table 2.2, where the number above the node denotes the activity duration.

A path in a network can be defined as a series of connected activities from the start to the end of the project. All activities (and consequently, all paths) must be completed to finish the project. Table 2.3 enumerates all possible paths of the example network of Fig. 2.12, with their corresponding total duration.

The earliest possible completion time of the project is equal to the longest path in the network. This path, referred to as the *critical path*, determines the overall project duration. Care must be taken to keep these activities on schedule, since delays in any of these activities result in a violation of the entire project duration.

The clever reader immediately recognizes the basic principle underlying the *Theory Of Constraints* (TOC) introduced by Dr. Eliyahu M. Goldratt in his book

Table 2.2 A fictitious project example with 12 nondummy activities

Activity	Predecessors	Duration (days)
1	–	0
2	1	6
3	1	5
4	1	3
5	3	1
6	3	3
7	3	2
8	4	1
9	2	4
10	5	3
11	7	1
12	6, 10, 11	3
13	8, 12	5
14	9, 13	0

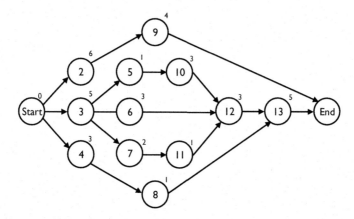

Fig. 2.12 The AoN example network of Table 2.2

Table 2.3 Enumeration of all possible paths of the project of Table 2.2	Path	Duration
	$1 \rightarrow 2 \rightarrow 9 \rightarrow 14$	10
	$1 \rightarrow 3 \rightarrow 5 \rightarrow 10 \rightarrow 12 \rightarrow 13 \rightarrow 14$	17
	$1 \rightarrow 3 \rightarrow 6 \rightarrow 12 \rightarrow 13 \rightarrow 14$	16
	$1 \rightarrow 3 \rightarrow 7 \rightarrow 11 \rightarrow 12 \rightarrow 13 \rightarrow 14$	16
	$1 \rightarrow 4 \rightarrow 8 \rightarrow 13 \rightarrow 14$	9

titled "The Goal"(Goldratt and Cox 1984), which is geared to help organizations continually achieve their goals. The main focus of this theory is to determine the most important constraint of a production system as the main driver of system performance and to give guidelines to protect this constraint in order to prevent loss of performance. Although the original book discussed the TOC in a production environment, it is a general management philosophy that can be applied to the basic project scheduling principles, amongst many others, discussed in this section. It basically consists of three steps, as follows:

1. What is your target/goal? The current scheduling objective is time.
2. What is the bottleneck constraint in your system? The critical path determines the target (time).
3. Protect the system constraint! In Chap. 5, a Schedule Risk Analysis is discussed as a tool to measure and understand the weakest parts (i.e. the constraints) of a project in order to protect them against unexpected events.

A detailed discussion of TOC is outside the scope of this book. In Chap. 10, this theory is used to add safety time in a resource-constrained project schedule as discussed in another book by Goldratt titled "Critical Chain" (Goldratt 1997).

It might be tempting to generate all possible paths of a project network in order to determine the longest path of a project. Unfortunately, the large amount of paths and consequently the required CPU-time to generate them render such a method inapplicable for networks with a realistic size. Therefore, software tools rely on a three step procedure in order to detect the critical path of a network, as follows:

1. Calculate the earliest start schedule
2. Calculate the latest start schedule
3. Calculate the slack for each activity

Earliest Start Schedule (ESS)

The earliest start es_i of each activity i can be calculated using forward calculations in the project network. The earliest start of an activity is equal to or larger than the earliest finish of all its predecessor activities. The earliest finish ef_i of an activity i is defined as its earliest start time increased with its duration estimate.

The earliest start times can be calculated using the following forward calculations, starting with the dummy start node 1:

$$es_1 = 0$$

$$es_j = max(es_i + d_i | i \in P_j)$$

and the earliest finish times are given by:

$$ef_i = es_i + d_i$$

It is easy to verify that the earliest start times of the project activities of Table 2.2 are given by $es_1 = 0$, $es_2 = 0$, $es_3 = 0$, $es_4 = 0$, $es_5 = 5$, $es_6 = 5$, $es_7 = 5$, $es_8 = 3$, $es_9 = 6$, $es_{10} = 6$, $es_{11} = 7$, $es_{12} = 9$, $es_{13} = 12$ and $es_{14} = 17$. The overall minimal project duration equals 17 time units.

Latest Start Schedule (LSS)

The latest finish lf_i of each activity i can be calculated in an analogous way, using backward calculations, starting from the project deadline δ_n at the dummy end node of the project. The latest finish of an activity is equal to or less than the latest start of all its successor activities. The latest start ls_i of an activity i is defined as its latest finish time decreased with its duration estimate.

The latest finish times can be calculated using the following backward calculations, starting with the dummy end node n:

$$lf_n = \delta_n$$

$$lf_i = min(lf_j - d_j | j \in S_i)$$

and the latest start times are given by:

$$ls_i = lf_i - d_i$$

Given the project deadline of 17 time units, calculated as the earliest start of the end dummy activity in the previous step, the latest start times of each activity are given by $ls_1 = 0$, $ls_2 = 7$, $ls_3 = 0$, $ls_4 = 8$, $ls_5 = 5$, $ls_6 = 6$, $ls_7 = 6$, $ls_8 = 11$, $ls_9 = 13$, $ls_{10} = 6$, $ls_{11} = 8$, $ls_{12} = 9$, $ls_{13} = 12$ and $ls_{14} = 17$.

Activity Slack/Float

The amount of slack associated with each activity is used to denote the free time of each activity within the ESS and LSS. It denotes the amount of time each activity can be delayed without violating the entire project duration. The slack (or float) of activity i can be calculated as

$$ls_i - es_i = lf_i - ef_i$$

Activities with zero slack cannot be delayed without affecting the entire project duration and are called critical activities. Hence, the *critical path* consists of a path of critical activities and is given by activities 1, 3, 5, 10, 12, 13 and 14 in Table 2.4.

Activities that lie on the critical path cannot be delayed without delaying the entire project duration. Since time is an important objective in scheduling, the critical path is what the project manager has to focus on. It helps the manager to calculate the minimum length of time in which the project can be completed and which activities should be prioritized to complete the project within its deadline. In order to finish a project on time, the critical path calculations help the project manager to focus on the essential activities to which attention and resources should be devoted. It gives an effective basis for the scheduling and monitoring of progress.

Table 2.4 The slack of the activities of the example project of Fig. 2.12

Activity	Slack
1	0
2	7
3	0
4	8
5	0
6	1
7	1
8	8
9	7
10	0
11	1
12	0
13	0
14	0

Gantt Charts

The Gantt chart is named after its originator Henry Gantt and displays a timetable for each activity of the project. Each activity is shown as a block or bar and drawn to scale in time. The timescale is usually drawn horizontally while the different activities are displayed on the vertical axis. This chart is used for scheduling and is often used in conjunction with the project network to show the technological dependencies between activities. Figure 2.13 shows an ESS Gantt chart of Table 2.2 along with the activity slack. The bars represent the earliest start and finish times of each activity of the example project. The gray lines following the activity bars represent the activity slack, and hence, shifting activities towards the end of these gray bars results in the corresponding LSS. Activities without slack (i.e. activities 1, 3, 5, 10, 12, 13 and 14) belong to the critical path and need the attention of the project manager.

Note that the introduction of generalized precedence relations (see previous chapter) might increase the complexity to find the critical path, but involves no fundamental difference in scheduling. However, some anomalies can occur when introducing these generalized precedence relations. Assume that, for illustrative purposes, the precedence relations between activity 5 and 10 and activity 10 and 12 change to a finish-finish and start-start relation, respectively, both with a minimal time-lag of 3 time units, i.e. $FF_{5,10}^{min} = 3$ and $SS_{10,12}^{min} = 3$. It is easy to verify that the critical path remains unchanged and still determines the entire project duration of 17 time units. However, the introduction of generalized precedence relations leads to counterintuitive results and sheds a new light on the philosophy of the critical path, activity crashing (see Chap. 3) and/or the effects of delays in critical activities. Indeed, decreasing the duration of the critical activity 10 from 3 time units to 1 time unit results in an increase of the project duration with 2 time units, as shown in Fig. 2.14 (activity 10 starts 2 time units later than in the schedule of Fig. 2.13). Hence, in the presence of generalized precedence relations, the general

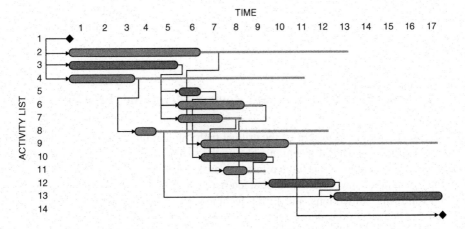

Fig. 2.13 The ESS Gantt chart of the example project and the activity slack

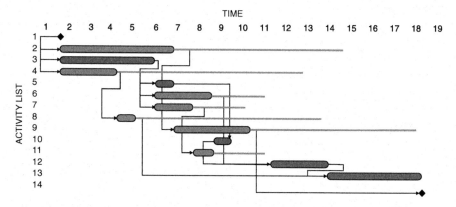

Fig. 2.14 The modified ESS Gantt chart of the example project and the activity slack

rule "increasing the duration of a critical activity (or delaying this activity) results in an increase of the project duration" is no longer applicable. Instead, decreasing the duration of a critical activity sometimes results in an increase of the project duration!

Resource Charts

In the previous sections, it is assumed that project activities do not require resources during their execution (or alternatively, the assumption is that the resources are unlimited in availability). In practice, activities in progress need resources that are limited in availability. These resources have been classified in two basic categories, renewable and nonrenewable resources, and will be discussed in further chapters.

In Part II of this book, resource charts will show that the presence of resources under a limited availability will lead to changes in the project schedule. The resource charts, which extend the Gantt charts to the presence of renewable resources, will modify the activity start times and will extend the critical path concept into a so-called "critical chain" approach.

2.4 Program Evaluation and Review Technique (PERT)

The previous sections described the critical path calculations that form the basis of both the PERT and CPM technique. Due to the strong similarities between the two scheduling techniques, it is often referred to as the PERT/CPM technique. However, both techniques have their own characteristics and need further explanation. In the following subsections, the PERT technique is described, which aims at the construction of a precedence feasible schedule in the absence of resources. The details of the critical path method (CPM) are reserved for Chap. 3, where the construction of a precedence feasible schedule with nonrenewable resources is discussed.

2.4.1 Three Activity Duration Estimates

In the previous section, it was assumed that the activity duration estimates, and the derived values for the earliest start, latest start, earliest finish and latest finish were all deterministic. In reality, this is seldom true and durations are often not known in advance. PERT has extended this deterministic approach in the face of uncertainty about activity times, and employs a special formula for estimating activity durations. The approach of PERT assumes that the activity duration estimates are done by someone who is familiar with the activity, and has enough insight in the characteristics of the activity. Hence, the technique requires three duration estimates for each individual activity, as follows:

- Optimistic time estimate: This is the shortest possible time in which the activity can be completed, and assumes that everything has to go perfect.
- Realistic time estimate: This is the most likely time in which the activity can be completed under normal circumstances.
- Pessimistic time estimate: This is the longest possible time the activity might need, and assumes a worst-case scenario.

Table 2.5 displays the three time estimates for the activities of the example project of Fig. 2.12. The optimistic time estimate is denoted by a, the pessimistic time estimate is denoted by b and m is used to refer to the realistic time estimate.

Table 2.5 Three time estimates for the activities of the project of Fig. 2.12

Activity	Optimistic a	Realistic m	Pessimistic b	t	σ
1	0	0	0	0	0
2	3	5	13	6	1.67
3	2	3.5	14	5	2
4	1	3	5	3	0.67
5	1	1	1	1	0
6	1	2	9	3	1.33
7	1	2	3	2	0.33
8	1	1	1	1	0
9	1	4	7	4	1
10	1	3	5	3	0.67
11	0.5	1	1.5	1	0.17
12	1	2.5	7	3	1
13	1	4	13	5	2
14	0	0	0	0	0

Fig. 2.15 A beta distribution used to express activity duration variability in PERT

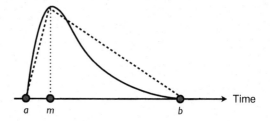

PERT assumes that each activity duration is a random variable between two extreme values (i.e. a and b) and follows a beta probability distribution. A typical beta distribution function and its triangular approximation is shown in Fig. 2.15. Note that the difference between m and b is often, but not necessarily larger than the difference between a and m to express positive skewness.

The expected time t of a beta distribution can be approximated by the weighted average that sums to one, as follows:

$$t = \frac{a + 4m + b}{6} \tag{2.1}$$

The standard deviation of an activity duration, which serves as a measure for risk, can be calculated using the philosophy of a three standard deviations interval, as follows:

$$\sigma = \frac{b - a}{6} \tag{2.2}$$

This calculation is indeed inspired by a so-called three sigma interval for the normal distribution. A three-sigma interval for the normal distribution is the interval between the average minus three times the standard deviation and the average plus three times the standard deviation, as exactly 99.73% of the observations lie in that interval. By calculating the standard deviation based on a similar interval as given in Eq. 2.2, PERT assumes that almost none of the observations (i.e. real activity durations) will lie outside the $[a, b]$ range.

2.4.2 Probability of Project Completion

The assumption that activity durations are random variables implies that the entire project duration is also a random variable. Hence, the entire project duration differs from the deterministic or expected project duration, due to the variability in the activity times as measured by its standard deviation. The PERT analysis allows to provide the following information:

- The expected entire project duration and the critical path.
- The probability to complete the project within a specified deadline.
- The deadline before which the project can be completed with a certain probability.

The PERT analysis calculates the expected critical path based on the expected duration of each activity. In the example project, the expected critical path $E(T)$ is equal to 17 time units and consists of the activities 1, 3, 5, 10, 12, 13 and 14. Since each activity is assumed to be a random variable following a beta probability distribution, the total expected duration $E(T)$ is also a random variable with a known distribution. This known distribution can be derived using the well-known *central limit theorem*.

> The central limit theorem states that, given a distribution with an average $E(T)$ and variance $Var(T)$, the sampling distribution of the mean approaches a normal distribution with an average $E(T)$ and a variance $Var(T)/n$ as n, the sample size, increases.

In the example project, the sample consists of the expected critical activities 1, 3, 5, 10, 12, 13 and 14 with each an average duration calculated earlier. Although the CLT as described above is formulated for the sampling distribution of the *mean*, the project completion time is simply the sum of the expected activity times for the critical path activities and hence, a total average duration of 17 time units can be calculated. Similarly, a total variance[1] that can be calculated as $Var(T) = 2^2 + 0^2 + 0.67^2 + 1^2 + 2^2 = 9.44$ and, consequently, the standard deviation equals $\sqrt{9.44} = 3.07$.

Consequently, the example project follows a normal distribution with an average total duration of 17 time units and a standard deviation of 3.07, i.e. $N(17; 3.07)$. Using normal tables, or the well-known "normdist" or "norminv" functions in Microsoft Excel, it is easy to verify the calculations below.

Probabilities: The probability that the example project has a total duration less than or equal to 20 time units equals

$$P(T \le 20) = P\left(\frac{T - 17}{3.07} \le \frac{20 - 17}{3.07}\right)$$
$$= P(z \le 0.976)$$
$$= 83.55\%$$

with z the symbol for the standardized value of the normal distribution.

Percentiles: The project duration T with a risk of exceeding of 10% is equal to the 90th percentile of the $N(17; 3.07)$ normal distribution and can be calculated as follows:

$$90\% \text{ percentile} \rightarrow z = 1.28 = \frac{T - 17}{3.07}$$
$$\rightarrow T = 20.9 \text{ time units (e.g. weeks)}$$

---

[1] Only activities on the expected critical path are taken into account.

Confidence Intervals: The project will have a total duration between approximately 10.8 and 23.1 time units with a probability of 95%, which can be calculated as a 2σ interval for the normal distribution. A more detailed statistical explanation can be found in any statistics handbook and is outside the scope of this book.

2.4.3 Beyond PERT

Despite the relevance of the PERT planning concept, the technique has often been criticized in literature. The PERT analysis implicitly assumes that all activities that are not on the critical path may be ignored by setting the activity durations to their average values. In realistic settings, projects have multiple critical paths instead of a single unique critical path. Moreover, in the stochastic setting, every noncritical path has the potential to become critical and hence the critical path would be the maximum of a set of possible critical paths. It is also assumed that the activity durations are independent random variables while in reality they can be dependent. These strict assumptions might lead to inaccuracies and has been the subject of a lot of research. In Chap. 5, the PERT technique is extended to Monte-Carlo simulation analyses, which allows to analyze the distribution of the critical path without the restricted PERT assumptions. For an overview of the pitfalls of making traditional PERT assumptions, the reader is referred to Elmaghraby (1977).

2.5 Conclusion

This chapter outlined the basic concepts of the definition and scheduling phases of a project's life cycle. The definition phase can be considered as the "what" phase since its main target is to determine what needs to be done in order to reach the project goal. It mainly consists of determining the main set of activities and precedence relations (modeled in a project network) and the responsibilities of the various project subparts. The scheduling phase, the "when" phase, constructs a timetable for the various project activities within a certain scheduling objective (which is assumed to be a time minimization objective in the current chapter), leading to a deterministic forecast of the earliest and latest activity start times and their slack within the minimal project duration.

In an attempt to add stochastic elements to the deterministic project schedule, the basic concepts of the PERT technique and an illustrative example have been discussed in the current chapter as a valuable tool to deal with a (low) degree of uncertainty in activity estimates. Although the basic concepts of the critical path scheduling approach have been outlined in this chapter, an overview of the main characteristics of the Critical Path Method (CPM), such as the activity time/cost trade-off function and the activity crashing possibility, is the subject of Chap. 3.

It should be noted that the usefulness of these scheduling methods should be put into the right perspective. Despite the relevance of introducing activity estimate variability in the project schedule under strict assumptions, the PERT principles have their inaccuracies and potential pitfalls. Consequently, the techniques discussed in this chapter are classified in the first quadrant (low uncertainty/low complexity) of the project mapping picture of Fig. 1.4. A project scheduling setting with higher degree of uncertainty is the topic of Chap. 5. A higher degree of complexity in project scheduling is mainly due to the introduction of a limited resource availability, which will be discussed in Part II of this book.

Chapter 3
The Critical Path Method

Abstract This chapter makes an effort to tighten the gap between the project scheduling literature and the needs of project managers and schedulers through the use of a practical computerized simulation game. Project managers are constantly confronted with the intricacy of scheduling a complex real-life problem in an efficient way when they often have little knowledge of the state-of-the-art in the algorithmic developments or inherent characteristics of the scheduling problem they solve. A game has been developed that serves as a training tool to help practitioners gain insight in project scheduling. The well-known critical path method (CPM) with activity time/cost trade-offs is introduced to the reader, and used as a project scheduling technique in the game.

3.1 Introduction to Literature

Project scheduling has been a research topic for many decades, leading to a project management body of knowledge containing a wide and diverse set of principles, tools and techniques. In recent years, several summary papers have given an overview of the past and current development in project scheduling literature (see, for example, the papers by Icmeli et al. (1993), Elmaghraby (1995), Özdamar and Ulusoy (1995), Herroelen et al. (1998) and Brucker et al. (1999)). These papers primarily focus on the modeling aspect and algorithmic developments necessary to schedule complex projects and parts of them will be discussed in later chapters of this book. A more recent experimental investigation of heuristic search methods to construct a project schedule with resources can be found in Kolisch and Hartmann (2006).

The wide diversity of project scheduling topics and research projects is reflected in two classification schemes developed by Brucker et al. (1999) and Herroelen et al. (1999). In these papers, the authors summarize and classify the main features and characteristics of various kinds of project scheduling problems according to project features, resource characteristics and scheduling objectives. Despite this ever growing amount of research on project scheduling, it has been shown in literature that there is a wide gap between the project management discipline and the research on project management, as illustrated by Delisle and Olson (2004), among many others.

This chapter makes an effort to tighten the gap between the project scheduling literature and the needs of project managers. Project managers are constantly confronted with the intricacy of scheduling a complex real-life problem in an efficient way when they often have little knowledge of the state-of-the-art in algorithmic developments. A Project Schedule Game (PSG) has been developed that serves as a training tool to help practitioners gain insight in project scheduling. The game is based on data from a real-life project from a water production center as an input (details about the real project are given in Chap. 4) but allows the incorporation of any project suggested by the participants. The purpose of the game is to get familiar with the well-known *discrete time/cost trade-off scheduling problem* as an inherent characteristic of the *Critical Path Method* (CPM), which will be discussed in detail throughout this chapter. The game helps to show the project manager how to cope with trade-offs between activity durations and their corresponding costs and creates an incentive to rely on academic research efforts and/or algorithmic procedures developed by many researchers in the field. The problem discussed in the current chapter can – similar to the previous chapter – be classified in quadrant 1 of Fig. 1.4.

The outline of this chapter is as follows. Section 3.2 gives an introduction to the Critical Path Method (CPM). Section 3.3 gives an overview of the features of the game. It discusses why managers can benefit from a project scheduling game and gives a short presentation of the real-life example project used in the PSG. Section 3.4 discusses the educational approach taken during a typical PSG class session. Section 3.5 draws overall conclusions.

3.2   Time/Cost Scheduling Trade-Offs

3.2.1   *Linear Time/Cost Relations*

Time/cost trade-offs in project scheduling find their roots in the Critical Path Method, developed between 1956 and 1959 at the Du Pont Company and at Remington Rand Univac (Kelley and Walker 1959; Walker and Sawyer 1959; Kelley 1961), which is originally based on an activity-on-the-arc network diagram. Since then, a never-ending amount of literature has focused on the extensions of this basic problem type. Basically, CPM assumes that the duration of project activities is a nonincreasing function of the amount of money used to perform this activity (i.e. money is considered here as a single nonrenewable resource; for more information on resources, see Chap. 7). This implies that the cost of an individual activity is a function of its duration, that is, by spending more (or less) nonrenewable

Fig. 3.1 The time/cost
trade-off of an activity

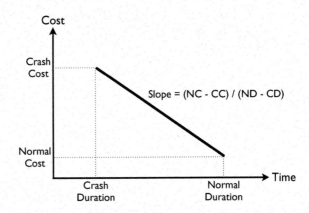

resources (money), the activity duration will decrease (or increase). Note that this chapter belongs to Part I of this book, where no resources are explicitly taken into account. In Chap. 7, a distinction will be made between renewable resources and nonrenewable (or consumable) resources and it will be shown that the presence of renewable resources (and *not* the presence of the nonrenewable resources that will be used in the current chapter) leads to an increase of the scheduling complexity. Consequently, the use of nonrenewable resources to incorporate a time/cost trade-off in project activities does not lead to a significant increase in the project scheduling complexity compared to the techniques of the previous chapter, which is exactly the reason why the CPM is discussed in this part of the book.[1]

A CPM project scheduling model assumes four pieces of information for each project activity, as follows:

- Normal Duration (ND): The maximum duration for the activity.
- Crash Duration (CD): The minimum duration for the activity.
- Normal Cost (NC): The cost associated with the normal duration.
- Crash Cost (CC): The cost associated with the crash duration.

The early time/cost trade-off models assumed the direct activity cost functions to be linear nonincreasing functions, as shown in Fig. 3.1. The objective was to determine the activity durations and to schedule the activities in order to minimize the project costs (i.e. the sum of the activity costs) within a specified project deadline. Therefore, the activity costs are a function of the activity durations, which are bounded from below (crash duration) and from above (normal duration). Consequently, the project manager needs to decide the optimal timing for each activity by selecting a time/cost combination for each activity. To that purpose, each

---

[1]Note that this classification can be subject to discussion. The discrete time/cost trade-off problem as discussed in Sect. 3.2.2 is known to be NP-hard, and hence, constructing an optimal schedule for this scheduling problem is known to be a very difficult problem. However, due to the absence of renewable resources, the problem is considered as easy (quadrant 1 of Fig. 1.4) relative to the resource-constrained projects of quadrant 3. Details are outside the scope of this book.

activity duration can be reduced to less than its normal duration, which is known as *activity crashing*. The slope of the time/cost curve determines the marginal crash cost per unit of time as follows:

$$\text{Unit Crash Cost} = \frac{\text{Normal Cost} - \text{Crash Cost}}{\text{Normal Duration} - \text{Crash Duration}}$$

Originally, the CPM has been modeled in an AoA network representation. Figure 3.2 shows an example AoA project network with five nondummy activities with each activity labeled with (CD, ND, UCC), with CD the crash duration, ND the normal duration and UCC the unit crash cost for each activity represented by arc (i, j).

The time/cost trade-off scheduling problem can be formulated by the following linear programming model (Elmaghraby 1977):

$$\text{Minimize} \sum_{(i,j) \in E} c_{ij} y_{ij} \tag{3.1}$$

subject to

$$t_i - t_j + y_{ij} \leq 0 \qquad\qquad \forall (i, j) \in E \tag{3.2}$$

$$cd_{ij} \leq y_{ij} \leq nd_{ij} \qquad\qquad \forall (i, j) \in E \tag{3.3}$$

$$-t_1 + t_n = \delta_n \tag{3.4}$$

The variable t_i is used to denote the realization time of event (node) i and the variable y_{ij} to denote the duration of activity (i, j). The parameter c_{ij} is used to represent the marginal cost of crashing activity i with one time unit (i.e. the slope of the activity time/cost line as calculated earlier by the Unit Crash Cost). The parameters cd_{ij} and nd_{ij} are used to denote the crash and normal duration of activity (i, j). The set E is used to refer to the set of project activities in an AoA format, represented by the edges in the network. Note that the model assumes that the cost of completing the project on normal time is already determined. The objective of the formulation minimizes the extra cost of crashing activities to durations lower than their normal duration. The cost of crashing is assumed to be a linear function of the activity duration varying between the crash and normal duration. The t_i variables

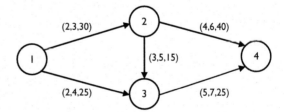

Fig. 3.2 A fictitious AoA network with five nondummy activities

are not restricted in sign, as shown by Elmaghraby (1977). Details are outside the scope of this book.

The optimal crashing cost for the example project of Fig. 3.2 with a predefined deadline of $\delta_n = 12$ is equal to 55. The activity durations are equal to 3, 4, 3, 6 and 6 for activities (1,2), (1,3), (2,3), (2,4) and (3,4).

Due to its inherent complexity and relevance in practice, numerous solution procedures for this CPM scheduling problem are proposed for other than linear activity cost functions, including concave, convex and general continuous activity cost functions. In the next section, a practical extension to discrete time/cost relations is discussed, which will be used in the PSG. Furthermore, in the remainder of this chapter, project networks will be represented by the AoN format instead of the AoA format.

3.2.2 Discrete Time/Cost Relations

A lot of procedures have also been developed for solving the discrete version of the scheduling problem in which the duration of project activities is a discrete, nonincreasing function of the amount of a single, nonrenewable resource committed to them. Figure 3.3 shows an example of a discrete activity time/cost profile containing five possible (time,cost) combinations. Each combination is referred to as an *activity mode* and the scheduling problem involves the selection of a set of execution modes for all project activities in order to achieve a certain objective. The problem has been studied under three possible schedule objectives, as follows:

- Deadline restriction: This CPM type involves the scheduling of all project activities in order to minimize the total cost of the project while meeting a given deadline.
- Budget restriction: This CPM version aims at minimizing the project duration without exceeding a given budget.

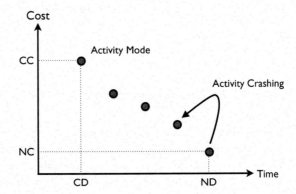

Fig. 3.3 A discrete time/cost trade-off for an activity

- Complete horizon: This CPM version combines the two previous ones and involves the generation of an efficient time/cost profile over the set of feasible project durations. That is, all the efficient points (T, C) so that, a project length T can be obtained with a cost limit C and, so that, no other point (T′, C′) exists for which both T′ and C′ are smaller than or equal to T and C.

Thanks to the relevance of this *discrete time/cost trade-off problem* (DTCTP) in practice, numerous researchers have investigated this problem. An Integer Programming (IP) formulation of the scheduling problem is outside the scope of this book. For more detailed information about problem formulations and solution methods, the reader is referred to papers written by Crowston and Thompson (1967), Crowston (1970), Robinson (1975), Billstein and Radermacher (1977), Wiest and Levy (1977), Hindelang and Muth (1979), Patterson (1979), Elmaghraby and Kamburowsky (1992), De et al. (1995, 1997), Demeulemeester and Herroelen (1996), Demeulemeester et al. (1998), and Skutella (1998). In the next sections, the DTCTP will be embedded in the simulation game, such that project managers can easily get acquainted with the scheduling problem, without knowing exact formulations or advanced solution methods.

3.3   The Project Scheduling Game

The *Project Scheduling Game* (PSG) is an IT-supported simulation game that illustrates the characteristics of scheduling a real-life project with discrete time/cost trade-offs in the project activities. The project is based on a sequence of activities for a large real-life project at the Vlaamse Maatschappij voor Watervoorziening, which aims at the expansion of the capacity to produce purified water (the data are based on the project description of Chap. 4). As explained in the previous section, the participant (manager) of the game has to construct a dynamic project schedule for the discrete time/cost trade-off problem. Indeed, by allocating nonrenewable resources (money) to a particular activity, the manager decides about the duration and corresponding cost of each network activity. The manager schedules the project with the negotiated project deadline in mind, focusing on the minimization of the total project cost.

3.3.1   Why Do Managers Need This Game?

It has been mentioned in Chap. 1 that a project typically goes through a number of different phases, which are often referred to as the project life cycle. Such a life cycle might consist of a project conception phase, a project definition phase, a phase in which the project has to be scheduled, the execution of the project, the controlling phase in which the progress of the project is monitored and the final termination of

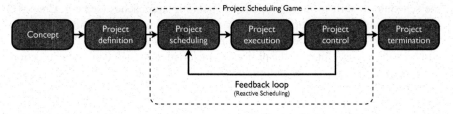

Fig. 3.4 The PSG project life cycle

the project. The project of the game, like any project, goes through these different phases. The conception and definition phases are assumed to be completed and serve as inputs to the simulation game. The project concept and the simulation process of the PSG are described in Sect. 3.3.3. The game simulates the scheduling, execution and control phases of the project, as shown in Fig. 3.4. Participants playing the game focus on the scheduling of the project (scheduling phase), receive feedback from the project control phase (feedback loop) and reschedule as the project is being executed. This approach is referred to as reactive scheduling (see Chap. 1).

The various algorithmic developments in literature dealing with the scheduling phase are strongly related with optimization modeling and require, therefore, the necessary skills and technical know-how (In literature, researchers often refer to the NP-hardness to denote the complexity of most scheduling problems (see, for example, Demeulemeester and Herroelen (2002)). Unfortunately, the manager who is in charge of the project often has little or no background in optimization and, consequently, unintentionally ignores the recent developments in the field. One of the major goals of this project scheduling game is to create a feeling of the inherent complexity of the project scheduling phase (even for projects in quadrant 1 of Fig. 1.4, which are labeled as rather easy, scheduling complexity issues arise) and to create an incentive to rely on the state-of-the-art developments by different universities. Indeed, research has revealed interesting insights in the crashing behavior of activity durations under different assumptions (linear, convex, concave, discrete or arbitrary time/cost trade-offs).

However, completely relying on algorithms to schedule real-life projects ignores the fact that uncertainty will occur. Indeed, due to unexpected events (a delay in an activity, a machine breakdown, a strike, an inaccurate estimate of resource usage, etc.) the execution of the project will differ from the original schedule. Periodically, the manager has to control the execution and adapt the preliminary schedule. A thorough understanding of the technical details and complexity of the scheduling mechanism is, therefore, indispensable. Consequently, the project manager has to update the project schedule of the game during the project's progress as new information arrives, and hence, considers the scheduling problem as a dynamic scheduling problem that needs modifications at regular time intervals. While the current approach has a clear focus on a *reactive scheduling* approach to deal with uncertainty, other approaches will try to analyze the risk during the construction of the schedule to shift to more *proactive scheduling* approaches (see e.g. Chap. 5). This proactive scheduling approach is not incorporated in the simulation game.

In the next section, the features of the real-life project used in the PSG business game are discussed. Note that the project characteristics discussed in the next section are a result of the project conception and definition and planning phase and are used as input for the manager (i.e., the player) who is now put in charge of scheduling the project.

3.3.2   The Project Data of PSG

The PSG requires project data consisting of a network with project activities and precedence relations, and multiple time/cost estimates for each activity. Moreover, project execution has to be simulated during the execution phase of the project, which requires input for uncertainty in the activity durations. Although this uncertainty aspect is unknown for those who play the game, it has to be defined by the game teacher in advance. While the software runs with any project that is correctly entered in the input screen of the game, a predefined project network is mostly used during the teaching sessions. The advantage of using predefined project data is twofold. On the one hand, it is less time consuming since entering time/cost data requires a tailoring step in order to be sure that the game reflects a realistic project setting. On the other hand, since both the project network and the uncertainty is known by the game developer, the optimal solution is known and available upon request, which can act as a validation tool that can be shown to the participants at the end of the game run (see Fig. 3.9 of Sect. 3.4).

The default project is based on project data obtained from the Vlaamse Maatschappij voor Watervoorziening (VMW), a Flemish water distribution company, which covers approximately 50% of Flanders, located in the northern region of Belgium. This company produces and delivers water by transforming surface water into drinkable water and distributing it to the customers. The VMW services 2.5 million customers with a pipeline network of 27,000 km and a yearly production of 140 billion liters of water.[2] The project aims at the expansion of the capacity to produce pure water and is the topic of Chap. 4.

In the definition phase, the organization defines the project objectives, the project specifications and requirements and the organization of the whole project. In doing so, the organization decides on how it is going to achieve these objectives. The VMW has decided to perform the project in two major steps. In a first step, it will focus on an extension of the storage capacity of treated water without expanding the production capacity of pure water. The latter is the subject of a second step that aims at an increase of the production capacity of pure water. For educational purposes, the game focuses only on a subpart of the whole original project.

---

[2]Data based on figures obtained in 2003.

The game takes the definition phase as an input and assumes that the organization has knowledge about the estimates of the durations and costs of the activities, and the precedence relations among these activities. The project scheduling game begins after this point of the project life cycle, taking the detailed description of the project as an input. The next step is to schedule the project in order to present a timetable for the project activities, which is under the responsibility of the game player. As previously mentioned, the game focuses on the construction of a precedence feasible schedule and the adaptation of this schedule during the execution and controlling phase, which is inevitable due to uncertain events.

Figure 3.5 displays the activity-on-the-node (AoN) network for the project. The project consists of 44 activities (and a dummy start and dummy end node), which can be divided into two main subprojects: the construction activities at the plant itself and all the remaining construction activities outside the plant. The project is different from the description of the original project (see Chap. 4), since it combines a number of activities into one domed activity for which time/cost trade-offs have been defined. This data is important since the game relies on the time/cost trade-off problem in order to illustrate the complexity issues of scheduling a real-life project. It is assumed that the structure of the network will remain unchanged throughout the simulation. This might differ from normal practice in which networks are often

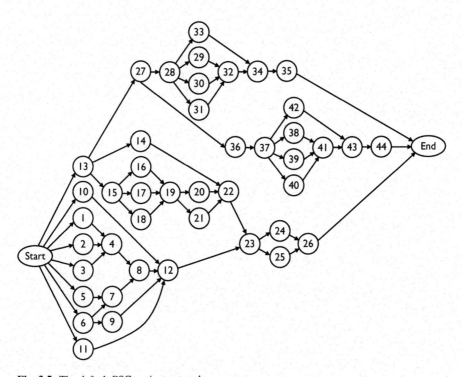

Fig. 3.5 The default PSG project network

changed substantially as the project progresses. A list of the project activities and their possible time/cost trade-offs is given at the end of this chapter in Table 3.1.[3]

In the next section, the project scheduling game is described in more detail, with a clear focus on the scheduling and controlling phases of the project life cycle.

3.3.3   Simulation Process of PSG

Each of the 44 individual activities shown in Fig. 3.5 must be finished to complete the capacity expansion project and this must be done in a sequence that does not violate the precedence relationships shown in the network diagram. As in real life, the activities that make up the total project do not have a single, fixed duration, but can vary with the amount of money that management spends (the so-called time/cost trade-off). The primary task for a project management team is to decide on the activity durations to be scheduled for each activity, taking into account costs and the project completion time. In addition, there are factors beyond control of management that can influence the length of an activity. During the project, occurrences such as strikes or acts of nature may cause some activities to be delayed beyond their planned duration. On the other hand, fortune may smile and result in an earlier-than-scheduled completion of some activities.

One of the unique features of the PSG is that it completely relies on the interaction between the scheduling, execution, and controlling phase (see Fig. 3.4) and makes use of the feedback loop in order to monitor the progress of a project. Indeed, during the execution phase the project has to be monitored and controlled. If deviations from the existing schedule occur, corrective actions have to be taken (previously referred to as reactive scheduling). Figure 3.6 displays the simulation process of the game indicating the inputs and outputs generated by the software and inputs needed by the user. In the following paragraphs, the various simulation steps of the figure are discussed in detail.

Start of the game: The game starts with an original schedule proposed by the game developer or the teacher entering new project data in which scheduled activity duration decisions have already been made. This results in an expected completion time T for the project, as well as a total cost for completing the project. The expected completion time is obtained by adding up the total time to complete the activities along the critical path in the network (as previously mentioned, the time/cost trade-off finds its roots in the critical path method). It is assumed that all weekends and holidays are also working days.[4] Total project cost is made up of the sum of the penalty cost (described below) and the planned activity costs for each of the 44 activities.

---

[3]The default project network is based on the project discussed in Chap. 4 but duration and cost combinations changed to other settings to model the time/cost trade-offs.

[4]No panic, it is only a game!

Table 3.1 An activity list for the PSG project with their time/cost trade-offs

ID	Activity description	Time (days)	Cost (€)
Construction activities at the water production center			
1	Obtain building license for architecture	(7)	(2,000)
2	Find contractor for architecture	(13)	(1,000)
3	Obtain environmental license	(10;11;12;13;14;15;16;17)	(7,970;7,650;7,400;7,200;7,036;6,900;6,784;6,684)
4	Execution of architectural work	(13;14;15;16)	(6,066;5,580;5,400;5,246)
5	Design equipment	(31;33)	(38,064;36,968)
6	Negotiations high voltage cabine (HVC)	(2;3)	(1,300;966)
7	Specification/Public tender/Fabrication	(12;14;15;16;19;20;21;22)	(8,000;7,822;7,600;7,500;7,332;7,262;7,200;7,142)
8	Execution	(20;21;22)	(7,500;7,352;7,222)
9	Additional work on cables for HVC	(14;15;16;17;19)	(17,570;17,332;17,124;16,940;16,630)
10	Updating existing high pressure room	(22)	(1,500)
11	Constructing pipes between installations	(11;12;13;14;15)	(100,908;93,332;86,922;81,428;76,666)
12	Coming into operation	(17;18;19)	(20,764;20,110;19,526)
Construction activities outside the water production center			
	Pipes from WPC to Eeklo		
13	First draft design	(10;11;13;14;15;16)	(40,000;38,180;35,384;34,284;33,332;32,500)
14	Find permission/contractor and construction pipeline	(15;16;17;18;19;20;21;22;23;24)	(39,332;37,250;35,410;33,776;32,314;31,000;29,808; 28,726;27,738;26,832)
15	Design	(11;12;13;14;15;16)	(15,544;15,166;14,846;14,570;14,232;14,124)
16	Find permission	(13;14;15;16;17;18;19)	(63,460;60,714;58,332;56,250;54,410;52,776;51,314)
17	Connection electricity	(15)	(7,500)
18	Specification equipment	(28;29;30;31;32;33;34; 35;36;37;38;39;40;41)	(70,000;68,274;66,666;65,160;63,750;62,424;61,176; 60,000;58,888;57,836;56,842;55,896;55,000;54,146)
19	Delivery equipment	(3;4;5)	(1,932;1,600;1,400)
20	Execution	(3)	(4,000)
			(continued)

Table 3.1 (continued)

ID	Activity description	Time (days)	Cost (€)
21	Fitting in communication system	(2;3)	(1,300;966)
22	Coming into operation	(17;18;19;20)	(12,822;12,666;12,526;12,284)
	Constructing pumps at Zelzate		
23	Design for connection electricity	(11;12;13;14;15;16;17;18)	(9,818;9,410;9,230;9,000;8,800;8,624;8,479;8,332)
24	Connection electricity	(8;9;10;11;12;14;15;16;17;18)	(16,000;15,332;14,800;14,362;14,000;13,482;13,200;13,000; 12,822;12,666)
25	Design/specification/delivery	(9;10;11;12;13;14;15;16;17;18)	(24,888;24,400;24,000;23,666;23,384;23,142; 22,932;22,750; 22,588;22,444)
26	Execution/coming into operation	(1)	(300)
	Constructing pumps and water tower at Eeklo		
27	First draft design	(13;14;15;16;17;18;19;20;21;22)	(18,538;18,284;18,066;17,874;17,704;17,554;17,420;17,300; 17,190;17,090)
28	Design	(15;16;18;19;20;21)	(14,532;14,374;14,110;14,000;13,900;13,808)
29	License request	(14;15;16;17;18;19;20;21;22)	(15,142;15,000;14,870;14,764;14,666;14,578;14,500;14,428; 14,362)
30	Specification and public tender	(16;17;18;20;21;23)	(21,750;21,528;21,332;21,000;20,856;20,608)
31	Environmental license and notification VLAREM	(15;16)	(18,400;18,250)
32	Realisation	(12;13;14;16;18;19)	(25,832;25,384;25,000;24,374;23,888;23,684)
33	Design/specification and request offer	(13;14;15;16;17;18;19;20;21)	(13,152;13,000;12,866;12,750;12,646;12,554;12,472;12,400; 12,332)

34	Execution	(14;15;16;17;18)	(27,284;27,066;26,874;26,704;26,554)
35	Coming into operation	(12;15;17)	(19,832;19,266;19,000)
	Constructing pumps at Waarschoot		
36	First draft design	(9;10;11;12;13;14;15;16;17;18)	(14,888;14,600;14,362;14,166;14,000;13,856;13,732;13,624; 13,528;13,444)
37	Design	(15;16;17)	(50,000;48,750;47,646)
38	File constructing license	(16;17;18)	(15,124;14,940;14,776)
39	Specification	(12;14;16;18;20;21)	(18,166;17,570;17,124;16,776;16,500;16,380)
40	File environmental license	(14;15;16;17;18;19;20)	(7,856;7,732;7,624;7,528;7,444;7,374;7,300)
41	Realisation	(15;17;18;19;21;22)	(18,666;17,882;17,554;17,262;16,760;16,544)
42	Design	(16;17;18;19;20)	(32,374;32,116;31,888;31,684;31,500)
43	Execution	(17;18;19;20;21;22)	(14,940;14,776;14,630;14,500;14,380;14,272)
44	Coming into operation	(10)	(1200)

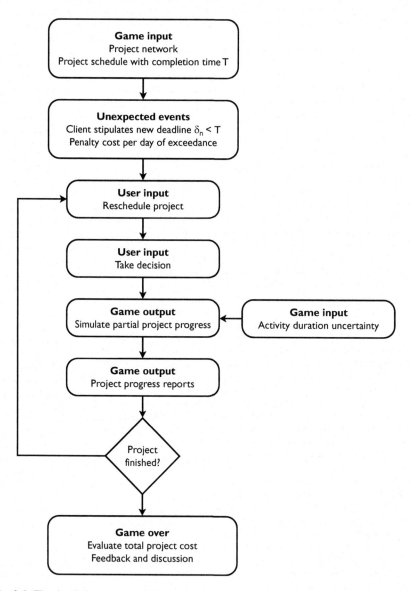

Fig. 3.6 The simulation process of the game

Unexpected events: At the start of the game, it is assumed that the manager faces a new target deadline δ_n, earlier than the project duration as initially proposed. If the project is not completed by this target deadline, a penalty cost will be imposed for each day of overrun. Shortening the entire project to bring the last project activity to completion by the target deadline may be accomplished by the expenditure of money, where necessary, to shorten various activities throughout the network.

The way money is spent (for overtime, additional workers, extra machinery, etc.) is not specified in this game.

Reschedule the project: Each project management team (i.e. the game user) is responsible for scheduling new activity durations, so that the project is completed at the lowest possible cost, where total cost is the sum of activity costs and delay costs. Consequently, the game focuses on the deadline problem of the time/cost trade-off problem, which involves the scheduling of project activities in order to minimize the total cost of the project while meeting a target deadline δ_n. Users have to select new activity modes for a subset of the project activities trying to complete the project schedule on or before the new target project deadline, aiming at minimizing the total project cost. Player decisions will establish new planned durations for some activities and will, therefore, change both the planned completion time of the project and its total cost. Decreasing activity durations will increase activity costs. The maximum activity cost for the project would result if all activities were planned at their shortest duration (the crash duration). Minimum activity cost, on the other hand, results when all activities have their longest duration (the normal duration). The difference between these two costs is the amount of resources that can be influenced by the management team's decisions.

Take decision: Upon a decision made by the user, the game simulates partial fictitious project progress. Since reality is fed with uncertainty, the game simulates uncertainty in the activity durations, leading to a project completion, which might differ from the expected project completion set by the user. These factors beyond the control of the user might mess up their original time and cost estimates of the project, and need to be carefully reviewed in order to bring the project back on track.

Evaluate project progress: After each decision, the computer will simulate the passage of a number of working days (execution phase, from t_i to t_{i+1} in Fig. 3.7) and will provide management with a list of all activities completed in that time period. PSG generates partial intermediate project progress reports indicating where changes in the original schedule took place. These reports, along with the Gantt

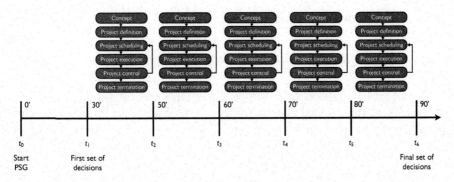

Fig. 3.7 The six decision moments of PSG

chart, must be used by the users to evaluate intermediate project progress and to adapt their previously made decisions. The computer will provide an explanation of any delays or early finishes that may have caused an activity to take a different duration than was scheduled by the project team. Before any set of decisions, the management team can change the scheduled duration for any activity that has not been completed. Obviously, the duration of a completed activity can no longer be altered by a management decision. This cycle of user decisions and project progress is repeated until the project is finished. Figure 3.7 gives a graphical illustration of the six different sets of decision steps in the game with the allocated time that a player receives to prepare his/her decision. The simulation ends after a predefined number of decision steps, within a predefined maximal allowable time limit. The default number of decision steps is equal to six, which need to be made within a 90 min time limit, but this can easily be changed by the teacher of the game.

Because of the large number of activities and huge amount of time/cost data needed during the scheduling task, a computer is used for the analysis. At any time it is possible to save and simulate scenarios before making a periodic decision, to return to the settings of the last decision, or to the settings of former saved scenarios.

3.3.4 Access to PSG Using ProTrack

The Project Scheduling Game can be accessed using the project scheduling tool ProTrack, which is discussed in Chap. 15. The best known solution for a given project can be obtained by submitting the project data to ProTrack's support webpage, using the serial number of the software version (only accessible by the teacher who needs a full version of ProTrack and not by users of the game). Moreover, teachers are encouraged to construct their own PSG data and submit their work on this support page to distribute with other PSG teachers. More details and specific features will be briefly discussed in Sect. 15.6.

3.4 Educational Approach

3.4.1 Simulation Seminar and Target Group

A traditional PSG session consists typically of three parts: a general introduction to the critical path method and the features of the project, the 90-min simulation (see previous section) and a closing part in which the distinct strategies used by the participants are discussed. The game focuses on the characteristics of allocating a scarce nonrenewable resource (money) to establish activity crashing, as well as on all basic project scheduling features (activity networks, earliest and latest start schedules, activity slack, etc.) of a large real-life project as discussed in Chap. 2.

It illustrates the difficulties a project manager faces when reactively scheduling and monitoring a large project. The game is particularly interesting for project managers, project schedulers and project team members and can be played individually or in groups of two or three participants.

3.4.2 Teaching Process

Each project management team should study the starting position and consider alternative courses of action for meeting the new required project completion date. While a complete analysis of the network is not essential at this point, the group should at least identify critical and subcritical paths and carefully investigate activities that are likely to be completed during the first decision report period (see Fig. 3.7). Once a decision has been made, activities completed during that period cannot be changed. During the simulation, the player is continuously confronted with a number of valuable concepts used in project scheduling, such as the earliest activity start/finish, the latest activity start/finish, the activity slack and the deadline slack. He or she must incorporate information with respect to these concepts to make periodic decisions based on a Gantt chart. Figure 3.8 shows the working screen of the player (the Gantt chart) on which decisions can be made. This screen shows:

- Activities of the current critical path of the resulting schedule.
- Possible changes in the activity duration (i.e., the activity time/cost trade-off).
- Activity slack.

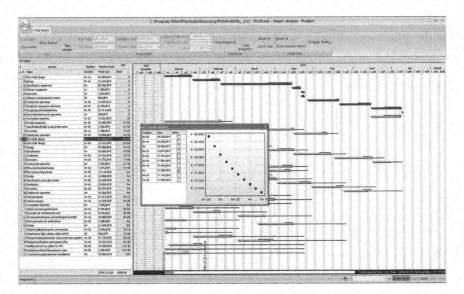

Fig. 3.8 The PSG Gantt chart in ProTrack

- The current decision moment.
- Expected project completion and the corresponding cost of the current schedule.

3.4.3 Performance Evaluation

Players are evaluated on the basis of the total cost of their final schedule. As stated earlier, total project cost is made up of the sum of the delay cost and the planned activity costs. This is illustrated in Fig. 3.9, which shows the complete optimal time/cost profile (the lowest possible cost for each possible completion time). The decreasing cost values when the project completion increases is the result of the time/cost trade-offs in the individual project activities. The increasing cost values from a certain project completion on is due to the penalty that needs to be paid when the project deadline δ_n is exceeded. Due to the combination of these two costs, players who are able to schedule the project within the target deadline δ_n do not necessarily generate the best overall schedule. Indeed, depending on the value of the penalty cost, it can be advantageous to schedule the project with a completion time δ_n^* longer than the target deadline δ_n, resulting in a penalty cost for each day overrun, but at a lower total cost. During the final discussion part of the session, the game players will be confronted with this result. Note that the final result of each participant can only lie on or above the optimal time/cost profile of Fig. 3.9.

3.4.4 Game Discussion

In the discussion following the game, performance of the teams is compared and participants are asked to describe the strategies they have followed. This leads them to a clear understanding of the meaning of the critical path and the impact of crashing activities on the critical path. Confronting the participants with the

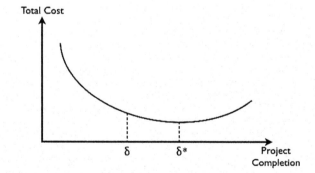

Fig. 3.9 The complete time/cost profile of the PSG project

minimum time/cost profile (as in Fig. 3.9) has proven to be very useful in this discussion.

Comparison of the results of the teams that have developed a clear strategy and those that have adopted a trial and error approach to the scheduling task illustrates the value of project scheduling techniques. Moreover, one typically observes that some teams try to optimize the project schedule over the entire project horizon at each decision phase, whereas other teams tend to focus on the first decision period only. The advantage of the former approach (reaching an optimal schedule) is then weighted against the advantage of the latter (maintaining stability in the project schedule and reaching higher efficiency in scheduling). The discussion may then turn towards the value of sophisticated scheduling in projects with high uncertainty.

The PSG is not unique. A well-known comparable game is CPSim (Piper 2005). CPSim is adapted from an exercise called CAPERTSIM that was developed by North American Aviation, Inc., Autonetics Education and Training Department. CAPERTSIM was available from the IBM SHARE library, and was adapted by the Harvard Business School in 1974 and renamed PLANETS II (*planning and network simulation*). The difference between PSG and the traditional project scheduling games, however, is the opportunity PSG provides to be played with any realistic project network tailored to the needs and wishes of the game players. The PSG can easily be extended to another project by simply changing the input file of the network under study. This makes it possible to tune the training to the participants' needs and to make the game very recognizable to the participant.

3.4.5   PSG as a Research Tool

Although the PSG is mainly described as an educational tool, it can, however, be used as a research tool. Experiments can be easily set up in which project managers schedule a project network with the game software. In these experiments, the software will observe the behavior of the managers and their preferences and strategies followed while repetitively scheduling the model. ProTrack's PSG will monitor and register all actions taken by the participants and provide a log file to the teacher. These log files can be analyzed to detect certain patterns or clusters of strategies leading to a similar output performance. Comparing performances across teams might allow the user to gain better understanding of the value of distinct project scheduling routines, under distinct types of projects and project environments. For example, it will be explored whether some scheduling strategies are more suited in project environments with low or high uncertainty.

The risk of the project can also be changed manually by the teacher of the game. While the participants have no idea about real project durations (which might differ from their chosen activity duration), the teacher can create alternative risk versions for different groups, allowing to investigate the influence of higher risk (activity duration uncertainty) on the overall performance of the different teams.

The introduction of the PSG was originally published in Vanhoucke et al. (2005), and a first research study has led to a paper by Wauters and Vanhoucke (2013). In this recent study, a student experiment based on data obtained from the game played at two universities and two management schools has been carried out. More precisely, a classification of student behaviour has been derived based on the collected data from 439 students who played the game. This experiment served as a basis to derive the most frequently used strategies used by the students. To that purpose, the authors presented a methodology for structuring the data that was made up of 5 components. By means of focus, activity criticality, ranking, intensity and the application of an action, different sets of actions could be applied. In reality, these actions are based on the assessment of two important dimensions, complexity and uncertainty. The appraisal of these two dimensions steered the logic of the proposed solution strategies into a different direction, resulting in two frequently used strategies. One strategy focuses on time, thus attempting to approximate the deadline, whereas the other strategy employs a cost-based focus.

A computer experiment has been carried out and during the analysis of the results, both time and cost aspects were taken into account. Moreover, in order to provide a fair comparison, the level of student effort, i.e. the time and effort the students spend on finding a good solution, was controlled throughout the computer experiment. The main results of an experimental study can be briefly summarized along the following lines. The results indicate that the time-based solution strategy performs particularly well when exceeding the deadline is heavily penalized. Furthermore, this strategy displays a more than competitive behaviour for highly uncertain project environments. On the other hand, the cost-based strategy is the best in class in low penalty environments and for projects containing many time/cost trade-offs. In those environments, the focus on costs and not on nearing the deadline (which is discouraged in the low penalty setting) proves advantageous. Apart from these main conclusions, a sensitivity analysis was carried out. This analysis focused on the sensitivity of the cost performance for a differing level of effort, the structure of the network and a varying degree of the deadline parameter. Increasing the level of effort exhibits a positive effect on the capability of the strategies. The network structure showed no significant impact on the performance of the solution strategies. Finally, both solution strategies showed a decreasing trend of their deadline deviation as the deadline parameter is increased.

3.5   Conclusions

In this chapter, a project scheduling game for the time/cost trade-off scheduling problem, known as the critical path method (CPM), has been presented. The project is a real-life project for a water production center in order to increase the production capacity of purified water. The individual player is presented with the task of scheduling the activities in time, taking into account the total project costs by carefully allocating money to a particular activity. In doing so, the player has six decision moments in which he or she decides about the duration and corresponding cost of each network activity. After the simulation, the total project cost of the resulting schedule is used as a performance evaluation. The ultimate target of the game is to bring the manager in contact with the different concepts of project scheduling in a practical way, to confront the manager with the inherent complexity that is involved in project scheduling, and to create an incentive to rely on algorithmic procedures or at least on state-of-the-art scheduling principles studied at different research institutes. Indeed, the game clearly illustrates that the scheduling phase of the project life cycle involves a series of decisions which requires a good knowledge about basic project scheduling techniques and a thorough understanding of the impact of decisions on the overall performance of the project.

Chapter 4
The VMW Project

Abstract The scheduling of activities over time has gained increasing attention with the development of the Critical Path Method (CPM) and the Program Evaluation and Review Technique (PERT), as discussed in the previous chapters. Since then, a large amount of solution procedures for a wide range of problem types have been proposed in the literature. In the previous chapters, it was implicitly assumed that the schedule objective is time, i.e. the construction of a precedence feasible schedule aiming at minimizing the total project duration. In a practical project setting, there often are many other scheduling objectives (a detailed description of different scheduling objectives is the topic of Chaps. 7 and 8) and consequently, many of the traditional time minimizing PERT/CPM procedures are not able to solve real life problems.

This chapter describes a capacity expansion project at a water production center (WPC) of the Vlaamse Maatschappij voor Watervoorziening (VMW) in Belgium and serves as an illustration of the use of scheduling algorithms and principles in a practical project environment without the presence of limited resources. The project aims at expanding the production capacity of pure water. It will be shown that scheduling the project with certain techniques will improve the financial status of the project. A modified version of the project description has been used for the project scheduling game of Chap. 3.

4.1 Introduction

The Vlaamse Maatschappij voor Watervoorziening (VMW) is a Flemish water distribution company, which covers approximately 50% of Flanders, located in the northern region of Belgium. The VMW services 2.5 million customers with

M. Vanhoucke, *Project Management with Dynamic Scheduling*,
DOI 10.1007/978-3-642-40438-2_4, © Springer-Verlag Berlin Heidelberg 2013

Fig. 4.1 Graphical scheme
of the production process
at the WPC of Kluizen

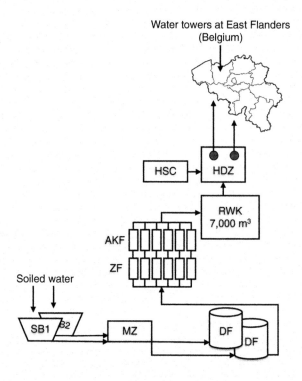

a pipeline network of 27,000 km and a yearly production of 140 billion liters
of water.[1]

This chapter describes the approach used to schedule a project at the water
production center of Kluizen (Belgium), which belongs to the VMW. This center
produces and delivers water by transforming surface water into drinkable water
and by distributing it towards its customers. Therefore, surface water is taken from
the area (with a total surface of $\pm 120 \, \text{km}^2$) around the WPC and is stored in
two open water reservoirs (spaarbekkens, SB1 and SB2) with a total capacity of
$11{,}000{,}000 \, \text{m}^3$. From this point on, a number of different steps are performed in
order to purge the water and make it drinkable. Figure 4.1 displays the different
steps of this production process without going into detail.

The filtering of the surface water consists of a number of filtering steps. These
are, in order of appearance, the micro sieving (microzeef, MZ), the decantation
filtering (decantatiefilter, DF), the filtering with sand (zandfilter, ZF) and the
carbon filtering (actief koolfilter, AKF). Chemical products are added at various
points during this process (e.g. $H_2SO_4, AlCl_3, NaOH, NaOCl$). At the end of
this water treatment process, the pure water is stored in a reservoir with treated
water (reinwaterkelder, RWK) which forms a buffer between the treatment and the

---

[1]Estimates based on data from the year 2003.

pumping phases. During the pumping phases, a number of pumps which are located in a high pressure room (hogedrukzaal, HDZ) disperse the water to the different regions in East Flanders. This HDZ is fed with energy coming from the high voltage cabin (hoogspanningscabine, HSC).

The storage capacity of the RWK amounts to $7.000\,m^3$ while the daily demand of pure water equals $30,000\,m^3$ or more (at peak moments, it amounts to $40,000\,m^3/day$). For this reason, an extension of the storage capacity of pure water is needed (referred to as subproject 1 in the remainder of this chapter). Moreover, forecasts made at the late 1990s of the daily demand indicated an increase to $59,000\,m^3/day$ in 2005 and $65,000\,m^3/day$ in 2013. Since the existing production center (as depicted in Fig. 4.1) then worked at almost 100% capacity, an extension was needed. This observation has led to the idea of building a new production center with a much higher capacity (referred to as subproject 2). Section 4.2 describes these two subprojects in more detail.

4.2 Description of the Project

This section briefly describes the two subprojects of the project at the WPC Kluizen, i.e. subproject 1, "An extension of the storage capacity of treated water" and subproject 2, "An increase of the production capacity to $70,000\,m^3/day$". The first subproject, as described in Sect. 4.2.1, consists of an increase of the storage capacity by building two extra reservoirs for treated water (RWK) which serve as buffers for pure water between the treatment and the pumping phases. In doing so, the WPC will be able to meet the daily demand of the customer much easier. However, it does not lead to the desired increase in the production capacity. In a second subproject, which is described in Sect. 4.2.2, the construction of the new production center must guarantee the desired production capacity of $70,000\,m^3/day$.

4.2.1 Subproject 1: Extension of the Storage Capacity of Treated Water

This first subproject consists of two steps, i.e. the building of the two reservoirs for treated water (RWK) at the production plant itself and the additional activities outside the production plant.

Activities at the Production Plant Itself

In order to increase the storage capacity of pure water, two new reservoirs for treated water (denoted by RWK1 and RWK2 in Fig. 4.2) have to be built, each with a

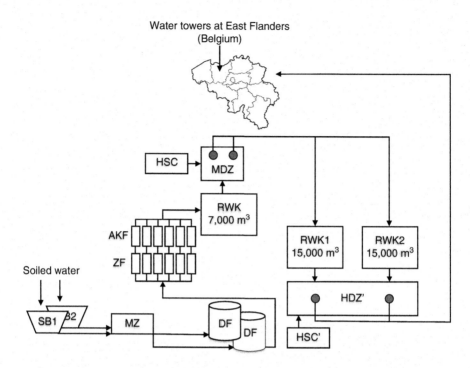

Fig. 4.2 Graphical scheme of the production process at the WPC of Kluizen and the new storage extensions (RWK1, RWK2, HDZ′ and HSC′)

capacity of 15,000 m³. Pumps in a new high pressure room (HDZ′) will assure the circulation of the pure water towards the customer, while the energy supply has to come from a new high voltage cabine (HSC′). The existing pumps located at the HDZ will be modified (in fact, they will be replaced by pumps with middle pressure capacity (middendrukzaal, MDZ)) in order to assure the flow of water towards the new reservoirs. Constructing pipes between these installations will complete this first step of subproject 1. Figure 4.2 gives a graphical representation of this first extension. Due to the new reservoirs for treated water RWK1 and RWK2, it will be much easier to satisfy peak moments in demand. The newly established installation will still not be able to produce much more than 30,000 m³/day.

A list of the detailed activities of these steps is depicted in Table 4.1 of the appendix. Each activity has an ID number and a task name. The duration and the cost of each activity are also given in this table. Figure 4.3 gives a network representation of the different tasks of this subproject. Note that the precedence relations between the activities are of the finish-start type (FS) with a time-lag of zero, unless it is indicated otherwise in the appendix. The total estimated cost of this step amounts to €7,483,905.51 or 301,900,000 BEF (BEF is the old currency used in Belgium at the time of the project baseline schedule construction with €1 = 40.3399 BEF).

Table 4.1 Description of the first step of subproject 1

Task	Task name	Duration (weeks)	Cost (BEF)
New RWK1 and RWK2 and HDZ (266,900,000 BEF)			
	Architecture		
1	Obtain building license	1	
2	Find contractor (available)	1	
3	Obtain environmental license	7	
4	Execution of work	130	196,900,000
	Equipment		
5	Design (available)	1	
6	Specification	8	
7	Public tender	16	
	Equipment		
8	Fabrication	50	
9	Execution of work	40	70,000,000
HSC (10,000,000 BEF)			
10	Negotiations with power distribution company	4	3,000,000
	Additional work on cables		
11	Design	10	
12	Specification	8	
13	Request offer	8	
	Realisation		
14	Fabrication	40	
15	Execution of work	12	7,000,000
16	Coming into operation	52	
Updating existing HDZ to MDZ (10,000,000 BEF)			
17	Design	10	
18	Specification	10	
19	Request offer	10	
	Realisation		
20	Fabrication	45	
21	Execution of work	26	10,000,000
22	Coming into operation	15	
Constructing pipes between installations (15,000,000 BEF)			
23	Design	26	
24	Specification	26	
25	Realisation	26	15,000,000
26	Coming into operation	10	

Activities Outside the Production Plant

The activities outside the production plant mainly focus on an optimal supply of the pure water to the customer. Therefore, a new pipeline has to be constructed from the WPC Kluizen to its customers (towns in the northern region of Flanders such as Eeklo and Waarschoot). Moreover, at some regions, WPC Kluizen is obliged to

Fig. 4.3 Network
representation of the work
completed at the production
plant WPC Kluizen

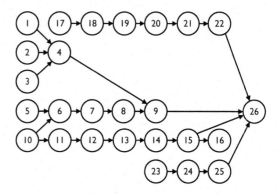

deliver a certain amount of water to another water distribution company TMVW
(Tussengemeentelijke Maatschappij Voor Watervoorziening) while at other regions
(e.g. Zelzate) the delivery is vice versa (WPC Kluizen receives an amount of water).
The main steps of this subproject can be summarized as follows[2]:

- The construction of a new pipeline between Kluizen and Eeklo.
- The delivery of water to the TMVW (i.e. building a measuring station and fitting
  it in the existing communication system).
- The construction of a pumping station (in order to increase the pressure of the
  water) at Zelzate.
- The construction of a pumping station (in order to increase the pressure of the
  water) that supplies a water tower in Eeklo.
- The construction of a pumping station (in order to increase the pressure of the
  water) in Waarschoot.

As before, a list of the detailed activities of these steps is depicted in Table 4.2
of the appendix. Figure 4.4 gives a network representation of the different tasks of
the second step of subproject 1. It has a total estimated cost of €5,032,238.55 or
203,000,000 BEF.

4.2.2   Subproject 2: Increase of the Production Capacity

The construction of the new production center with a desired production capacity
of 70,000 m³/day is a capital-intensive project with a total estimated cost equal
to ±€13,150,751.49 or 530,500,000 BEF. It mainly consists of three steps, i.e.
building the carbon filters (actief koolfilters, AKF), establishing an alternative
system for the decantation filtering and the treatment of waste.

In a first step, 12 new carbon filters (denoted by AKF in Fig. 4.5) will be built
in two phases. In a first phase, three carbon filters will be built, while in a second
phase the remaining nine carbon filters will be installed.

---

[2]Eeklo, Kluizen, Waarschoot and Zelzate are small villages or towns in the Eastern part of Flanders.

Table 4.2 Description of the second step of subproject 1

Task	Task name	Duration (weeks)	Cost (BEF)
Pipes from Kluizen to Eeklo (170,000,000 BEF)			
27	First draft design	26	
28	Find permission and contractor	70	
29	Construct pipeline	52	170,000,000
30	Coming into operation	4	
Water supply to TMVW (1,500,000 BEF)			
31	Design	4	
32	Find permission	26	
33	Connection electricity	26	
	Equipment		
34	Specification equipment	12	
35	Delivery equipment	26	1,000,000
36	Execution	10	
37	Fitting in communication system	2	500,000
38	Coming into operation	2	
Constructing pumps at Zelzate (2,500,000 BEF)			
39	Design for connection electricity	4	
40	Connection electricity	10	400,000
41	Design	1	
42	Specification	8	
43	Request offer	8	1,500,000
44	Delivery	30	
45	Execution	15	600,000
46	Coming into operation	4	
Constructing pumps and building water tower at Eeklo (24,000,000 BEF)			
47	First draft design	8	
48	Design	15	
49	File building license	5	
50	Request building license	26	
51	Specification	10	
52	Public tender	18	
53	File environmental license	5	
54	Notification VLAREM	1	
55	Realisation	75	16,000,000
56	Design	4	
57	Specification	10	
58	Request offer	8	
	Execution		
59	Fabrication	30	
60	Equipment	20	8,000,000
61	Coming into operation	8	

(continued)

Table 4.2 (continued)

Task	Task name	Duration (weeks)	Cost (BEF)
Constructing pumps at Waarschoot (5,000,000 BEF)			
62	First draft design	8	
63	Design	15	
64	File constructing license	5	
65	Request constructing license	26	
66	Specification	10	
67	Public tender	18	
68	File environmental license	5	
69	Notification VLAREM	1	
70	Realisation	52	
71	Design	4	
72	Specification	10	
73	Request offer	8	
	Execution		
74	Fabrication	30	
75	Equipment	10	5,000,000
76	Coming into operation	4	

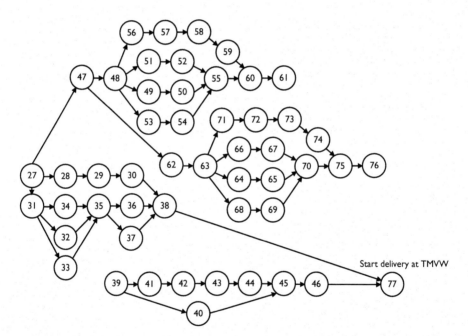

Fig. 4.4 Network representation of the work completed outside the production plant WPC Kluizen

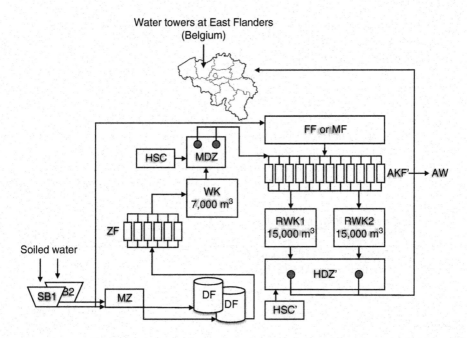

Fig. 4.5 Graphical scheme of subproject 2: Increase in capacity

In a second step, an alternative technique for the rather old-fashioned decantation filtering step (see Fig. 4.1) has to be selected. The two alternatives are:

- Membrane processes (membraanfilter, MF) employ a semi-permeable (selective) membrane and a driving force (pressure, concentration, etc.) across the membrane to separate target constituents from a feed liquid. Water passes through the membrane, forming a treated water stream (permeate) and leaving behind the other constituents in a concentrate. Different types of membrane processes can remove dissolved and colloidal constituents in the size range of 0.0001–$1\,\mu$m. The commercially available membrane processes include micro-filtration, ultra-filtration, reverse osmosis, membrane electrolysis and diffusion dialysis. The technologies operate differently, and each is best suited for specific applications. They are all useful for separation of molecular mixtures.
- Air flotation techniques (flotatiefilter, FF) are used to remove insoluble contaminants from a solvent. The removal is based on the adhesion of dissolved air at the contaminants, after which it will come to the surface of the liquid.

The total cost of this step amounts to €7,560,752.50 or 305,000,000 BEF for the first alternative and €5,577,604.31 or 225,000,000 BEF for the second alternative. This chapter only considers the first alternative. Similar results with respect to the proposed schedules of Sect. 4.3 have been obtained in the case of the second alternative.

The third step deals with the sludge treatment (afvalverwerking, AW) and has a total estimated cost of €991,574.09 or 40,000,000 BEF. The sludge is disposed of in containers after being thickened and desiccated.

The results of subproject 2 are depicted in Fig. 4.5. This figure reveals that the original reservoir for treated water (RWK) with a capacity of 7,000 m^3 now serves as a reservoir for nontreated water (waterkelder, WK) since the AKF is removed from the picture. Consequently, the water stored in this WK still has to pass the AKF' step before being stored in RWK1 or RWK2. In the long run, the new water production center must replace the old production center of Fig. 4.1. When this is the case, the nontreated water will flow directly from SB1 and SB2 to the first filtering step, i.e. step FF or MF. A detailed activity list of these steps is depicted in Tables 4.3 and 4.4

Table 4.3 Description of the first step of subproject 2

Task	Task name	Duration (weeks)	Cost (BEF)
Carbon filters (AKF), phase 1 (85,500,000 BEF)			
78	First draft design AKF (2 alternatives)	4	
79	Design AKF	10	
80	Specification AKF	8	
81	Building license procedure	26	500,000
82	Public tender	10	25,000,000
83	Execution building reservoir for AKF	52	
84	Design carbon filter	10	
85	Determine number of filters	0	
86	Specification	6	
87	Request offer	8	
	Equipment AKF		
88	Fabrication materials	26	
89	Execution of work	26	20,000,000
90	Request offer	8	
	Carbon filters		
91	Construction filters	40	
92	Delivery filters	2	35,000,000
93	Delivery Carbon	2	5,000,000
94	Coming into operation AKF	8	
Carbon filters (AKF), phase 2 (100,000,000 BEF)			
95	Determine number of carbon filters	0	
96	Specification	4	
97	Request offer	10	
	Equipment AKF		
98	Fabrication materials	26	
99	Execution of work	26	10,000,000
100	Request offer	10	
	Carbon filters		
101	Construction filters	40	
102	Delivery filters	2	90,000,000
103	Coming into operation AKF	4	

Table 4.4 Description of the second step of subproject 2

Task	Task name	Duration (weeks)		Cost (BEF)	
		Alt. 1	Alt. 2	Alt. 1	Alt. 2
	Water treatment (membrane or air flotation) (305,000,000 BEF for alternative 1 and 225,000,000 BEF for alternative 2)				
104	First draft design flotation filtering	0.2	26		
105	First draft design and specification of architecture	20	52		
106	Public tender	14	18		
107	Preparation building license	10	26		
108	Request building license	26	26		
109	Preparation environmental license	10	26		
110	Request environmental license	26	26		
111	Realization architecture for flotation or membrane technique	156	104	200,000,000	40,000,000
112	Design for flotation/membrane technique	20	26		
113	Specification	10	10		
114	Request offer	8	10		
	Equipment for flotation/membrane technique				
115	Fabrication	52	52		
116	Execution of work	52	52	70,000,000	150,000,000
	Connection installations				
117	Design	26	26		
118	Specification	26	26		

(continued)

Table 4.4 (continued)

Task	Task name	Duration (weeks)	Cost (BEF)
119	Realisation	26	20,000,000
	Automation		
120	Design	20	
121	Request offer automation	12	
122	Realization equipment	40	15,000,000
123	Coming into operation (flotation or membrane technique)	12	
Waste treatment (40,000,000 BEF)			
124	First draft design	15	
125	Design	40	
126	Specification	15	
127	Obtain environmental and building license	26	
128	Design and specification	16	
129	Realisation architecture	52	20,000,000
130	Realisation	40	
131	Execution of work	26	20,000,000
	Connect installations		
132	Design	26	
133	Specification	26	
134	Realisation	26	
135	Coming into operation (installation)	10	
136	Coming into operation (extra production)	52	

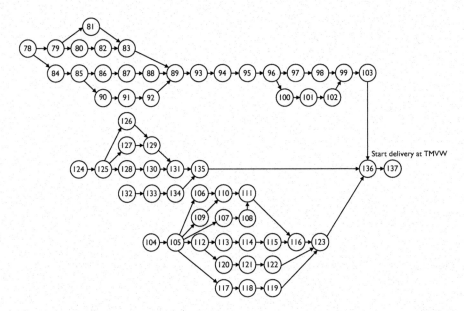

Fig. 4.6 Network representation of the three steps to increase the production capacity

of the appendix. Figure 4.6 gives a network representation of the different tasks of this project.

4.2.3   Work Breakdown Structure

Figure 4.7 shows a Work Breakdown Structure for the VMW project up to the work package level. Each work package can be further subdivided in the individual project activities as discussed earlier in Chap. 2. The activities have not been displayed in this picture but can be found in the tables of the appendix.

This illustrative WBS was used to assign responsibilities to the work items. The project manager had an overall view on the project, while two individual persons were responsible for the "storage extension" and "increase production capacity" subprojects.

4.3   Analysis of the Project

4.3.1   Features of the Project

The project under study is the subject of a widely discussed topic in the project scheduling literature. It involves the scheduling of project activities in order to maximize *the net present value (npv)* of the project in the absence of resource constraints.

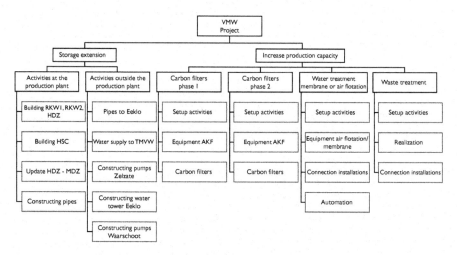

Fig. 4.7 The WBS for the VMW project up to the work package level

This observation finds its motivation by the following statement by Herroelen et al. (1997):

> When the financial aspects of project management are taken into consideration, there is a decided preference for the maximization of the net present value of the project as the more appropriate objective, and this preference increases with the project duration.

Since the project is a very capital-intensive project (total estimated cost exceeds the value of €25,000,000.00) with a total project duration of approximately 7 years, the maximization of the net present value seems the appropriate objective function. This problem is classified in the project scheduling literature as the max-*npv* problem and can be formulated as follows:

$$\text{Minimize} \sum_{i=1}^{137} c_i e^{-\alpha(s_i + d_i)} \tag{4.1}$$

subject to

$$s_i + l_{ij} \leq s_j \qquad \forall (i, j) \in A \tag{4.2}$$

$$s_0 = 0 \tag{4.3}$$

$$s_{137} \leq 362 \tag{4.4}$$

$$s_i \in int^+ \qquad \forall i \in N \tag{4.5}$$

where the variables d_i, c_i and s_i denote the duration, the cost at the completion of the activity and the start time, respectively, of an activity i. The set of arcs, A, represents the precedence constraints of a project (with a time-lag l_{ij} as defined in Sect. 2.2.3) while α represents the discount rate. Note that the minimal time-lags of the project equal zero ($FS_{i,j}^{min} = 0$ and consequently, $l_{ij} = d_i$) unless otherwise indicated. Extra arcs are added to the project for activities with ready times $r_i \neq 0$, i.e. $FS_{0,i}^{min} = r_i$ or $l_{0i} = r_i$. The objective function in Eq. 4.1 maximizes the net present value by compounding the value of each activity towards the beginning of the project as follows: $c_i e^{-\alpha(s_i+d_i)}$. More details on the way cash flows are discounted using a discount rate α will be given later in Sect. 7.3.3. The constraint set given in Eq. 4.2 maintains the precedence relations with time-lag l_{ij} among the activities. Equation 4.3 forces the dummy start activity 0 to start at time zero and Eq. 4.4 limits the project duration to the project deadline of 362 weeks (in fact, the project started at February 1, 1999 and had to be finished by the start of 2006). Equation 4.5 force the variables to be nonnegative integer values.

For more information and a solution procedure for the max-*npv* problem, the reader is referred to Vanhoucke et al. (2001b) (minimal time-lag precedence constraints) and Vanhoucke (2006a) (maximal time-lag precedence constraints). In Chap. 7, the maximization of the net present value in project scheduling is discussed in detail within the presence of resource constraints.

Figure 4.8 displays an activity-on-the-node network representation of the entire project. Remark that the nodes with a cost $c_i < 0$ are colored in black. Grey nodes represent activities that are required to finish as early as possible. Remark that these activities always present an end activity of a subset of connected activities, which has to finish as soon as possible.

In the remainder of this chapter, alternative schedules will be proposed, each having a different scheduling objective. In Sect. 4.3.2, the activities are scheduled as soon as possible and the net present value is calculated. Section 4.3.3 presents some modifications to the schedule in order to increase the net present value of the project. Section 4.3.4 proposes a robust schedule that combines the advantages of both schedules.

4.3.2 Earliest Start Schedule

Figure 4.9 displays illustrative Gantt charts for activities 39–46 (constructing a pump at Zelzate), which propose schedules in which all activities are performed as soon as possible (Fig. 4.9a, an earliest start schedule (ESS)) and as late as possible (Fig. 4.9b, a latest start schedule (LSS)). The bars represent the schedule of each activity in time while the lines are used to represent the slack of each activity. This activity slack is calculated under the assumption that activity 46 of Fig. 4.8 still has to be performed as soon as possible. Consequently, an activity with label "as soon as possible" has a slack of zero since it is assumed that a shift in these activities is not allowed.

The earliest start schedule of the complete project has a net present value of €−4,358,606.90 of −175,825,766.24 BEF (an illustrative weekly discount rate $\alpha = 0.01\%$ is used). The schedule has the advantage that there are still quite a number of activities that can be shifted forward in time (towards the deadline)

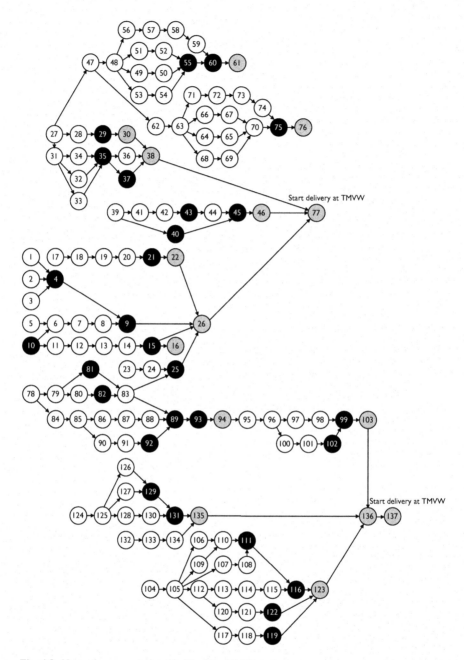

Fig. 4.8 Network representation (AoN) of the VMW project

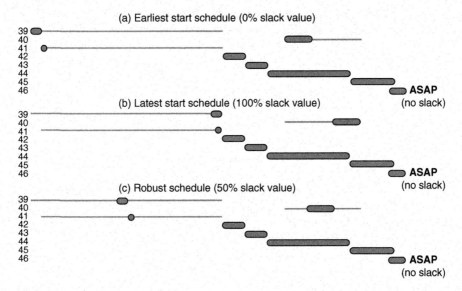

Fig. 4.9 Three different schedules for a subpart of subproject "constructing a pump at Zelzate" (see Table 4.2). (**a**) Earliest start schedule (0% slack value); (**b**) Latest start schedule (100% slack value); (**c**) Robust schedule (50% slack value)

without violating the project deadline. The length of the shift is represented by the grey lines in the Gantt charts of Fig. 4.9. This means that, when something unexpected happens (and it always does), which causes delays in the activities, there is a chance that the project deadline of 362 weeks (at the beginning of 2006) will still be met. This is, of course, not true for delays in activities scheduled on the critical path (given the project deadline δ_n of 362 weeks).

4.3.3   Maximizing the Net Present Value

In Sect. 4.3.1, it has been shown that the project can be categorized as a max-*npv* problem that aims at scheduling projects in time to maximize the net present value. This net present value scheduling objective relies on the intuitive idea that positive cash flows should be scheduled as early as possible while negative cash flows should be scheduled as late as possible within the precedence constraints. Indeed, it is known from financial theory that the time value of money can play an important role in decision making processes. As a consequence, a euro received today is more valuable than a euro to be received in some future time period, since the euro today can be invested in order to earn interest.

With this in mind, a schedule is proposed in which all activities for which $c_i < 0$ are scheduled as late as possible within the precedence constraints, without delaying the activities with a label as soon as possible. This leads to the illustrative Gantt chart of Fig. 4.9b in which all activities are shifted towards the end of the grey line. In doing so, the grey activities are still scheduled as soon as possible, as required.

This schedule has a net present value of €−4,173,596.31 of −168,362,457.85 BEF, which constitutes an *npv* increase of €185,010.85 when applying the second schedule. Despite this gain in the net present value, the proposed schedule is very sensitive to unexpected events during the project. Almost every activity has been scheduled as late as possible, which may cause an increase in the project deadline if one of these activities will be delayed.

As a summary, this section illustrates that the quality of the baseline schedule depends on the scheduling objectives set by the project manager. In Chaps. 7 and 8, various scheduling objectives will be discussed in detail. In the next section, an approach that combines the advantages of both schedules is described. This schedule results in a relatively high net present value, which does not rapidly run into trouble when something unexpected happens.

4.3.4 Robust Schedule

Since uncertainty is what typifies projects, a new schedule is proposed that combines the advantages of both former approaches of Sects. 4.3.2 and 4.3.3. In Sect. 4.3.2, all activities are scheduled as soon as possible, while the activities of the schedule of Sect. 4.3.3 are scheduled at their latest finish times, leaving no slack at all. In the new proposed schedule, the activities with $c_i < 0$ are delayed towards their latest finish times, under the restriction that each activity still needs a fraction of its slack of the earliest start schedule. In doing so, the philosophy of maximizing the net present value is combined with the idea of providing the activities with sufficient slack in order to prevent the violation of the project deadline when something unexpected happens.

More specific, the slack is calculated for each activity as the difference of the earliest finish time and latest finish time schedule (the grey lines as shown in Fig. 4.9). Then, a slack value is determined for each activity, which is a fraction of the original slack. Finally, each activity is shifted, starting from its earliest finish time, as far as possible towards its latest finish, taking the slack value into account. This process is repeated for different slack values resulting in different scheduling scenarios.

In the bottom schedule of Fig. 4.9, the activities have been shifted towards their latest finish time (in order to increase the net present value of activities 40, 43 and 45). Each activity has a slack value equal to 50% of the original grey lines of the top schedule. In doing so, the net present value of this subproject increases and the schedule can still handle some unexpected things (such as activity delays or any other unexpected event).

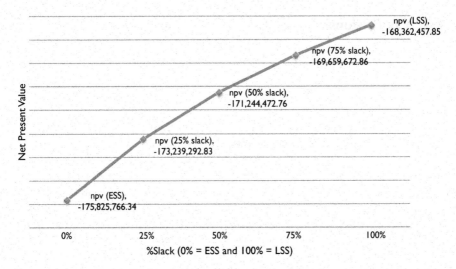

Fig. 4.10 The net present values (in BEF) for different schedules with different degrees of the %Slack

Figure 4.10 shows the different net present values of the project under different schedules. The net present value for the %Slack = 0% corresponds to the Earliest Start Schedule (ESS) of Sect. 4.3.2 (with a minimal *npv*) while the net present value for the %Slack = 100% corresponds to the Latest Start Schedule (LSS) of section schedule 4.3.3 (with a maximal *npv*). The values in-between correspond to schedules with a net present value between these two extremes. The fact that all net present values are negative does not mean that the project has to be rejected. In the project, only negative cash flows have been considered (from the perspective of the owner of the project). The resulting positive cash flows (once the project will be completed) are known to exceed the total investment costs and, consequently, are not considered in the schedule of the project.

Remark that only activities that have a positive slack in Fig. 4.8 have been shifted towards the deadline. It is also possible to allow a shift for other activities, such as the activities with label as soon as possible. For example shifting the finish time of activity 61 and 76 to the deadline will not lead to an increase of the project duration. These shifts would lead to a further increase in the net present value. The project data (in ProTrack format) and a full net present value analysis (in MS Excel) of the real project data can be downloaded from www.or-as.be/books. As a summary, this section illustrates that the optimization of the net present value can be in conflict with the protection of the total project duration. Therefore, the insertion of extra slack, as a kind of safety time buffer, protects the project duration from unexpected changes in the activity duration estimates without harming the net present value too much. In Chap. 10, a formalized way of buffer insertions in project baseline schedules will be discussed in detail.

4.4   Conclusions

This chapter discussed a project scheduling problem at the Vlaamse Maatschappij voor Watervoorziening in Kluizen, Belgium. This project aims at expanding the production capacity of water in East Flanders. It is a very capital-intensive project with a duration of approximately 7 years.

Since the net present value lies at the very heart of every budgeting and investment problem, it has been shown that the net present value is schedule-dependent. In fact, both an earliest and latest start schedule have been proposed where each schedule has its own advantages. The former performs worst with respect to the net present value but is less sensitive to changes in the original activity durations. The latter has the opposite effect: it maximizes the net present value but runs into trouble as soon as an activity is delayed. With this in mind, some schedules have been proposed, which are combinations of the two in order to maximize the net present value of the project under the restriction that each activity must have a certain amount of slack, if possible. While this chapter mainly served as an illustration of the relevance of a scheduling objective different from the project time minimization, Chaps. 7 and 8 elaborate on various other scheduling objective extensions for projects that need to be executed within the presence of limited resource availabilities. Moreover, this chapter also illustrated that a clever use of safety time buffers is needed in order to protect the project deadline from unexpected changes in the duration estimates of the activities. Buffer insertion techniques to protect the project deadline from variation in the project progress are discussed in Chap. 10.

4.5   Appendix

This appendix gives a detailed description of the activities of the different steps in the project and technical details about the precedence relations. The files can be downloaded from www.or-as.be/books and can be opened in the ProTrack software tool (see Chap. 15). Note that all precedence relations are minimal finish-start relations with a time-lag of zero and there are no ready times, except in cases where it is indicated.

Table 4.1 displays the activities of the first step (activities at the production plant) of subproject 1 consisting of (1) building RWK1, RWK2 and HDZ', (2) building HSC', (3) updating existing HDZ to MDZ and (4) constructing pipes as described in Sect. 4.2.1. All relations are of the $FS_{i,j}^{\min} = 0$ type except for $FS_{4,9}^{\min} = -30$, $FS_{9,26}^{\min} = -8$, $FS_{21,22}^{\min} = -10$ and $FS_{22,26}^{\min} = -8$. All ready times $r_i = 0$ except for $r_3 = 4$, $r_6 = 11$, $r_{11} = 53$, $r_{17} = 43$, $r_{19} = 63$ and $r_{23} = 46$. This step has a total estimated cost of €7,483,905.51 = 301,900,000 BEF.

The details of the second step (activities outside the production plant) of subproject 1 are shown in Table 4.2. It consists of (1) constructing pipes from

Kluizen to Eeklo, (2) the water supply to TMVW, (3) constructing pumps at Zelzate, (4) constructing pumps and building a water tower at Eeklo and (5) building pumps at Waarschoot as described in Sect. 4.2.1 with a total estimated cost of €5,032,238.55 = 203,000,000 BEF. All relations are of the $FS_{i,j}^{min} = 0$ type except for $FS_{27,31}^{min} = 26$, $FS_{40,45}^{min} = -4$, $SS_{47,62}^{min} = 10$, $FS_{48,56}^{min} = 36$, $FS_{55,60}^{min} = -8$, $FS_{63,71}^{min} = 20$ and $FS_{70,75}^{min} = -8$. All ready times $r_i = 0$ except for $r_{31} = 73$, $r_{34} = 102$, $r_{37} = 44$, $r_{40} = 92$, $r_{42} = 70$ and $r_{47} = 35$.

The list of activities of subproject 2 (increase of the production capacity) is shown in Tables 4.3 and 4.4. Table 4.3 consists of building carbon filters in (1) phase 1 and (2) phase 2 as described in Sect. 4.2.2 while Table 4.4 consists of subproject 2 consisting of (3) the treatment of water and (4) the treatment of waste as described in Sect. 4.2.2. The total estimated costs amount to €13,150,751.16 = 530,500,000 BEF for the first alternative (membrane processes) and €11,167,603.29 = 450,500,000 BEF for the second alternative (air flotation techniques, this second alternative is not treated in this chapter since it would lead to the same conclusions with respect to the schedule alternatives of Fig. 4.10). All relations are of the $FS_{i,j}^{min} = 0$ type except for $FS_{83,89}^{min} = -10$, $FS_{94,95}^{min} = 52$, $FS_{103,136}^{min} = -40$, $FS_{111,116}^{min} = -26$ and $FS_{129,131}^{min} = -12$. All ready times $r_i = 0$ except for $r_{82} = 42$, $r_{84} = 32$, $r_{85} = 106$, $r_{95} = 259$, $r_{105} = 53$, $r_{106} = 70$, $r_{120} = 205$, $r_{124} = 149$, $r_{132} = 205$ and $r_{136} = 308$.

Chapter 5
Schedule Risk Analysis

Abstract The interest in activity sensitivity from both the academics and the practitioners lies in the need to focus a project manager's attention on those activities that influence the performance of the project. When management has a certain feeling of the relative sensitivity of the various activities on the project objective, a better management focus and a more accurate response during project tracking or control should positively contribute to the overall performance of the project.

The technique known as Schedule Risk Analysis (SRA) connects the risk information of project activities to the baseline schedule and provides sensitivity information of individual project activities as a way to assess the potential impact of uncertainty on the final project duration and cost.

5.1 Introduction

Since the introduction of the well-known PERT and CPM techniques in the late 1950s in project scheduling, research on measuring a project's sensitivity has increasingly received attention from both practitioners and academics. This interest is inspired by the observation that a schedule obtained by the PERT/CPM principles assumes that the durations and precedence relations of the project activities are known with certainty. Reality, however, is flavored with uncertainty, which renders the critical path method inapplicable for many real life projects. Consequently, despite its relevance in practice, the PERT/CPM approach often leads to under-estimating the total project duration, which obviously results in time overruns in practice. This occurs for the following reasons:

- The activity durations in the critical path method are single point estimates that do not adequately address the uncertainty inherent to activities. The PERT method extends this to a three point estimate, but still relies on a strict predefined way of analyzing the critical path.

M. Vanhoucke, *Project Management with Dynamic Scheduling*,
DOI 10.1007/978-3-642-40438-2_5, © Springer-Verlag Berlin Heidelberg 2013

- Estimates about time and cost are predictions for the future, and human beings often tend to be optimistic about it or, on the contrary, often add some reserve safety to protect themselves against unexpected events.
- The topological structure of a network often implies extra risk at points where parallel activities merge into a single successor activity.

Motivated by the common knowledge that the traditional critical path analysis gives an optimistic project duration estimate, measuring the project sensitivity and the ability to forecast the final duration during its execution have become key parameters for project managers. The remainder of this chapter puts a strong focus on the sensitivity of a project's duration as a result of variability in the individual activity durations and not on the cost sensitivity of project activities. Obviously, a risk analysis can also be performed on the cost dimension of a project in order to detect the cost sensitivity of individual project activities on the total cost outline of a project. Since the total activity cost is mostly a weighted sum of its required resources, Sect. 7.6 elaborates on the cost calculations of project activities. Using the cost calculations presented there, the variations of activity durations discussed in the current chapter have an immediate effect on the total activity cost, resulting in cost sensitivity information of the project activities.

Measuring the duration sensitivity of project activities is referred to as *Schedule Risk Analysis* (SRA, Hulett (1996)), which can be considered as an extended version of the PERT/CPM scheduling principles towards a higher degree of uncertainty. Consequently, throughout this chapter, it is assumed that project scheduling and risk analysis need to be integrated for projects lying in quadrant 2 of the project mapping Fig. 1.4.

The outline of this chapter can be summarized as follows. Section 5.2 reviews the four basic steps of a schedule risk analysis study and highlights the central role of the baseline project schedule. In Sect. 5.3, four different sensitivity measures to calculate the duration sensitivity of project activities are discussed. Section 5.4 shows an illustrative example and discusses strengths and weaknesses of these activity sensitivity measures. In Sect. 5.5, the relevance of SRA is put in a practical project tracking and performance measurement setting, and general conclusions of a research study are drawn. Section 5.6 gives a chapter summary and draws general conclusions.

5.2   Schedule Risk Analysis

In this section, the four steps of a successful schedule risk analysis are described. Figure 5.1 gives a graphical overview of an SRA study, which will be outlined into detail along the following paragraphs.

The first step requires a scheduling phase to construct a baseline schedule that serves as a point of reference during the three remaining steps. In a second step,

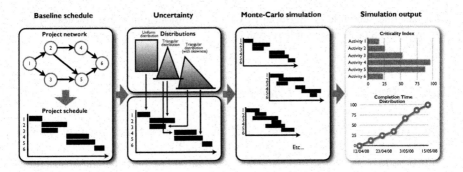

Fig. 5.1 The four steps of a schedule risk analysis

uncertainty needs to be defined resulting in activity duration range estimates. The third step requires an extensive Monte-Carlo simulation run to simulate project progress based on the uncertainty estimates. In a final step, results are reported through sensitivity measures, which require knowledge and understanding of their meaning as well as interpretation for the specific project. This is an important step since metrics without understanding lead to useless results. Beware to always interpret the results of a schedule risk analysis in the light of the characteristics of the project under study.

In the following four subsections, these four steps will be discussed in detail.

5.2.1   Step 1. Baseline Scheduling

When appropriate methods are chosen and the uncertainty of their result is estimated, then the result may be compared to some expected outcome, or to a guideline, standard or baseline level. Both the PERT and CPM methods calculate the shortest path of a project network, the critical path, based on the network logic and the activity duration estimates made by the project manager. However, since estimates are often, if not always, subject to a margin of error, people feel more comfortable with a range of possible project outcomes rather than with a single point estimate like the critical path length. Moreover, the black-and-white view of the CPM methods on the critical activities should be more refined since noncritical (critical) activities have the potential to become critical (noncritical) during the progress of the project.

Consequently, the project baseline schedule serves as a point of reference to which the simulated real project progress of step 3 is compared to. Although it is generally accepted that it is very unlikely that everything will go according to plan, the baseline schedule plays a central role in a schedule risk analysis and the lack of it would lead to incomparable data or even biased results. The construction

of a baseline schedule is the topic of Chap. 2 (without renewable resources) and
Chaps. 7 and 8 (with renewable resources).

5.2.2   Step 2. Risk and Uncertainty

Risk management requires analytical skills and basic knowledge of statistics, which
is often perceived as mathematically complex and sometimes theoretical and far
from practice. However, a basic understanding of probability and distribution
functions allows the project manager to better estimate the effects of unexpected
events on the project outcome. The level of detail of an SRA can be varied according
to the level of expertise in mathematics and statistics, as described along the
following lines.

- Statistical expert: Formulas for statistical distribution functions and their cumulative counterparts need to be known and understood.
- Basic knowledge of statistics: A basic knowledge about the statistical terminology and the willingness to rely on easy-to-use software tools like Microsoft Excel
  or graphical supported risk distribution tools allow the project manager to easily
  set up a schedule risk analysis. The use of basic three-point estimates for risk as
  an easy approximate alternative for the complex statistical distributions makes
  schedule risk analysis understandable to a broad audience.
- Statistics for dummies: The classification of project activities in easy-to-
  understand and well-defined risk classes brings the schedule risk analysis
  technique to the work floor accessible for people who have never heard about
  any statistical analysis.

These three levels of statistical expertise, and their impact on the way SRA is
done, are briefly outlined in the following three paragraphs.

Statistical Expertise: An expert in statistics is expected to have a profound
knowledge of the formulas and characteristics of statistical distribution functions.
Once the parameters of these functions are known, one can easily transform any
distribution function into a cumulative distribution function (CDF), which allows
the generation of a random number from this function. Consider, as an example,
the use of an exponential distribution. The cumulative distribution function of
a random variable X that follows an exponential distribution can be given by
$P(X \leq x) = 1 - e^{-\lambda x}$ with $\frac{1}{\lambda}$ the mean of the exponential distribution. When u is used
as a parameter to denote the cumulative probability $P(X \leq x)$, which obviously lies
between 0 and 1, one can have:

$$u = 1 - e^{-\lambda x} \rightarrow x = -\frac{1}{\lambda} ln(1 - u)$$

u can be replaced by a random generated number from the interval $[0,1[$, obtained by e.g. the RAND() function in Microsoft Excel, which leads to a randomly generated number from an exponential distribution with an average equal to $\frac{1}{\lambda}$ (see Sect. 5.2.3).

The validity of this exact distribution approach in reality is often questionable due to uniqueness of the project or lack of data about the specific probability distributions. However, the method can be used in research environments where the influence of various project parameters on the project outcome is measured under different scenarios by varying the parameters of well-known statistical probability distributions.

Basic Statistical Knowledge: Risk is often measured through a degree of skewness as a measure of the asymmetry of the probability distribution of a real-valued random variable. The skewness measures can be easily used to express risk as follows:

- No risk: the activity entails no risk and the duration is a single point estimate (i.e. the estimate used in the baseline schedule).
- Triangular distribution

  - Symmetric: The activity is subject to risk within a certain range, with worst case and best case scenarios symmetric above and below the average.
  - Skewed to the right: The activity is subject to risk within a certain range, where activity delays are more likely than early activity durations.
  - Skewed to the left: The activity is subject to risk within a certain range, where early activity durations are more likely than activity delays.

Dummy in Statistics: When statistical knowledge is not available by risk analysts, a simple risk classification to classify project activities into a small set of predefined risk categories representing relative distributions often is a valuable alternative. Each distribution has a certain class name and a well-defined meaning of risk, and each activity can be assigned to each of these classes while a software simulation engine does the rest and provides risk measures for each individual activity.

An example of a risk classification is given below. The reader should note that both the names and the meaning of each risk class are only for illustrative purposes, and can vary along the characteristics of the project, the culture of the company, the wishes and needs of the project team, and many more. Moreover, each risk class is linked to a certain probability distribution, and consequently, these risk classes serve as easy-to-understand tools to define probability distributions that will be used during the Monte-Carlo simulation runs.

- Variation: The activity time estimate is quite reliable, but might be subject to little unexpected changes.
- Foreseen Uncertainty: The activity time estimate is quite reliable, unless a known risk factor shows up. A typical example is a quite reliable time estimate of the project activity, which can be subject to a delay if weather conditions (i.e. the known risk factor) are worse than expected.

- Unforeseen Uncertainty: The activity time estimate is not very reliable and might vary between two extremes.
- Chaos: The activity time estimate is a rough average prediction, and can differ very much from the original prediction in two extremes: much lower or much higher than expected.

5.2.3   Step 3. Monte-Carlo Simulation

Figure 5.2 shows the basic underlying principle of a Monte-Carlo simulation run used in a schedule risk analysis. A simulation run generates a duration for each project activity given its predefined uncertainty profile, as follows:

1. Generate a continuous uniform random number from the interval [0,1[.
2. Add the number as the u parameter in the CDF function and search for the corresponding real activity duration.
3. Replace the baseline duration by the newly generated number and recalculate the critical path.

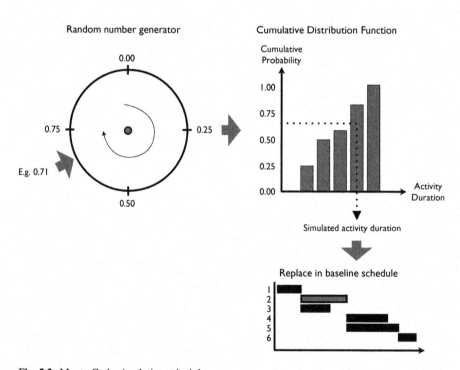

Fig. 5.2 Monte-Carlo simulation principle

This Monte-Carlo approach is used to generate activity durations that might differ from their original baseline values, leading to a change in the set of critical activities and a total real project duration that might differ from its baseline planned duration. The effect of these changes is measured in the next and last step of an SRA run.

5.2.4 Step 4. Results

During each simulation run, the simulation engine has recorded all project schedules and critical paths during the simulated project progress in order to be able to measure the degree of activity sensitivity on the project objective. The output of a schedule risk analysis is a set of measures that define this degree of activity criticality and sensitivity. These measures refine the black-and-white view of the critical path (which defines that an activity is either critical or not) to a degree of sensitivity, as follows:

- Criticality Index (CI): Measures the probability that an activity is on the critical path.
- Significance Index (SI): Measures the relative importance of an activity.
- Schedule Sensitivity Index (SSI): Measures the relative importance of an activity taking the CI into account.
- Cruciality Index (CRI): Measures the correlation between the activity duration and the total project duration, in three different ways:
  - CRI(r): Pearson's product-moment correlation coefficient.
  - CRI(ρ): Spearman's rank correlation coefficient.
  - CRI(τ): Kendall's tau rank correlation coefficient.

Each measure gives the manager an indication of how sensitive the activity is towards the final project duration. Next to the sensitivity measures, an SRA simulation also provides the probability of the project finish over time, expressed in a "cumulative project duration" graph as shown in Fig. 5.3. The values for the sensitivity measures are available upon completion of the simulation run and are used as triggers to focus on the risky activities, which probably require higher attention in order to achieve successful project fulfilment. The specific calculations of each sensitivity measure are discussed in the next section.

5.3 Sensitivity Measures

In this section, the four activity based sensitivity measures are reviewed. The CI, SI and CRI indices are originally discussed in Williams (1992) while the SSI is published in PMBOK (2004). More detailed information can be found in

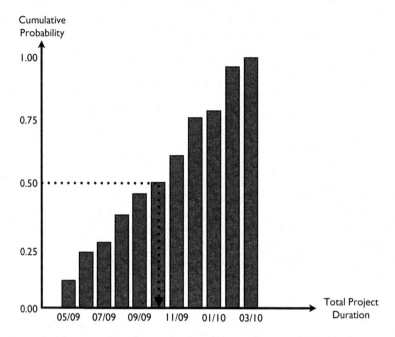

Fig. 5.3 Cumulative project duration graph

Vanhoucke (2010b). The following notation will be used throughout the presentation of the sensitivity measure formulas:

nrs	Number of Monte-Carlo simulation runs (index k)
d_i	Duration of activity i
	(superscript k will be used to refer to the d_i of simulation run k)
tf_i	Total float of activity i
	(superscript k will used to refer to the tf_i of simulation run k)
RD	Total real project duration (as a result of a simulation run)
	(superscript k will used to refer to the RD of simulation run k)

5.3.1   Criticality Index CI

The criticality index measures the probability that an activity lies on the critical path. It is a simple measure obtained by Monte-Carlo simulations, and is expressed as a percentage denoting the likelihood of being critical. The CI of activity i can be given as follows:

$$CI = \Pr(tf_i = 0). \tag{5.1}$$

with $\Pr(x)$ the abbreviation used to denote the probability of x.

Although the criticality index has been used throughout various studies and implemented in many software packages, the CI often fails in adequately measuring the project risk. The main drawback of the CI is that its focus is restricted to measuring probability, which does not necessarily mean that high CI activities have a high impact on the total project duration. As an example, it is perfectly possible that an activity with a very low duration always lies on the critical path (i.e. CI = 100%), although it will have a low impact on the total project duration due to its negligible duration.

A simulation-based estimator of CI, denoted by $\widehat{\text{CI}}$, can be calculated easily as the frequency of an activity i being critical over all simulation runs $k = 1, \ldots, nrs$, as follows:

$$\widehat{\text{CI}} = \frac{1}{\text{nrs}} \sum_{k=1}^{\text{nrs}} \mathbf{1}(\text{tf}_i^k = 0), \tag{5.2}$$

where in general the indicator function $\mathbf{1}(.)$ is defined by

$$\mathbf{1}(G) \equiv \begin{cases} 1, & \text{if } G \text{ is true,} \\ 0, & \text{if } G \text{ is false.} \end{cases} \tag{5.3}$$

5.3.2 Significance Index SI

In order to better reflect the relative importance between project activities, the sensitivity index of activity i has been formulated as follows:

$$\text{SI} = E\left(\frac{d_i}{d_i + \text{tf}_i} \cdot \frac{\text{RD}}{E(\text{RD})}\right) \tag{5.4}$$

with $E(x)$ used to denote the expected value of x. The SI has been defined as a partial answer to the criticism on the CI. Rather than expressing an activity's criticality by the probability concept, the SI aims at exposing the significance of individual activities on the total project duration. In some examples, the SI seems to provide more acceptable information on the relative importance of activities. Despite this, there are still examples where counterintuitive results are reported.

A simulation-based estimator of SI is given by

$$\widehat{\text{SI}} = \frac{1}{\text{nrs}} \sum_{k=1}^{\text{nrs}} \left(\frac{d_i^k}{d_i^k + \text{tf}_i^k}\right) \left(\frac{\text{RD}^k}{\overline{\text{RD}}}\right). \tag{5.5}$$

with $\overline{\text{RD}}$ the average of all RD values over all simulation runs, i.e. $\frac{1}{\text{nrs}} \sum_{k=1}^{\text{nrs}} \text{RD}^k$.

5.3.3   Cruciality Index CRI

A third measure to indicate the duration sensitivity of individual activities on the total project duration is given by the *correlation* between the activity duration and total project duration. This measure reflects the relative importance of an activity in a more intuitive way and measures the portion of total project duration uncertainty that can be explained by the uncertainty of an activity.

This measure can be calculated by using the Pearson's product-moment, the Spearman's rank correlation or Kendall's tau rank correlation, as described along the following lines.

(a) A simulation-based estimator of *Pearson's product-moment* of activity i can be calculated as follows:

$$\widehat{\text{CRI}}(r) = \frac{\sum_{k=1}^{\text{nrs}}(d_i^k - \bar{d}_i)(\text{RD}^k - \overline{\text{RD}})}{\text{nrs}\,\sigma_{d_i}\sigma_{\text{RD}}} \tag{5.6}$$

with σ_{d_i} and σ_{RD} the population standard deviations of variables d_i and RD,[1] given by

$$\sigma_{d_i} = \sqrt{\frac{\sum_{k=1}^{\text{nrs}}(d_i^k - \bar{d}_i)^2}{\text{nrs}}} \text{ and } \sigma_{\text{RD}} = \sqrt{\frac{\sum_{k=1}^{\text{nrs}}(\text{RD}^k - \overline{\text{RD}})^2}{\text{nrs}}}. \tag{5.7}$$

This correlation metric is a measure of the degree of linear relationship between two variables. However, the relation between an activity duration and the total project duration often follows a nonlinear relation. Therefore, Cho and Yum (1997) propose to use nonlinear correlation measures such as the Spearman Rank correlation coefficient or Kendall's tau measure. These nonlinear measures can be calculated as follows:

(b) The *Spearman's Rank Correlation* assumes that the values for the variables are converted to ranks and the differences between the ranks of each observation on the two variables are then calculated. A simulation-based estimator is given by

$$\widehat{\text{CRI}}(\rho) = 1 - \frac{6\sum_{k=1}^{\text{nrs}}\delta_k^2}{\text{nrs}(\text{nrs}^2 - 1)} \tag{5.8}$$

where δ_k is the difference between the ranking values of d_i and RD during simulation run k, i.e. $\delta_k \equiv rank(d_i^k) - rank(\text{RD}^k)$ for $k = 1, \ldots, \text{nrs}$.

(c) *Kendall's tau rank correlation* index measures the degree of correspondence between two rankings as follows:

---

[1] Alternatively, the sample standard deviations can be used, given by $s_{d_i} = \sqrt{\frac{\sum_{k=1}^{\text{nrs}}(d_i^k - \bar{d}_i)^2}{\text{nrs}-1}}$ and $s_{\text{RD}} = \sqrt{\frac{\sum_{k=1}^{\text{nrs}}(\text{RD}^k - \overline{\text{RD}})^2}{\text{nrs}-1}}$.

$$CRI(\tau) = \frac{4P}{\text{nrs}(\text{nrs} - 1)} - 1 \qquad (5.9)$$

where P is used to represent the number of concordant pairs[2] of the d_i and RD variables.

A simulation-based estimator is given as follows:

$$\widehat{CRI}(\tau) = \left[\frac{4}{\text{nrs}(\text{nrs} - 1)} \sum_{k=1}^{\text{nrs}-1} \sum_{\ell=k+1}^{\text{nrs}} \mathbf{1}\left\{(d_i^\ell - d_i^k)(\text{RD}^\ell - \text{RD}^k) > 0\right\} \right] - 1. \quad (5.10)$$

5.3.4 Schedule Sensitivity Index SSI

The Project Management Body Of Knowledge (PMBOK 2004) mentions quantitative risk analysis as one of many risk assessment methods and proposes to combine the activity duration and project duration standard deviations (σ_{d_i} and σ_{RD}) with the criticality index. It is referred to as the Schedule Sensitivity Index (SSI). The measure is equal to

$$\text{SSI} = \left[\sqrt{\frac{\text{Var}(d_i)}{\text{Var}(\text{RD})}} \right] \cdot \text{CI} \qquad (5.11)$$

and its corresponding simulation-based estimator is given by

$$\widehat{\text{SSI}} = \frac{\sigma_{d_i} \cdot \widehat{\text{CI}}}{\sigma_{RD}}. \qquad (5.12)$$

5.4 Sensitivity Examples

5.4.1 A Fictitious Project Example

This section discusses the use of the sensitivity measures on a fictitious project example displayed in Fig. 5.4. The numbers above each node are used to refer to the activity duration estimates. Table 5.1 shows five fictitious simulated scenarios for the example project network. Each scenario is characterized by a set of activity

---

[2]Let (x_i, y_i) and (x_j, y_j) be a pair of (bivariate) observations. If $x_j - x_i$ and $y_j - y_i$ have the same sign, the pair is *concordant*, if they have opposite signs, the pair is *discordant*.

Fig. 5.4 An example project
(Source: Vanhoucke 2010a)

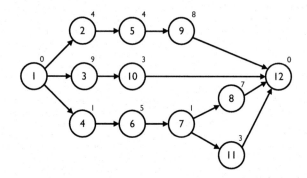

Table 5.1 Five simulation scenarios to perform a schedule risk analysis

Scenario	2	3	4	5	6	7	8	9	10	11	RD
1	6	11	1	4	3	2	8	8	5	4	18
2	7	14	1	4	5	1	8	11	5	5	22
3	6	16	1	7	8	1	11	14	6	5	27
4	4	14	1	7	5	1	9	9	5	3	20
5	6	17	2	6	9	2	13	12	4	4	26
Average	5.8	14.4	1.2	5.6	6	1.4	9.8	10.8	5	4.2	22.6
StDev.	0.98	2.06	0.40	1.36	2.19	0.49	1.94	2.14	0.63	0.75	3.44

Table 5.2 The sensitivity measures for all activities obtained through a schedule risk analysis

	2	3	4	5	6	7	8	9	10	11
CI	0.80	0.00	0.20	0.80	0.20	0.20	0.20	0.80	0.00	0.00
SI	0.94	0.82	0.36	0.94	0.61	0.38	0.72	0.97	0.62	0.30
CRI (r)	0.27	0.93	0.49	0.52	0.96	0.14	0.83	0.97	0.09	0.50
CRI (ρ)	0.30	0.88	0.50	0.50	0.88	0.13	0.73	1.00	0.30	0.60
CRI (τ)	0.20	0.60	0.40	0.20	0.60	0.60	0.40	1.00	0.20	0.20
SSI	0.23	0.00	0.02	0.32	0.13	0.03	0.11	0.50	0.00	0.00

durations and a total real project duration RD. Note that scenario 1 corresponds to the Gantt chart presented later in Fig. 12.13.

Table 5.2 displays the values for all sensitivity measures and Table 5.3 displays the intermediate calculations required to calculate the sensitivity measures.

The sensitivity measures are calculated for illustrative purposes for activity 2 of the example network.

Criticality Index CI: The rows of Table 5.3 with label "critical (yes/no)" display for each scenario whether the activity is critical or not, and are used to calculate the criticality index. As an example, the CI for activity 2 is equal to $CI = \frac{4}{5} = 0.80$.

Significance Index SI: The activity float (row "Total Float") is necessary to calculate the significance index as $SI = \left(\frac{6}{6+0} * \frac{18}{22.6} + \frac{7}{7+0} * \frac{22}{22.6} + \frac{6}{6+0} * \frac{27}{22.6} + \frac{4}{4+0} * \frac{20}{22.6} + \frac{6}{6+2} * \frac{26}{22.6}\right)/5 = 0.94$.

Cruciality Index CRI: The cruciality index CRI can be calculated using the three formulas:.

- **CRI (r):** The CRI (r) measure is calculated as CRI $(r) = \frac{1}{5*0.98*3.44} * (6 - 5.8) *$ $(18 - 22.6) + (7 - 5.8) * (22 - 22.6) + (6 - 5.8) * (27 - 22.6) + (4 - 5.8) *$ $(20 - 22.6) + (6 - 5.8) * (26 - 22.6) = 0.27$.

- **CRI (ρ):** In order to avoid errors resulting from nonlinearities, the CRI (ρ) and CRI (τ) require a transformation of the original data into a ranking. In case of tied ranks, the same rank is given to each of the equal values as the average of their positions in the ranking. As an example, placing the activity durations of activity 2 in increasing order for all scenarios results in the following scenario

  $$\overbrace{4 - 1 - 3 - 5}^{tie\ break} - 2$$

  sequence $4 - 1 - 3 - 5 - 2$ corresponding to a ranking [2,5,3,1,4] for scenarios [1,2,3,4,5]. However, tie breaks occur for scenarios 1, 3 and 5. In this case, the average is taken of their ranking values as $\frac{2+3+4}{3} = 3$, resulting in the ranking [3,5,3,1,3] as shown in the rows with label "ranking (tie breaks)" of Table 5.3. Consequently, the CRI (ρ) measure uses these rankings to calculate the δ values and is equal to CRI $(\rho) = 1 - 6 * \frac{(3-1)^2+(5-3)^2+(3-5)^2+(1-2)^2+(3-4)^2}{5*(5^2-1)} = 0.30$.

- **CRI (τ):** The CRI (τ) measure relies on the Kendall τ coefficient in which the P value can be calculated rather easily by re-ordering the ranks in increasing

Table 5.3 Intermediate calculations for the sensitivity measures

	Scenario	2	3	4	5	6	7	8	9	10	11	RD
Critical	1	Yes	No	No	Yes	No	No	No	Yes	No	No	–
(yes/no)	2	Yes	No	No	Yes	No	No	No	Yes	No	No	–
	3	Yes	No	No	Yes	No	No	No	Yes	No	No	–
	4	Yes	No	No	Yes	No	No	No	Yes	No	No	–
	5	No	No	Yes	No	Yes	Yes	Yes	No	No	No	–
Total	1	0	2	4	0	4	4	4	0	2	8	–
float	2	0	3	7	0	7	7	7	0	3	10	–
	3	0	5	6	0	6	6	6	0	5	12	–
	4	0	1	4	0	4	4	4	0	1	10	–
	5	2	5	0	2	0	0	0	2	5	9	–
Ranking	1	3	1	2.5	1.5	1	4.5	1.5	1	3	2.5	1
(tie breaks)	2	5	2.5	2.5	1.5	2.5	2	1.5	3	3	4.5	3
	3	3	4	2.5	4.5	4	2	4	5	5	4.5	5
	4	1	2.5	2.5	4.5	2.5	2	3	2	3	1	2
	5	3	5	5	3	5	4.5	5	4	1	2.5	4
Ranking	1	3	1	2.5	1.5	1	4.5	1.5	1	3	2.5	1
(re-ordered)	4	1	2.5	2.5	4.5	2.5	2	3	2	3	1	2
	2	5	2.5	2.5	1.5	2.5	2	1.5	3	3	4.5	3
	5	3	5	5	3	5	4.5	5	4	1	2.5	4
	3	3	4	2.5	4.5	4	2	4	5	5	4.5	5
	P	4	8	3	6	8	2	7	10	4	6	–

order of the RD ranking values (the rows with label "ranking (re-ordered)" of Table 5.3). The P value is then calculated by counting for each scenario how many ranking values displayed below the current scenario are higher than the ranking for the current scenario. For example, in scenario 1, only 1 ranking value (i.e. for scenario 2) below scenario 1 is higher than the current ranking value, and hence, the contribution to P is 1. For scenario 4, three ranking values displayed below this scenario have a higher ranking value, and hence, its contribution to P equals 3. Consequently, the P value for activity 2 is equal to $1 + 0 + 3 + 0 + 0 = 4$ and CRI $(\tau) = |\frac{4*4}{5*(5-1)} - 1| = 0.20$. Alternatively, the value can be calculated using Eq. 5.10.

Schedule Sensitivity Index SSI: The schedule sensitivity index can be calculated as $SSI = \frac{0.98*0.80}{3.44} = 0.23$.

5.4.2 Counterintuitive Examples

In this section, a short critical review is given on the use of three of the four sensitivity measures as a summary from various sources in the literature. It will be shown that each of the following three sensitivity measures, CI, SI and CRI has their own weaknesses, which might lead to anomalies and counterintuitive results. Quite a number of extensions have been proposed to deal with these weaknesses, but only partial answers have been given in these studies. A detailed study of these sensitivity extensions is outside the scope of this book, and the interested reader is referred to the different sources in the literature (see e.g. Cho and Yum (1997), Elmaghraby et al. (1999), Elmaghraby (2000), Gutierrez and Paul (2000), Kuchta (2001), and Williams (1992)).

The use of the criticality index CI has been criticized throughout literature since it is based on probabilistic considerations, which are very far from management's view on the project. Moreover, the metric only considers probabilities, while it is generally known that the risk of an activity depends on a combination of probability and impact. The latter is completely ignored in the CI value, as illustrated in Fig. 5.5. The figure shows a parallel project network (the unnumbered nodes are used to denote the start and end dummy activities) with the possible durations and the corresponding probabilities denoted above each node. Obviously, activity 1 has the highest potential impact on the project duration since it might lead to a project with a total duration of 100 time units. However, the CI of activity 1 is equal to 1%, which is much lower than the CI = 99% of activity 2. Consequently, the values for the sensitivity measures are not always intuitively clear, and they might lead to strange and counterintuitive conclusions.

Although the SI and CRI measures have been proposed to reflect the relative importance of an activity in a better way than the CI, they can, however, both

Fig. 5.5 A parallel two
nondummy activity example
network (SP = 0) (Source:
Williams 1992)

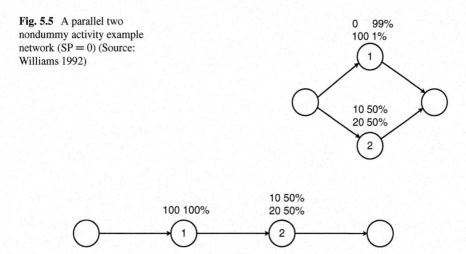

Fig. 5.6 A serial two nondummy activity example network (SP = 1) (Source: Williams 1992)

produce counterintuitive results as illustrated by means of the example network
of Fig. 5.6. Clearly, activity 1 has the largest impact on the project duration and
$E(\text{RD}) = 115$. However, the SI values are equal for both activities and hence no
distinction is made between the sensitivity of both activities. Indeed, the SI is equal
to $100\% * \frac{100}{100} * \frac{115}{115} = 1$ for activity 1 and to $50\% * \frac{10}{10} * \frac{110}{115} + 50\% * \frac{20}{20} * \frac{120}{115} = 1$
for activity 2. Even worse, the CRI values show an opposite risk profile for both
activities. The CRI measure shows only the effect on the risk of the total project
and, consequently, if the duration of an activity is deterministic (or stochastic but
with very low variance), then its CRI is zero (or close to zero) even if the activity is
always on the critical path. The CRI value for activity 1 is equal to 0% (no variation)
while it is equal to $\frac{(10-15)*(110-115)+(20-15)*(120-115)}{2*5*5} = 1$ for activity 2.

5.5   Schedule Risk Analysis in Action

Schedule risk analysis needs, like any risk assessment method, to be used to study
and understand the risk inherent to the specific project. However, the different
sensitivity measures discussed in this chapter might give different values for the
same project and hence require interpretation before they can be blindly used to
support decisions. Project managers can benefit from schedule risk analysis only if
they understand the meaning of the various sensitivity measures for their specific
project in order to provide better and more realistic time and cost forecasts and
to support better decisions during a project's progress. In the next sections, the
sensitivity measures are discussed as a tool to support the project tracking process
to trigger corrective actions in case the project runs into trouble.

5.5.1   Project Tracking

It has been mentioned earlier that the critical path offers a black-and-white view
on the project activities which leads to an extreme view on the importance of the
various activities during project tracking: an activity deserves attention when it is
critical or can be ignored when it is not. The extensions to sensitivity measures
discussed in this chapter allow the project manager to refine his/her focus on the
project in order to take appropriate corrective actions during project tracking. Rather
than having a yes/no measure, it allows to set an action threshold to distinguish
between important and less important activities. The use of schedule risk analysis
and its activity sensitivity measures to guide the project tracking phase of the project
life cycle is known as *bottom-up project tracking*.

Although project tracking or control is the subject of Part III of this book, Fig. 5.7
can be used to illustrate how sensitivity information of project activities (in this case,
the CRI(r) of Table 5.2) can be used in a dynamic project tracking environment and
how an action threshold can be set to trigger corrective actions in case of problems.
This action threshold defines the degree of control, which can vary between no
control and full control, and is shown by the vertical dotted line on the figure. All
activities with a CRI(r) value higher than or equal to this line are said to be highly
sensitive activities that require attention during the tracking process and corrective
actions in case of delays. In the example case of the figure, the action threshold
has been set at 60% such that only the most sensitive activities 2, 5, 7 and 8 with
a CRI(r) value higher than 0.60 need to be considered during the tracking process.
These highly sensitive activities (activities 2, 5, 7 and 8 at the bottom of the WBS
tree) require full attention and action when necessary. All other activities are said to
be insensitive and require less or no attention during project progress.

5.5.2   Network Topology

The bottom-up tracking approach is a project tracking system that classifies project
activities in a sensitive/insensitive distinction based on sensitivity measures obtained
by an SRA study. However, in order to guarantee timely and effective corrective
actions in case of project problems, these sensitivity measures should be able to
classify the right activity into the right class. The validity of the four sensitivity
measures discussed in this chapter for a bottom-up tracking system has been
investigated in a large simulation study of Vanhoucke (2010b) and Vanhoucke
(2011) and the following conclusions could be made:

- Network topology: The bottom-up tracking approach is particularly relevant
  when projects contain more parallel activities, and less attractive for serial
  activity project networks. The serial/parallel structure of a project network can
  be measured by the SP (Serial or Parallel) or the OS (Order Strength) indicators
  discussed later in Sect. 8.3.1. The study has also shown that a top-down project

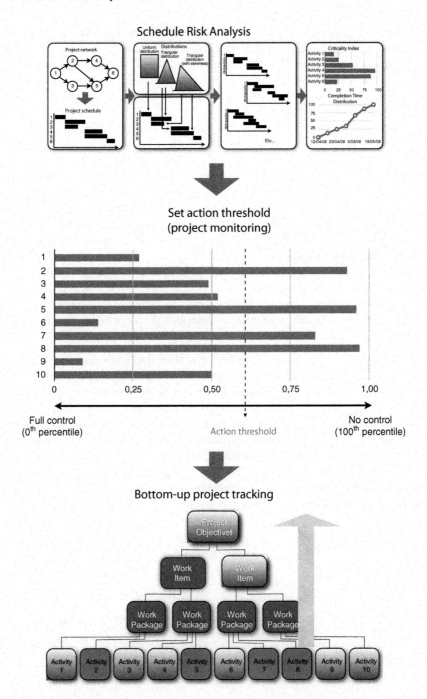

Fig. 5.7 Action thresholds during project tracking using SRA activity information

tracking (as the opposite of the previously mentioned bottom-up project tracking) approach using general project performance measures instead of relying on sensitivity information of individual activities brings a reliable project tracking alternative for more serial activity networks. The impact of network topology measures on the accuracy of top-down and bottom-up tracking approaches will be discussed in Chap. 13.

- The Schedule Sensitivity Index SSI performs best in a bottom-up tracking approach, followed by the CRI(r) and CRI(ρ) measures, when the project contains a lot of activities in parallel (i.e. when SP values are low). Even when action thresholds are set to high values to stimulate a less time consuming tracking approach, the total contribution of corrective actions to the highly sensitive activities remains relatively high. Since high action thresholds for the SSI measure lead to a relative small set of project activities that are said to be important, this means that a small subset of activities is responsible for a high project duration variance.
- When a project contains more and more serial activities (high SP values), the CI, SI and CRI(r) measures perform rather poor, as they are not able to select a small subset of activities to take significant corrective actions. Only the SSI performs reasonably well, leading to significant contributions when taking the appropriate corrective actions.

The influence of the network topology has been implicitly described in earlier SRA studies in the literature. It is recognized that a project with multiple parallel paths has almost always a higher probability to be overrun than a serial activity project network. This is known as "merge bias"(MacCrimmon and Ryavec 1967). This can be easily illustrated on two simplified projects as displayed in Fig. 5.8. Activities 1 and 2 have duration estimates that are, for the sake of simplicity, assumed to consist of three single point estimates with an equal probability, i.e. $d_i = 3, 4$ or $5, i = \{1, 2\}$ with a probability of 33%. Activity 3 has a fixed duration equal to 4. Since average activity durations are equal to 4 time units for all activities, both average critical paths are equal to 8 time units.

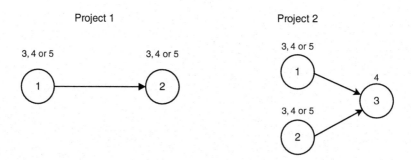

Fig. 5.8 Two projects with serial (*left*) and/or parallel (*right*) activities

Table 5.4 The effect of multiple parallel paths: the merge bias

Act 1	Act 2	Act 3	CP_1	CP_2
3	3	4	6	7
4	3	4	7	8
5	3	4	8	9
4	3	4	7	8
4	4	4	8	8
4	5	4	9	9
5	3	4	8	9
5	4	4	9	9
5	5	4	10	9
4	4	4	8	8.44

However, when risk is taken into account, the project duration might be different from the average deterministic critical path. Clearly, path merge points, i.e. project activities with multiple predecessor activities, will lead to an increase in project risk, as can be illustrated with the example projects in Table 5.4. The table shows all possible durations for each project activity and the corresponding project critical path for project 1 (CP_1) and project 2 (CP_2). The table shows that the second project duration is always longer than the first one, with an average project duration of 8.44 (bottom row), which is one time unit longer than the deterministic critical path of 8.

Consequently, it should be clear that for real projects, which contain multiple parallel paths and merge points, the deterministic critical path, which is based on average project duration estimates, is often not a realistic estimate of the total project duration. A schedule risk analysis identifies and quantifies this merge bias and highlights the real critical components of a project taking ranges of activity estimates into account.

5.6 Conclusion

This chapter discussed the features of a schedule risk analysis (SRA) in project scheduling and reviews the four basic steps: (1) create a baseline schedule, (2) define uncertainty as ranges in activity durations (and costs), (3) perform a Monte-Carlo run to simulate project progress and (4) report sensitivity measures and interpret the results. The chapter discussed the relevance of four activity based sensitivity measures: the criticality index CI, the sensitivity index SI, three variants of the cruciality index CRI and the schedule sensitivity index SSI, and illustrates their use on a fictitious project example. Finally, a simulation study has been briefly summarized to illustrate the usefulness of these sensitivity measures in practice. The study aimed at investigating whether the activity sensitivity measures are able to distinguish between highly sensitive and insensitive project activities in order to steer the focus of the project tracking and control phase to those activities that are likely to have the most beneficial effect on the project outcome.

The chapter should be relevant to practitioners since it provides general guidelines where the focus of a project manager should be during the project tracking phase. The results show that a bottom-up project tracking approach could lead to reliable results and that its use depends on the topological structure of the underlying project network. More precisely, the results show that it is particularly useful for parallel project networks where detailed activity sensitivity information is required at the lowest WBS levels during project tracking in order to support corrective actions when the project runs into trouble. Consequently, project managers need a certain feeling of the relative sensitivity of the individual activities on the project objective, in order to restrict the management focus to only a subpart of the project while still being able to provide an accurate response during project tracking to control the overall performance of the project. In Part III of this book, this bottom-up project tracking process is outlined and discussed into detail.

Chapter 6
The Mutum-Paraná II Bridge Project (A)

Abstract The case description of this chapter can be considered as an integrated exercise to get acquainted with the scheduling principles discussed in previous chapters. It assumes the construction of a baseline schedule and knowledge of basic critical path scheduling principles, and allows the extension to basic calculations of risk in order to provide a supportive tool for taking protective actions. It can be extended to various other scheduling settings, such as the extension to a computerized schedule risk analysis, the incorporation of other scheduling objectives, etc. In this chapter, only the case description is given. The solution and the educational approach depend on the wishes and needs of the students who solve the case and teacher who can act as the moderator during the case teaching session.

6.1 Introduction

The second longest river in South America after the Amazon, the Paraná River joins with the Paraguay and Uruguay Rivers before emptying into the Ro de la Plata estuary on its way to the Atlantic Ocean. The river begins its 3,032-mile (4,879-km) course in east-central Brazil. The Paraná flows mainly among high plateaus through Paraguay and Argentina.

The Brazilian company Curitiba Pontes Ltd. has been awarded for the construction of the Mutum-Paraná II bridge over the river Paraná. The river Paraná in Argentina is the last obstacle in a big highway construction project. This highway was a promise from the government to the poor people of the interior to link their region to Buenos Aires. Therefore large investments were made to stimulate the economy.

M. Vanhoucke, *Project Management with Dynamic Scheduling*,   101
DOI 10.1007/978-3-642-40438-2_6, © Springer-Verlag Berlin Heidelberg 2013

6.2 The Team Meeting

José Silva Coelho, the manager of this project, was very pleased with the announcement and called an early morning meeting to share his preliminary thoughts with his
team. While Carlos and Orlando were looking carefully at the technical details of the
project, José eagerly opened the meeting. He was confident that the company should
be able to start at the beginning of the year (January 2nd, 2012) in order to meet the
deadline. Although a specific deadline was not yet negotiated, José believed that
the project should be finished at the end of February 2013 (February 25th, 2013).
He believed that a weekly penalty clause of €15,000 would be a reasonable and
realistic estimate.

Carlos Garez has been working as a construction engineer for 10 years for
the same company. He knew that the unstable ground could cause severe delays.
The Paraná had some very unstable river banks because of the swirling water. He
estimated that the chance of the ground being unstable at both sides was 50%. Extra
stabilization activities would then be needed, leading to a severe increase of the
preparatory work (activity 1). The stabilization of these river banks would take 10
extra weeks if the river banks mainly consisted of clay (70%), but could go up to 15
weeks if the river banks consisted of quicksand (30%).

Maria Mota Pereira, the account manager of Curitiba Pontes Ltd., was surprised
by the early start proposal of José, but quickly realized that he would not tolerate any
start delay whatsoever. Therefore, she decided to warn the whole team for a possible
cost increase for the total mobilization, excavation and demobilization activities
(activities 2 to 16). Since there is a small chance (1 out of 5) that the cranes, needed
to perform these activities, could only be released from another project by the end
of April, she proposed to delay the project till then.

Orlando Carvalheiro, the resource manager of the company, was also aware that
José would not tolerate any delay and replied that this extra mobilization cost would
not lead to severe cost increases, as long as this resource constraint was carefully
taken into account. Maria replied that alternative machines to temporarily replace
the unavailable cranes until the end of April would cost €250 per week. Orlando
was not pleased with that limited information about the resources, and interrupted
by saying that other cost considerations were also important. He immediately
mentioned the overhead expense of €250 per week that would be incurred in case
of any project delay.

The technical details of the project are given in the next subsection of this case.

6.3 The Project

The bridge is a composite steel-concrete construction for a highway spanning a river
and a small ravine. It consists of a concrete paving slab supported by seven steel
girders that are placed on three reinforced concrete abutments. The river flows on the

right-hand side between abutments 2 and 3. Each of the abutments rests on a heavy concrete footing supported by steel piles in the ground. A steel guardrail is mounted on each side of the bridge. Figure 6.1 shows the highway bridge profile with the three abutments (two outside abutments and one middle abutment). Figure 6.2 displays a cross section of the highway bridge, showing the various steel girders.

First, some preparatory work (activity 1) has to be performed and the equipment has to be moved into place. As soon as the necessary preparations have been performed (6 weeks after the start of activity 1) the mobilization of the pile rigs 1, 2 and 3 (activity 2, 3 and 4) can be started together with the excavation of the abutments 1, 2 and 3 (activity 5, 6 and 7). The mobilization of the piles can be done in 1 week, the excavation of the abutments 1 and 3 will take 4 weeks. The excavation of abutment 2 will need 6 weeks to complete. When the excavations are completed, the piles can be driven into the ground. This job can be done in 1 week for piles 1 and 3 (activity 8 and 10). The middle pile (activity 9) will need an extra week to complete.

Next, the pile rigs can be demobilized and removed (activities 11, 12 and 13). This will take 1 week. At the same time, the company can start to make the concrete footings (activities 14, 15 and 16). Each activity includes the delivery of the forms for the concrete footing, the pouring of the concrete and the stripping of the footing. The footing between the river and the ravine will take 7 weeks to complete

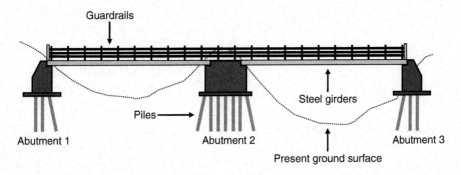

Fig. 6.1   The highway bridge – profile

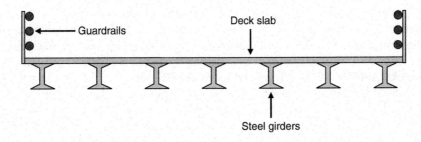

Fig. 6.2   The highway bridge – cross section

Table 6.1 The project
activities for the
Mutum-Paraná II
bridge project (A)

ID	Activity description
1	Preparatory Work and Move in
2	Mobilize Pile Rig 1
3	Mobilize Pile Rig 2
4	Mobilize Pile Rig 3
5	Excavate Abutment 1
6	Excavate Abutment 2
7	Excavate Abutment 3
8	Drive Piles Abutment 1
9	Drive Piles Abutment 2
10	Drive Piles Abutment 3
11	Demobolize Pile Rig 1
12	Demobolize Pile Rig 2
13	Demobolize Pile Rig 3
14	Forms, Pour and Strip Footing 1
15	Forms, Pour and Strip Footing 2
16	Forms, Pour and Strip Footing 3
17	Forms, Pour and Strip Abutment 1
18	Forms, Pour and Strip Abutment 2
19	Forms, Pour and Strip Abutment 3
20	Backfill Abutment 1
21	Backfill Abutment 2
22	Backfill Abutment 3
23	Set Girders and Forms Deck 1-2
24	Set Girders and Forms Deck 2-3
25	Pour Deck
26	Saw Joints
27	Strip Deck and Rub Concrete
28	Clean Up and Final Inspection

(activity 15). The other footings can be finished in 5 weeks. When the concrete footings are in place, the forms for the abutments can be inserted, the concrete can be poured and the abutments can be stripped. These three activities can be considered as one activity for each abutment. For the outside abutments (activity 17 and 19) this will take 7 weeks. The middle abutment will take 10 weeks to be finished. Once finished, the backfilling of the abutments (activities 20, 21 and 22) can be started. This will take 3 weeks to complete for the outside abutments. Backfilling abutment 2 (activity 21) will take 5 weeks. Between the 3 abutments, the company will put two sets of steel girders and will install the forms for the deck. Activity 23 (set girders and forms deck 1-2) can start as soon as activity 17 and 18 are finished and will take 6 weeks. Activity 24 (set girders and forms deck 2-3) can start as soon as activity 18 and 19 are finished and will take 8 weeks. When the girders are put in place and the forms for the deck are ready, the company can pour the deck (activity 25), which will take 2 weeks to complete. Then, it can start to strip the deck and rub the concrete (activity 27), which will take 5 weeks to complete. Simultaneously, the joints can be sawed (activity 26), which can be finished in 4 weeks. The last

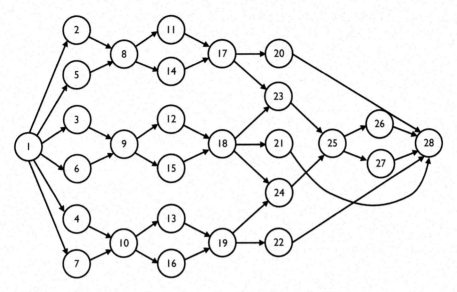

Fig. 6.3 The project network for the Mutum-Paraná II bridge project (A)

activity is the clean up and final inspection (activity 28). This job will take 7 weeks and can only start after the backfilling of the abutments is finished. Moreover, it is necessary that activity 26 (saw joints) and activity 27 (strip deck and rub concrete) are completed. The detailed description and the technological successive relations are indicated in Table 6.1 and Fig. 6.3. All precedence relations are assumed to be minimal finish-start relations with a time-lag of zero.

6.4   The Team Proposals

Five proposals were submitted by the members of the team. A wrap-up meeting will be scheduled next week to decide the best alternative to cope with the situation:

- Proposal 1: Orlando knows that the activity "strip deck and rub concrete (27)" can be expedited by the use of a sophisticated machine. Using this machine would decrease the activity duration from 5 weeks to 2 weeks, at an additional total cost of €100.
- Proposal 2: Maria proposes to halve the duration of any of the "excavations of the abutments (5, 6 and 7)" activities, which costs the company €500 per abutment.
- Proposal 3: The activity "forms, pour and strip abutment 2 (18)" can be expedited by the help of extra pile driver men and equipment operators. The minimal duration is 5 weeks, at an additional cost of €5,000 per week.
- Proposal 4: An option proposed by the whole team is to expedite the "backfilling of the abutments (20, 21 and 22)" to 50% of the original duration. Would

you agree on decreasing the duration of these activities, when the total cost of expediting these activities is €5,000?

- Proposal 5: José thinks the whole team panics too easily and proposes to take no special action. He believes that the project, although subject to a number of risk factors, can be performed with success without severe cost problems. Next week, there is a new meeting anyway, and Orlando will come up with new and detailed information then. What do you think about that?

Part II
Scheduling with Resources

Chapter 7
Resource-Constrained Project Scheduling

Abstract Resource-constrained project scheduling is a widely discussed project management topic which has roots in and relevance for both academic and practical oriented environments. Due to its inherent problem complexity, it has been the subject of numerous research projects leading to a wide and diverse set of procedures and algorithms to construct resource feasible project schedules. Thanks to its practical value, many of the research results have found their way to practical project management projects. This chapter gives an overview of the project scheduling efforts and needs in order to bring the academics closer to real life projects and vice versa. It gives an extensive overview on the use of resources in dynamic scheduling problems and discusses various scheduling objectives to optimize the schedule to the wishes and needs of the company or project owner. The chapter also gives a set of techniques to validate the quality of the resource feasible baseline schedules and highlights some important features and characteristics that should be taken into account when using scheduling tools.

7.1 Introduction

This chapter elaborates on the critical path based scheduling approach discussed in Part I of this book where it is assumed that resources are not taken into account when scheduling projects. However, project activities are executed by resources (usually people) which mostly have a limited availability over the complete time horizon of the project. This chapter puts a detailed emphasis on these resources required to execute the project activities.

Resource-constrained project scheduling is the process of constructing a project schedule within the limited amount of resources available. It requires the examination of the possible unbalanced use of resources over time to resolve over-allocations (the so-called resource conflicts) when more resources are required than available. The critical path based scheduling methods of the previous part will often schedule certain activities simultaneously. When more resources such as machines or people are needed than there are available, these activities will have to be rescheduled concurrently or even sequentially to resolve the resource constraints. Resource-constrained project scheduling is the process of resolving these resource conflicts under different scheduling objectives.

The outline of this chapter is as follows. Section 7.2 gives a brief description of the two main resource classes used in resource-constrained project scheduling. Section 7.3 discusses various resource-constrained project scheduling types under different scheduling objectives. It will be shown that each scheduling objective serves another practical project purpose and determines the main characteristics of the project scheduling approach. In Sect. 7.4, easy and quick scheduling techniques are presented to construct the resource-constrained project schedules under the different objectives. Section 7.5 puts the assumptions into perspective and extends the scheduling results of previous sections to more practical oriented settings. Section 7.6 discusses how the total activity cost, as a weighted sum of the costs for the activities and their resource assignments, can be calculated. Section 7.7 draws general chapter conclusions.

7.2 Resources

In the previous sections, it is assumed that project activities do not require resources during their execution (or alternatively, the assumption is that the resources are unlimited in availability). In practice, activities need resources during their execution, that are limited in availability. These resources have been classified in two basic categories.

- *Nonrenewable or consumable resources* are available on a total project basis, with a limited consumption availability for the entire project. Typical examples are money, raw materials, energy, . . .
- *Renewable resources* are available on a period-by-period basis, i.e. the available amount is renewed from period to period. Only the total resource use at every time instant is constrained. Typical examples are manpower, machines, tools, equipment, space, . . .

Doubly-constrained resources are a combination of the two previous categories, and are constrained per period (e.g. per period cash flows) as well as for the overall project (e.g. total expenditures, overall pollution limits, . . .).

In this chapter, the resource focus is restricted to the use of renewable resources with a limited availability, since they are responsible for an increase in the scheduling complexity. The use of nonrenewable resources has been previously discussed in Chap. 3, with the trade-off between the activity duration and its corresponding cost, which is clearly a nonrenewable resource. The current chapter and Chaps. 8 and 9 elaborate on project scheduling techniques under low uncertainty and high complexity (see quadrant 3 of Fig. 1.4). Chapter 10 extends this complex scheduling approach to higher degrees of uncertainty.

7.3 Scheduling Objective

The scheduling phase aims at the construction of a timetable to determine the activity start and finish times in order to optimize a certain predefined scheduling objective. Although the minimization of the project lead time is probably the most important objective during the scheduling phase, other scheduling objectives are often crucial from a practical point of view. While the focus of Chap. 2 was on resource-unconstrained project scheduling with the minimization of the total project time as the only scheduling objective, the current chapter will add two important extensions. First, project scheduling tools and techniques are presented with the presence of limited availability of renewable resources and, second, extensions will be made to various other scheduling objectives, each of them classified in one of two main scheduling objective classes.

7.3.1 Regular and Nonregular Objectives

Scheduling activities over time implies the optimization of a certain objective function. These objective functions (often referred to as measures of performance) are numerous and often complex. Moreover, when several objectives are relevant at the same time, it is quite possible that a trade-off will be present since the objective functions are often conflicting. Trade-offs between scheduling objectives can be taken into account using two general principles. In the *multi-criteria* case, the different measures must be ranked according to certain criteria in order to specify in which order they should be considered. The *multi-objective* case combines or weighs the different kinds of objectives. During the past decades, a huge number of different scheduling objectives were treated in the project scheduling literature (for an overview, see Icmeli et al. (1993), Elmaghraby (1995), Özdamar and Ulusoy (1995), Herroelen et al. (1998) and Brucker et al. (1999)). Since time is a crucial factor in the global market, the vast majority of the project scheduling methodologies presented in the literature have been developed with the objective of minimizing the project length subject to precedence as well as resource constraints. The measure is attractive from a practical point of view. As an example, Shtub et al. (1994) stated that successful companies will be those that learn to make and deliver goods and services faster than their competitors do. Nowadays, the factor time has become a critical element in the so-called time-based competition.

Nevertheless, the focus on the minimization of the duration of the project ignores some realistic and very important factors. Factors such as costs, quality, risk, safety and maintainability are sometimes much more relevant than solely the time aspect of projects. Besides the minimization of the project duration, an almost endless list of possible measures of performance is treated in the literature. Objectives such as minimizing direct costs, risks or expenditures for material, equipment or labor, or maximizing revenues, safety, quality, etc. play an important role in practical scheduling problems. According to Pinnell and Busch (1993), the quality of a project can be measured by time (how long it takes), cost (within the budget) and how well the project conforms to specifications. A survey of variants and extensions of the resource-constrained project scheduling problems can be found in Hartmann and Briskorn (2010). Taking these observations into account, the objective functions are classified into two distinct classes: regular measures of performance and nonregular measures of performance.

A *regular measure of performance* (also referred to as early completion measures) is a nondecreasing (in the case of a minimization problem) or a nonincreasing (in the case of a maximization problem) function of the activity finish times. According to French (1982) it means that, when R is a regular function of $f_1, f_2, \ldots, f_n$, such that $f_1 \leq f_1', f_2 \leq f_2', \ldots, f_n \leq f_n'$, then

$$R(f_1, f_2, \ldots, f_n) \leq R(f_1', f_2', \ldots, f_n') \text{ (minimization problem)}$$

or

$$R(f_1, f_2, \ldots, f_n) \geq R(f_1', f_2', \ldots, f_n') \text{ (maximization problem)}$$

with f_i the finish time of activity i and n the number of activities in a project.

The minimization of the project duration is undoubtedly the most popular regular measure of performance. Other examples of regular measures of performance are the minimization of the mean flow-time, the mean lateness, the mean tardiness and the number of activities that are tardy. The logic of this type of measure lies in the fact that it will never be beneficial to delay an activity towards the end of the project when only the precedence constraints are considered and consequently without considering the constraints on the resources. Therefore, when two feasible project schedules have been constructed such that each activity under the first schedule finishes no later than the corresponding finish time in the second schedule, then the first schedule is at least as good as the second schedule. In recent years, scheduling problems with *nonregular measures of performance* (also referred to as free completion measures) have gained increasing attention. A nonregular measure of performance is a measure for which the above definition does not hold. This implies that delaying an activity may result in an improvement of the performance measure. Practical applications of nonregular measures of performance often introduce financial aspects of project management. Such financial aspects may take the form of cash flows related to the activities of a project, penalty costs related to the due dates of the activities, quality costs, and many more. The project scheduling objectives described in Sects. 7.3.3, 7.3.4 and 8.2 are all nonregular measures of performance.

Similar to Part I of this book, it is assumed that a project consists of a set of activities N, numbered from a dummy start node 1 to a dummy end node n, between which precedence relations exist. For the sake of simplicity, it is assumed that all precedence relations are minimal finish-start relations with a time-lag of zero, unless otherwise indicated. Moreover, there are K renewable resources with a_k ($1 \leq k \leq K$) the availability of resource type k over the complete scheduling horizon and with r_{ik} ($1 \leq i \leq n, 1 \leq k \leq K$) as the resource requirements of activity i with respect to resource type k. No nonrenewable resource constraints are taken into account, unless otherwise indicated. The start and end dummy activities representing the start and finish of the project have a duration and a renewable resource requirement equal to zero. A project network is represented by a topologically ordered activity-on-the-node format where A is the set of pairs of activities between which a finish-start precedence relationship with time lag 0 exists. It is assumed that the graph $G(N, A)$ is acyclic. A schedule is defined by an n-vector of start times $s = (s_1, \ldots, s_n)$, which implies an n-vector of finish times $f(f_i = s_i + d_i, \forall i \in N)$. A schedule is said to be feasible if the precedence and resource constraints are satisfied. The objective of the scheduling problem type differs along the subsections, as described hereunder.

7.3.2 Time Minimization

The critical path calculations of Chaps. 2 and 3 ignore the limited availability of renewable resources. However, when the use of renewable resources is limited in availability, the construction of a feasible schedule with a minimal entire project duration might be a complex task. The presence of limited renewable resources often results in resource over-allocations (or resource conflicts) at certain points in time where more resources are needed than actually available. In this case, activities need to be shifted in time in order to resolve the resource conflict and to make the schedule both precedence as well as resource feasible. A resource conflict occurs when there is at least one period $]t - 1, t]$ for which $\exists k \leq K : \sum_{i \in S(t)} r_{ik} > a_k$, where $S(t)$ denotes the set of activities in progress in period $]t - 1, t]$.

Table 7.1 is an extended version of Table 2.2 containing information of the activity use of a single renewable resource which is assumed to be available for 10 units (i.e. $a_1 = 10$). The columns with the cash flow and resource group are irrelevant for this section and can be ignored. The network logic of the table is graphically displayed in an activity-on-the-node network of Fig. 7.1 with each number above the node denoting the activity duration and the number displayed below each node the resource demand. The resource graph of the ESS is given in Fig. 7.2. If the availability of the example project equals $a_1 = 10$, then there are resource over-allocations of the single renewable resource type at periods $]0, 3]$ and $]5, 10]$ (as an example, the set of activities in progress at period $]2, 3]$ is equal to $S(3) = \{2, 3, 4\}$). In order to resolve these resource conflicts, some activities that incur such a conflict need to be shifted forwards in time.

This problem is known as the *Resource-Constrained Project Scheduling Problem* (RCPSP), which can be formally stated as follows. A set of project activities is to be scheduled within a minimal project duration and subject to the precedence relations and a set of renewable resource types. It is mentioned earlier that a schedule is said

Table 7.1 Activity and resource data for the example project of Fig. 7.1

Activity	Predecessors	Duration	Resource use	Cash flows (€)	Resource group
1	–	0	0	0	–
2	1	6	7	−50	A
3	1	5	1	50	B
4	1	3	5	−50	–
5	3	1	6	−100	–
6	3	3	1	10	–
7	3	2	2	−10	B
8	4	1	2	20	–
9	2	4	8	100	A
10	5	3	6	0	–
11	7	1	2	−50	B
12	6, 10, 11	3	6	50	B
13	8, 12	5	8	100	–
14	9, 13	0	0	1,000	–

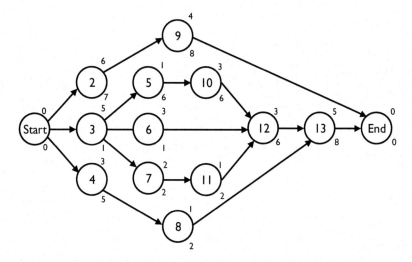

Fig. 7.1 The AoN example network of Table 7.1

to be feasible if the precedence *and* the renewable resource constraints are satisfied. Consequently, the objective of the RCPSP is to find a feasible schedule such that the total project duration (often referred to as the schedule makespan) s_n is minimized. A conceptual formulation for the RCPSP can be given as follows:

$$\text{Minimize } s_n \tag{7.1}$$

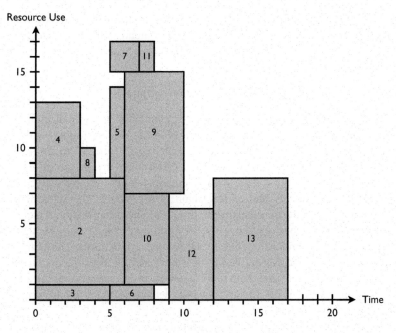

Fig. 7.2 Resource graph for earliest start schedule (ESS)

subject to

$$s_i + d_i \leq s_j \qquad\qquad \forall (i,j) \in A \qquad\qquad (7.2)$$

$$\sum_{i \in S(t)} r_{ik} \leq a_k \qquad\qquad k = 1,\ldots, K; t = 1,\ldots, T \qquad (7.3)$$

$$s_1 = 0 \qquad\qquad\qquad (7.4)$$

$$s_i \in int^+ \qquad\qquad i = 1\ldots, n \qquad\qquad (7.5)$$

The objective in Eq. 7.1 minimizes the entire project duration by minimizing the start time of the dummy end activity. The constraint set given in Eq. 7.2 maintains the finish-start precedence relations with a time-lag of zero among the activities. Equation 7.3 are used to model the limited availability of the renewable resources. It stipulates that the sum of the resource requirements of all activities in progress at time period $]t - 1, t]$ is not allowed to exceed the availability of the renewable resource over the complete time horizon of the project T. Equation 7.4 forces the dummy start activity, and hence the project, to start at time zero. Equation 7.5 ensure that the activity start times assume nonnegative integer values.

In the remainder of this section, it is assumed that each activity follows a "fixed duration" mode, i.e. the time estimates (in duration units, above the node) and resource demand (in units, below the node) cannot be changed during scheduling.

In Sect. 7.5, this assumption will be extended to a "fixed work" mode where the product of both estimates, the so-called work content, is fixed but the individual estimates for the activity duration and resource unit demand can change, respecting the following equation:

$$\text{Work} = \text{Duration} * \text{Units}$$

Figure 7.3 displays the optimal resource chart with a minimal entire project duration of 25 time units. The presence of renewable resources with limited availability increases the minimal critical path length from 17 to 25 time units. The minimal length of the project is now determined by the so-called *critical chain*, which replaces the critical path calculations when resources are limited in availability. Consequently, the critical chain of a project is the set of dependent activities that defines the minimal project duration. These dependencies include both technological precedence relations (like the traditional critical path calculations) as well as resource dependencies (due to the limited availability). The critical chain is similar to a resource-constrained critical path and requires the attention of the project manager. The critical chain of the example project consists of the dependent set of activities 2, 4, 5, 9, 10, 12 and 13, which determines the minimal entire project duration of 25 time units.

Note that the problem formulation without Eq. 7.3 boils down to the ordinary critical path calculations of Chap. 2. The logical extension from minimal precedence relations with a zero time-lag to generalized precedence relations leads to an increase in schedule problem complexity. In the conceptual formulation, the Eq. 7.2 will be replaced by the generalized precedence relations of Bartusch et al. (1988) as discussed in Sect. 2.2.3 as follows:

$$s_i + l_{ij} \le s_j \qquad\qquad \forall (i, j) \in A$$

Since the introduction of renewable resources will lead to an increase of the entire project duration (the entire project duration might remain unchanged when

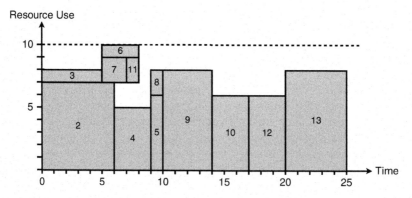

Fig. 7.3 Feasible resource graph with minimal time

Table 7.2 Four renewable resources for the example project of Fig. 7.1

Activity	Duration	Resource 1	Resource 2	Resource 3	Resource 4
1	0	0	0	0	0
2	6	7	15	2	6
3	5	1	8	4	8
4	3	5	8	3	3
5	1	6	15	2	6
6	3	1	13	0	3
7	2	2	16	2	0
8	1	2	9	4	4
9	4	8	12	5	5
10	3	6	17	5	0
11	1	2	10	2	5
12	3	6	5	5	4
13	5	8	10	3	7
14	0	0	0	0	0

no resource conflicts occur in the critical path schedule), the critical path is a lower bound for the entire project duration under the presence of renewable resources. Obviously, the introduction of additional renewable resource types will further increase the total project duration. Consider, for example, Table 7.2 where the example project is subject to four renewable resource types with a limited availability of $a_1 = 10, a_2 = 20, a_3 = 8, a_4 = 10$.

It can be shown that the use of renewable resources under limited availability leads to an increase in the project duration. In the example, the project duration increases when iteratively taking the resources into account, from 25 (only resource 1 is taken into account) to 31 (resources 1 and 2), 33 (resources 1, 2 and 3) and 36 (all resources).

For illustrative purposes, Fig. 7.4 displays the four resource graphs with a project duration of 36 time units. In the remainder of this chapter, a single renewable resource type is used to illustrate all project scheduling objectives, without loss of generality.

7.3.3 Net Present Value Maximization

In Chap. 4 of this book, it is already mentioned that, when the financial aspects of project management are taken into consideration, there is a decided preference for the maximization of the net present value (*npv*) of the project as the more appropriate objective, and this preference increases with the project duration (Herroelen et al. 1997). This criterion is based on a very simple principle: accept the project if the *npv* is greater than or equal to zero and reject it when the *npv* is less than zero. In this *accept-reject decision* mechanism, the value of the cash flows (either cash inflows or cash outflows) will be compounded towards time zero by

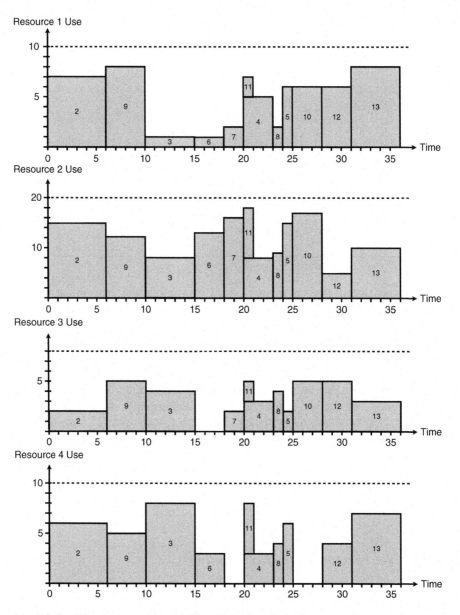

Fig. 7.4 Feasible resource graphs with four renewable resources

means of a discrete discount rate r as follows:

$$npv = cf_{10} + \sum_{i=2}^{n} \sum_{t=1}^{\infty} \frac{cf_{it}}{(1+r)^t}$$

where cf_{it} denotes the cash flows associated with activity i at the end of period t. Notice that cf_{10} denotes the initial cash flow for the dummy start activity 1 at the end of period zero, which usually takes the form of an initial investment when the project starts. When a continuous discount factor α is introduced, the *npv* can be calculated as follows:

$$npv = cf_{10} + \sum_{i=2}^{n}\sum_{t=1}^{\infty} cf_{it}e^{-\alpha t}$$

Various assumptions concerning the cash flows cf_{it} are presented in the literature. A lot of research has focused in the case where the cash flows are independent of the finish time of the corresponding activity. In that case, a terminal value of each activity upon completion can be calculated by compounding the associated cash flows cf_{it} towards the end of the activity, i.e. terminal cash flow $c_i = \sum_{t=1}^{d_i} cf_{it}e^{\alpha(d_i - t)}$. This terminal value is assumed to be independent of the time of completion of the corresponding activity. Figure 7.5 shows an illustrative example of an activity with a baseline duration of 5 weeks and a cash flow prediction of €−10, €−30, €−50, €−40 and €200 for weeks 1–5. These cash flows (positive and negative) are assumed to be independent of the start time of the activity, and therefore, the total value can be compounded to a single cash flow value $c_i = -10e^{0.05*4} - 30e^{0.05*3} - 50e^{0.05*2} - 40e^{0.05*1} + 200e^{0.05*0} = €55.62$ when using a discount rate of $\alpha = 0.05$. The compounded values are still independent from the start and finish time of the activity and will be used in the further calculation of the net present value of the project schedule.

Research work has also been done on the case where activity cash flows are dependent on the finish times of the corresponding activities, resulting in a large number of different time dependencies. Examples are given along the following lines:

- Progress payments: The cash outflows occur when an activity is completed as a result of cost of resources, materials, etc. whereas cash inflows are incurred as progress payment at the end of some time period (e.g. each month) for the work completed during this fixed time period. For references in the literature, the reader is referred to Kazaz and Sepil (1996), Sepil and Ortac (1997) and Vanhoucke et al. (2003).
- Linear dependent cash flows: Cash flows are assumed to be linearly dependent or a nonincreasing step function in time. Linear time-dependent cash flow functions occur in situations where penalties are involved. This means that the contractor

Fig. 7.5 Independent activity cash flows can be represented by a single cash flow value using discount rates

€ -10	€ -30	€ -50	€ -40	€ 200

=

€ 0	€ 0	€ 0	€ 0	€ 55.62

will receive the activity cash flows as agreed from the owner of the project (which can be negative to the contractor after cost reductions) if the schedule meets the targets. Penalties can be imposed for each activity which grow linearly in time, i.e. for every day that the activity finish time is later than its earliest finish time. For references in the literature, the reader is referred to Etgar and Shtub (1999) and Vanhoucke et al. (2001b).

- Cash flow payment problem: Up to now, it is assumed that the amount of cash flow is known at the scheduling phase for each individual activity. In practice, both the amount and timing of activity cash flows (given a certain total predefined project budget) must be determined simultaneously. This so-called payment scheduling problem of simultaneously determining the amount and timing of progress payments in order to maximize the net present value reduces to distributing payments over the duration of the project. This scheduling problem has been studied by, among others, Dayanand and Padman (1997, 2001a,b).

- Equitable solution: The net present value for a contractor is not the same as the net present value for the client of the project. Indeed, cash inflows for the contractor are, in the extreme, cash outflows for the client. A so-called equitable project schedule is a schedule where both the contractor and the client deviate from their respective ideal solutions (i.e. the net present value of the schedule) by an equal percentage. A reference in the literature can be found at Ulusoy and Cebelli (2000).

In this section, the activity cash flows are assumed to be independent of their time of occurrence. Extensions to time-dependent cash flows lead to an increase in scheduling complexity, but do not fundamentally change the underlying scheduling approach. These extended scheduling problems are outside the scope of this chapter. The *resource-constrained project scheduling problem with discounted cash flows* (RCPSPDC) where cash flows are assumed to be time-independent can be conceptually formulated as follows:

$$\text{Maximize} \sum_{i=1}^{n} c_i e^{-\alpha(s_i + d_i)} \tag{7.6}$$

subject to

$$s_i + d_i \le s_j \qquad\qquad \forall (i, j) \in A \tag{7.7}$$

$$\sum_{i \in S(t)} r_{ik} \le a_k \qquad\qquad k = 1, \ldots, K; t = 1, \ldots, T \tag{7.8}$$

$$s_1 = 0 \tag{7.9}$$

$$s_n \le \delta_n \tag{7.10}$$

$$s_i \in int^+ \qquad\qquad i = 1 \ldots, n \tag{7.11}$$

The objective in Eq. 7.6 maximizes the net present value of the project by discounting the terminal activity cash flows c_i towards the beginning of the project. The constraint set given in Eq. 7.7 maintains the finish-start precedence relations among the activities. The limited availability of the renewable resources is modeled by Eq. 7.8. Equation 7.9 forces the dummy start activity, and hence the project, to start at time zero while Eq. 7.10 limits the project duration to a negotiated project deadline δ_n. Equation 7.11 ensure that the activity start times assume nonnegative integer values.

Figure 7.6 displays the optimal resource-feasible schedule for the example project of Table 7.1 with a discount rate $\alpha = 0.01$, a project deadline $\delta_n = 25$ and activity cash flows given in Table 7.1 that occur at the finish of the activity (i.e. the values are assumed to be equal to c_i as a discounted value of all its cf_{it} values). The resource-constrained project scheduling problem with the use of activity cash flows is very similar to the classical RCPSP since it only differs in its objective function. The objective is to schedule all the activities in order to maximize the net present value of the project, without violating the precedence or resource constraints and subject to a given deadline. The simple translation of the *npv*-philosophy into project scheduling is to schedule all activities with a positive cash flows as soon as possible and to delay all activities with a negative cash flow as late as possible towards the deadline. Notice that the finish times of activities 4, 5, 7, 8 and 11 have been shifted to the project deadline compared to the time objective and activities 9 have been scheduled earlier, which has resulted in an overall improvement of the objective value. In fact, it leads to an improvement for activities 4, 5, 7, 9 and 11 and a deterioration for activity 8. The total net present value equals $npv = -50e^{(-0.01*6)} + 50e^{(-0.01*5)} - 50e^{(-0.01*13)} - 100e^{(-0.01*14)} + 10e^{(-0.01*8)} - 10e^{(-0.01*16)} + 20e^{(-0.01*14)} + 100e^{(-0.01*10)} + 0e^{(-0.01*17)} - 50e^{(-0.01*17)} + 50e^{(-0.01*20)} + 100e^{(-0.01*25)} + 1,000e^{(-0.01*25)} = $ €833.65, which is an improvement of the net present value of €12.95 for the schedule of Fig. 7.3. Note that the project duration is equal to 25, which is the minimal duration possible (see previous section). Thanks to a big lump

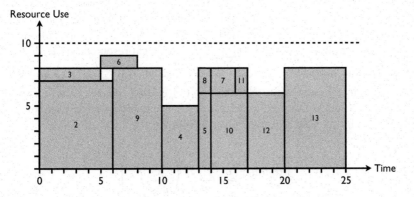

Fig. 7.6 Feasible resource graph with maximal *npv*

sum payment for the dummy end activity of €1,000, this would also have been the case, even if the deadline constraint $\delta_n \leq 25$ would have been omitted.

The importance of the net present value in project scheduling has been described in a paper by Herroelen et al. (1997). In this paper, the use of the max-*npv* objective over a relatively short period of time is seriously questioned. Furthermore, the max-*npv* objective also seems to be questionable under conditions of uncertainty. Consequently, the relevance of the max-*npv* objective is limited to those situations where the time value of money is to be taken into consideration. It is clear that this is the case in capital intensive projects with a sufficiently long duration, significant cash flows, high interest rates and high costs of capital. This may be the case in the construction industry but is certainly not the case in production environments with a time horizon of days or weeks.

7.3.4   Resource Leveling

Both the RCPSP and the RCPSPDC aim at the construction of a precedence and resource feasible schedule with a certain objective (time and *npv*, respectively). When over-allocations of resources occur (known as the so-called resource conflicts), they are resolved by shifting activities further in time. However, none of the previous problem types explicitly takes the resulting pattern of total resource use over time into account, and hence, project schedules with very irregular resource use (peak demands as well as low resource demands) are a matter of degree. The *resource-leveling project scheduling problem* (RLPSP) aims at the construction of a precedence and resource feasible schedule within a predefined deadline with a resource use that is as level as possible within the project horizon. In order to avoid jumps from peaks to low resource demands, the total use of all resources needs to be balanced over the total schedule horizon.

The RLPSP involves the scheduling of project activities in order to level the use of the renewable resources subject to technological precedence relations and a predefined project deadline. Often, no explicit resource availability is taken into account, although many projects are simply subject to a maximum resource availability as specified in the previous scheduling objectives. The objective function depends on the total resource use $\sum_{i \in S(t)} r_{ik}$ for each resource type k during the complete time horizon $t = 1, \ldots, \delta_n$, denoted as $f_k \left(\sum_{i \in S(t)} r_{ik} \right)$ and can be formulated in different ways. Note that $f_k(x)$ is used to refer to a function that depends on x and is not used to refer to a finish time of an activity. A conceptual formulation for the RLPSP can be given as follows:

$$\text{Minimize} \sum_{k=1}^{K} \sum_{t=1}^{\delta_n} f_k \left(\sum_{i \in S(t)} r_{ik} \right) \qquad (7.12)$$

subject to

$$s_i + d_i \leq s_j \qquad\qquad \forall (i, j) \in A \qquad\qquad (7.13)$$

$$\sum_{i \in S(t)} r_{ik} \leq a_k \qquad\qquad k = 1, \ldots, K; t = 1, \ldots, \delta_n \qquad (7.14)$$

$$s_1 = 0 \qquad\qquad\qquad\qquad\qquad\qquad\qquad\qquad (7.15)$$

$$s_n \leq \delta_n \qquad\qquad\qquad\qquad\qquad\qquad\qquad\qquad (7.16)$$

$$s_i \in int^+ \qquad\qquad i = 1, \ldots, n \qquad\qquad\qquad (7.17)$$

The objective in Eq. 7.12 is a general formulation to express a preference for a balanced use of resources over the scheduling horizon. All other constraints modeled by Eqs. 7.13–7.17 are similar to the scheduling problems of previous sections. The objective function of this formulation can take many forms and measures how leveled the resource use is. Common expressions are as follows:

$$f_k \left(\sum_{i \in S(t)} r_{ik} \right) = w_k \left(\sum_{i \in S(t)} r_{ik} \right)^2$$

$$f_k \left(\sum_{i \in S(t)} r_{ik} \right) = w_k \left(\sum_{i \in S(t)} r_{ik} - a_k \right)^2$$

$$f_k \left(\sum_{i \in S(t)} r_{ik} \right) = w_k \left| \sum_{i \in S(t)} r_{ik} - a_k \right|$$

$$f_k \left(\sum_{i \in S(t)} r_{ik} \right) = w_k \left| \sum_{i \in S(t)} r_{ik} - \sum_{i \in S(t-1)} r_{ik} \right|$$

The first equation measures the leveling objective as a total weighted sum of the squared resource use, with a weighting factor w_k that depends on the importance of resource k. Expressions 2 and 3 take an explicit resource availability into account, and weigh the absolute or squared deviation of the resource use from a given resource availability a_k. The last expression weighs the variation of the resource use from period to period and hence aims at the minimization of the resource use jumps over time. Figure 7.7 shows a feasible project schedule where the use of the renewable resource is more or less leveled. It can be easily verified that the values for the four objective functions are equal to 1,411, 171, 63 and 14 (under the assumption that $w_1 = 1$), respectively.

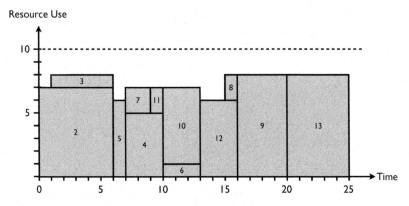

Fig. 7.7 Feasible resource graph with leveled resource use

7.4   Scheduling Methods

Resource-constrained project scheduling has been a research topic for many decades, resulting in a wide variety of optimization procedures that differ in objective functions, activity assumptions, resource constraints and many more. The main focus on the total project time minimization has led to the development of various exact and heuristic procedures for scheduling projects with tight renewable resource constraints where the well-known resource-constrained project scheduling problem (RCPSP) clearly took the lead. This problem type of Sect. 7.3.2 aims at minimizing the total duration of a project subject to precedence relations between the activities and the limited renewable resource availabilities and is known to be NP hard (Blazewicz et al. 1983). Extensions to other objective functions (see e.g. the scheduling objectives discussed in Sects. 7.3.3, 7.3.4 and 8.2), alternative resource constraints (to nonrenewable and doubly-constrained resources), multiple activity modes, etc. often result in highly complex optimization problems and have been studied in the literature by many authors. For an extensive overview of resource-constrained project scheduling procedures in the literature, the reader is referred to the research handbook written by Demeulemeester and Herroelen (2002).

The vast majority of resource-constrained scheduling procedures can be classified in two categories: exact and heuristic procedures. Exact procedures aim at finding the best possible solution for the scheduling problem type and are therefore often restricted to small projects under strict assumptions. This class of optimization procedures is widely available in the literature but is not discussed in this book. The second class of scheduling procedures aims at finding good, but not guaranteed to be optimal schedules for more realistic projects (i.e. under different assumptions and for larger sizes) in a reasonable (computational) time. Although these procedures do not guarantee an optimal solution for the project, they can be easily embedded in any scheduling software tool due to their simplicity and generality to a broad range of different projects.

In the remaining sections of this chapter, *constructive heuristic procedures* will be discussed to schedule resource-constrained projects under various scheduling objectives. Sections 7.4.1, 7.4.2 and 7.4.3 are devoted to techniques to construct and assess project schedules with regular measures of performance (in casu, the RCPSP with time minimization) while Sect. 7.4.4 presents a general technique for project scheduling problems under nonregular measures of performance.

7.4.1 Constructive Heuristics

Priority rule based scheduling is a simple and quick scheduling method used to construct project schedules under a regular measure of performance. A priority rule based heuristic is a single-pass method to construct a feasible schedule based on two components: a priority rule and a schedule generation scheme. A *priority rule* is used to select the next activity during the heuristic search process. Therefore, a priority rule requires a priority list that ranks all project activities in a certain order. A *schedule generation scheme* aims at the generation of a feasible schedule by extending the partial schedule (i.e. a schedule where only a subset of the activities has been assigned a start and finish time) in a stage-wise fashion. Hence, the heuristic priority-based procedure consecutively selects project activities from the constructed priority list and schedules them according to the rules of the schedule generation scheme. These two components are discussed along the following subsections.

Priority Rules

A priority rule determines the activity that is selected next during the heuristic search process, and results in a priority list in which the activities are ordered such that the network structure has been preserved. This means that no activity should be ordered before one of its predecessors. In what follows, four classes of priority rules are discussed, and a number of examples for each class is given. A fifth class is mentioned as a combined version of the four classes. The alert reader can extend each class to many other priority rules.

1. Activity based priority rules: Construction of a priority list is based on the characteristics of the project activities. The most straightforward characteristic is the duration of an activity.
2. Network based priority rules: The priority list is constructed based on the network logic, i.e. the set of activities and their precedence relations.
3. Critical path based priority rules: Critical path based scheduling information is used to construct the priority list.
4. Resource based priority rules: Priority lists are constructed based on the network logic and the resource information.

Table 7.3 Various priority rules used to construct a schedule for the example project of Fig. 7.1

Priority rule	Priority list	SSGS	PSGS
Activity based rules			
Shortest Processing Time (SPT)	[4,8,3,5,7,11,6,10,12,13,2,9]	27	25
Longest Processing Time (LPT)	[2,3,9,4,6,7,5,10,8,11,12,13]	25	25
Network based rules			
Most Immediate Successors (MIS)	[3,2,4,5,6,7,8,9,10,11,12,13]	25	25
Most Total Successors (MTS)	[3,5,7,4,6,10,11,2,8,12,9,13]	27	25
Least nonrelated Jobs (LNRJ)[a]	[3,5,7,10,11,6,12,4,8,13,2,9]	27	25
Greatest Rank Positional Weight (GRPW)[b]	[3,2,6,4,8,5,10,9,7,11,12,13]	25	25
Critical path based rules			
Earliest Start Time (EST)	[2,3,4,8,5,6,7,9,10,11,12,13]	25	25
Earliest Finish Time (EFT)	[4,8,3,2,5,7,6,11,10,9,12,13]	25	25
Latest Start Time (LST)	[3,5,6,7,10,2,4,11,12,8,13,9]	27	25
Latest Finish Time (LFT)	[3,5,7,6,10,11,4,8,12,2,9,13]	27	25
Minimum Slack (MSLK)	[3,5,10,6,7,11,12,2,9,4,8,13]	27	26
Resource based rules			
Greatest Resource Demand (GRD)	[2,9,4,3,5,10,7,6,8,11,12,13]	25	25
Greatest Cumulative Resource Demand (GCRD)	[2,9,3,5,10,6,4,8,7,11,12,13]	25	25

[a] A job (activity) is not related to another job if there is no precedence related path between the two activities in the project network
[b] The GRPW is calculated as the sum of the duration of the activity and the durations of all its immediate successors

5. Composite priority rules: A weighted combination of previous priority rules is used to construct the priority list.

Table 7.3 gives an incomplete list of priority rules from each of the first four classes for the example project of Fig. 7.1. The solution obtained by using a serial (SSGS) and parallel (PSGS) schedule generation schemes, discussed hereafter, is also reported.

Schedule Generation Schemes

A schedule generation scheme determines the way in which a feasible schedule is constructed by assigning start times to the project activities. A serial schedule generation scheme (SSGS) follows an activity-incrementation approach while a parallel schedule generation scheme (PSGS) makes use of a time-incrementation scheme.

Using a *serial schedule generation scheme*, the priority values can be used to construct a project schedule by scheduling each activity one-at-a-time and as soon as possible within the precedence and resource constraints. Consequently, the SSGS scans the priority list and selects at each stage the next activity from the priority list in order to schedule it at its first possible start time without violating both the precedence and resource constraints.

A *parallel schedule generation scheme* iterates over the time horizon of the project (instead of the priority list) and adds activities that can be scheduled at a certain predefined moment in time. It selects at each decision point t the eligible activities and assigns a scheduling sequence of these eligible activities according to the priority list. At each decision point, the eligible activities are scheduled with a start time equal to the decision point (on the condition that there is no resource conflict). Activities that cannot be scheduled due to a resource conflict are skipped and become eligible to schedule at the next decision point t', which equals the earliest finish time of all activities active at the current decision point t.

Figure 7.8 displays the solution obtained by using the serial (top) and parallel (bottom) schedule generation schemes using the SPT priority rule, resulting in a project duration of 27 and 25 time units, respectively. The assignment of activities to the project schedule using a parallel schedule generation scheme is illustrated in Table 7.4. The set of eligible activities for each time decision point t is ranked according to the SPT rule, and activities are added to the schedule at time point t in the order given by the 'Ranked' column and in case it does not lead to a resource conflict.

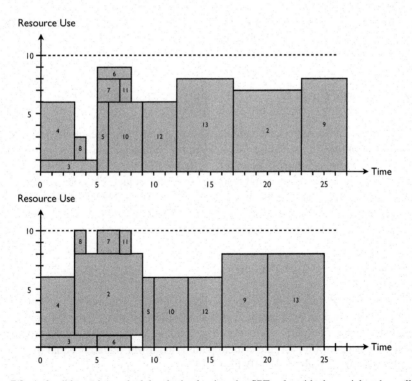

Fig. 7.8 A feasible project schedule obtained using the SPT rule with the serial and parallel schedule generation schemes

Table 7.4 The parallel
schedule generation scheme
procedure to obtain the
bottom schedule of Fig. 7.8

t	Eligible	Ranked	Scheduled
0	{2,3,4}	{4,3,2}	{3,4}
3	{2,8}	{8,2}	{2,3,4,8}
4	–	–	{2,3,4,8}
5	{5,6,7}	{5,7,6}	{2,3,4,6,7,8}
7	{5,11}	{5,11}	{2,3,4,6,7,8,11}
8	{5}	{5}	{2,3,4,6,7,8,11}
9	{5,9}	{5,9}	{2,3,4,5,6,7,8,11}
10	{9,10}	{10,9}	{2,3,4,5,6,7,8,10,11}
13	{9,12}	{12,9}	{2,3,4,5,6,7,8,10,11,12}
16	{9,13}	{9,13}	{2,3,4,5,6,7,8,9,10,11,12}
20	{13}	{13}	{2,3,4,5,6,7,8,9,10,11,12,13}

It should be noted that the calculations of the rankings using the priority lists as shown in Table 7.3 take the precedence relations into account. For this reason, the SPT rule displays activity 13 before activity 2 (shorter duration) and activity 2 before activity 9 (precedence relation), although activity 9 has a shorter duration than activity 13. When using the SPT rule for constructing a feasible schedule with the parallel generation scheme (Table 7.4), activity 9 has been scheduled earlier than activity 13 (shorter duration). When the original list of Table 7.3 should have been used, activity 13 would have been scheduled before activity 9. Both approaches lead to a total project duration of 25 time units.

7.4.2 Lower Bounds

The purpose of lower bound calculations is to validate the quality of project schedules obtained by software tools or simple methods such as the priority rule based scheduling techniques presented earlier. While these heuristics were able to quickly present a precedence and resource feasible project schedule, a bound does not construct a feasible schedule but instead calculates a lower bound on the minimal project duration (upper bound in case of maximization problem). In the following subsections, three lower bound calculations will be explained.

Critical Path Based Lower Bound

Since the critical path method ignores the resource constraints and constructs an earliest start schedule with minimal project duration by only taking the precedence relations into account, it is obviously a lower bound on the RCPSP schedule. In the example project of Fig. 7.1, the critical path based lower bound is equal to 17 units resulting from the path "1-3-5-10-12-13-14".

Resource Based Lower Bound

The resource based lower bound ignores the precedence relations of the project network and can therefore be considered as an inverse calculation of the critical path based lower bound. Since each activity is characterized by a duration and a renewable resource demand per resource type k, it can be expressed as an activity work content $r_{ik}d_i$. The work content, expressed in man-hours, man-days or man-weeks can be used to calculate a lower bound on the total project duration, as follows:

$$\max_k \left\lceil \frac{\sum_{i=1}^{n} r_{ik}d_i}{a_k} \right\rceil$$

where $\lceil x \rceil$ is used to calculate the smallest integer that is larger than x.

The resource based lower bound for the example project of Fig. 7.1 can be calculated as follows ($k = 1$): The numerator is equal to $6 * 7 + 5 * 1 + 3 * 5 + 1 * 6 + 3 * 1 + 2 * 2 + 1 * 2 + 4 * 8 + 3 * 6 + 1 * 2 + 3 * 6 + 5 * 8 = 187$ and hence the lower bound equals $\lceil \frac{187}{10} \rceil = 19$.

Critical Sequence Lower Bound

The critical sequence lower bound is a combination of the two previous lower bounds since it simultaneously considers both the precedence relations as well as the renewable resource constraints. The calculation of this bound consists of four steps, as follows:

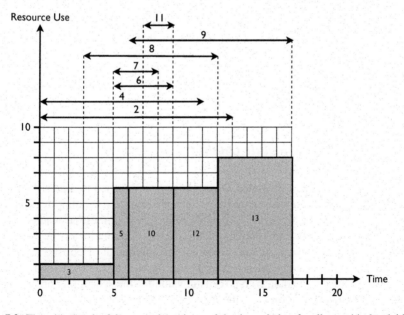

Fig. 7.9 The critical path of the example project and the time window for all noncritical activities

Table 7.5 Intermediate
calculations to obtain the
critical sequence lower bound
value

Activity	d_i	es_i	lf_i	e_i	$d_i - e_i$
2	6	0	13	5	1
4	3	0	11	3	0
6	3	5	9	3	0
7	2	5	8	2	0
8	1	3	12	1	0
9	4	6	17	0	4
11	1	7	9	1	0

1. Consider a critical path in the network.
2. Determine for each noncritical activity i how many time periods e_i this activity
   can be scheduled consecutively in parallel with the activities on the critical path
   (between its es_i and lf_i).
3. Set $e_i = \min(e_i, d_i)$ for each noncritical activity.
4. Increase the critical path length with the maximum of all $d_i - e_i$ values for the
   noncritical activities to obtain the critical sequence lower bound.

Figure 7.9 shows the critical activities 3, 5, 10, 12 and 13 resulting in a critical
path with length of 17 time units. The remaining activities are displayed by means
of an arc, showing their time window between their es_i and lf_i given the critical
path length.

Table 7.5 displays the calculations of the e_i and shows the increase in the critical
path length when each activity is individually added to the critical path schedule of
Fig. 7.9. As an example, activity 2 can only be scheduled in parallel with the current
critical path for 5 time units without violating the renewable resource constraints,
while its duration is equal to 6. Consequently, $d_2 - e_2 = 6 - 5 = 1$ which means that
the critical path length of 17 will increase by 1 time unit when introducing activity 2
in the schedule. All e_i and $d_i - e_i$ calculations are made for each noncritical activity
individually (see the table) and the largest $d_i - e_i$ value is added to the current
critical path value for the calculation of the lower bound. In the example, the critical
sequence lower bound is equal to $17 + \max(d_i - e_i) = 17 + (d_9 - e_9) = 17 + 4 = 21$
time units.

7.4.3 Assessing Schedule Quality

It has been mentioned earlier that lower bounds can be used to assess the quality
of a project schedule constructed by a software tool, a scheduling technique or
any other procedure. Since lower bounds often report infeasible results (due to
e.g. resource conflicts or violations of the precedence relations), they lead to a
scheduling objective value that is unrealistically optimistic. Heuristic scheduling
techniques, on the contrary, such as priority rule based scheduling methods, provide
a resource feasible schedule with a realistic value for the scheduling objective, but
with an unknown deviation from the theoretically best possible schedule. The gap
between the two values for the scheduling objective gives an indication about the

Fig. 7.10 Assessment of the project schedule quality

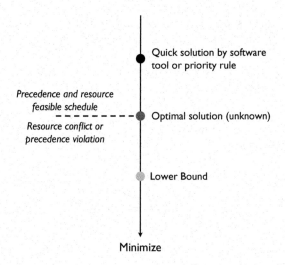

Quick solution by software tool or priority rule

Precedence and resource feasible schedule

Optimal solution (unknown)

Resource conflict or precedence violation

Lower Bound

Minimize

room for improvement, as shown in Fig. 7.10 for a minimization objective (such as time for the RCPSP).

In case of the example project of Fig. 7.1, the best solution obtained by all priority rule based scheduling rules can be considered as an upper bound for the total project duration, and equals 25 time units. The best lower bound is equal to 21. In this example, the gap between the two bounds does not provide much information. It might give the (false) impression that the heuristic solution can be further improved to lower values than 25, however, it has been shown earlier that this is not possible since it is the optimal minimal project duration. More advanced lower bound calculations, or other project network examples, might lead to smaller gaps and more precise estimates about the heuristic solution quality.

7.4.4 Other Scheduling Methods

Burgess and Killebrew Algorithm

The serial and parallel schedule generation schemes discussed in Sect. 7.4.1 are used to transform a priority rule into a resource feasible earliest start schedule aiming at minimizing a regular scheduling objective, e.g. the total project duration. However, since many of the real-life scheduling objectives are different from the time objective (see the previous sections of this chapter), another schedule generation scheme that is able to construct project schedules that deviate from a resource feasible earliest start schedule would be useful in case of a nonregular scheduling objective. The Burgess and Killebrew (B&K) algorithm presented in this section is a general, easy and effective algorithm to transform a priority rule into a project schedule where the variability in resource use is minimized (expressed by the resource leveling scheduling objective discussed in Sect. 7.3.4). It relies on the main characteristic of nonregular scheduling objectives, i.e. delaying an activity in time might lead to an improvement in the scheduling objective. The pseudo code of the B&K algorithm to transform a predefined priority rule into a resource feasible project scheduling with a resource leveling objective can be displayed as follows:

> Schedule all activities at their early start time: $s_i = es_i$
> while change $= 1$
>   For each activity i from the first one in the priority list to the last
> $CB = \infty$
>   For each possible start time t of activity i from s_i to ls_i
>   Calculate the scheduling objective O_{it}
>   If $O_{it} \le CB$ then $CB = O_{it}$ and $s_i^{best} = t$
>   If $s_i^{best} \ge s_i$ then $s_i = s_i^{best}$ and change $= 1$

with

s_i	Current start time of activity i
es_i	Earliest start time of activity i
ls_i	Latest start time of activity i (given the s_i of all successor activities!)
O_{it}	Scheduling objective value when activity i starts at time t
	$=$ calculation of the nonregular objective value when all other activities remain unchanged in the schedule
CB	Scheduling objective value of current best schedule found
s_i^{best}	Best start time of activity i
$change$	0/1 variable denoting a change or not
	$=$ defines the stop criterion of the while loop in the B&K algorithm

The reader should have noted that the B&K algorithm does not explicitly take the renewable resource constraints into account. The aim of the algorithm is to schedule the project activities in time such that the variability of resource use is leveled to the best possible, without constraining the maximal use per time specified in a resource availability.

The B&K algorithm can be illustrated on the example project of Fig. 7.1 where the scheduling objective is to level the use of resources. It is assumed that the scheduling objective is calculated as $f_k(\sum_{i \in S(t)} r_{ik}) = (\sum_{i \in S(t)} r_{ik})^2$ which measures the leveling objective as a total sum of the squared resource use, with a weighting factor $w_k = 1$. The priority rule used is a randomly generated priority list equal to [12, 10, 3, 4, 2, 8, 13, 11, 7, 6, 9, 5] (start and end nodes are excluded from the list). The earliest start times of the nondummy activities are equal to $es_2 = 0, es_3 = 0, es_4 = 0, es_5 = 5, es_6 = 5, es_7 = 5, es_8 = 3, es_9 = 6,$ $es_{10} = 6, es_{11} = 7, es_{12} = 9$ and $es_{13} = 12$ (see Fig. 7.2). The current start times of all activities are initially set to their earliest start times. It is assumed that a project deadline of 25 is set, and the latest start times are calculated as $ls_2 = 0, ls_3 = 0, ls_4 = 0, ls_5 = 5, ls_6 = 6, ls_7 = 5, ls_8 = 11, \quad ls_9 = 21, ls_{10} = 6,$

$ls_{11} = 8, ls_{12} = 9$ and $ls_{13} = 20$. Note that these latest start times are not calculated as done in Chap. 2 using backward calculations, but instead are calculated *given* the current start times of all successor activities. As an example, ls_9 is equal to 21, since it has no successors (except the dummy end activity 14 which starts and ends at the project deadline 25) while ls_{12} is equal to 9 since its successor activity 13 currently starts at $s_{13} = 12$. Consequently, the latest start times need to be continuously updated when activities shift in time. The B&K procedure runs as follows (only activities that are shifted in time are shown):

Run 1: $ls_2 = 0, ls_3 = 0, ls_4 = 0, ls_5 = 5, ls_6 = 6, ls_7 = 5, ls_8 = 11, ls_9 = 21, ls_{10} = 6, ls_{11} = 8, ls_{12} = 9$ and $ls_{13} = 20$. The current schedule has a total objective value of 2,289. This value is calculated as the sum of the squared resource use for all activities shown in Fig. 7.2 and is equal to $13^2 + 13^2 + 13^2 + 10^2 + 8^2 + 16^2 + 17^2 + 17^2 + 14^2 + 14^2 + 6^2 + 6^2 + 8^2 + 8^2 + 8^2 + 8^2 + 8^2$.

- Shift activity 8 from 3 to 11 and update $ls_4 = 8$ and $ls_8 = 11$
- Shift activity 13 from 12 to 20 and update $ls_8 = 19, ls_{12} = 17$ and $ls_{13} = 20$
- Shift activity 11 from 7 to 8 and update $ls_7 = 6$ and $ls_{11} = 8$
- Shift activity 9 from 6 to 16 and update $ls_2 = 10$ and $ls_9 = 21$

Run 2: $ls_2 = 10, ls_3 = 0, ls_4 = 8, ls_5 = 5, ls_6 = 6, ls_7 = 6, ls_8 = 19, ls_9 = 21, ls_{10} = 6, ls_{11} = 8, ls_{12} = 17$ and $ls_{13} = 20$. The current schedule has a total objective value of 1,797.

- Shift activity 12 from 9 to 13 and update $ls_6 = 10, ls_{10} = 10, ls_{11} = 12$ and $ls_{12} = 17$
- Shift activity 10 from 6 to 10 and update $ls_5 = 9$ and $ls_{10} = 10$
- Shift activity 4 from 0 to 7 and update $ls_4 = 8$
- Shift activity 8 from 11 to 15 and update $ls_4 = 12$ and $ls_8 = 19$
- Shift activity 11 from 8 to 9 and update $ls_7 = 7$ and $ls_{11} = 12$
- Shift activity 7 from 5 to 6 and update $ls_7 = 7$
- Shift activity 6 from 5 to 6 and update $ls_6 = 10$
- Shift activity 5 from 5 to 6 and update $ls_3 = 1$ and $ls_5 = 9$

Run 3: $ls_2 = 10, ls_3 = 1, ls_4 = 12, ls_5 = 9, ls_6 = 10, ls_7 = 7, ls_8 = 19, ls_9 = 21, ls_{10} = 10, ls_{11} = 12, ls_{12} = 17$ and $ls_{13} = 20$. The current schedule has a total objective value of 1,419.

- Shift activity 3 from 0 to 1 and update $ls_3 = 1$
- Shift activity 7 from 6 to 7 and update $ls_7 = 7$
- Shift activity 6 from 6 to 10 and update $ls_6 = 10$

Run 4: $ls_2 = 10, ls_3 = 1, ls_4 = 12, ls_5 = 9, ls_6 = 10, ls_7 = 7, ls_8 = 19, ls_9 = 21, ls_{10} = 10, ls_{11} = 12, ls_{12} = 17$ and $ls_{13} = 20$. The current schedule has a total objective value of 1,411.

- No further shifts could be found. The schedule is given in Fig. 7.7.

7.5   Scheduling Extensions

In the previous sections, a number of implicit assumptions have been made during the scheduling of activities, such as a fixed activity duration and resource use, no splitting possibilities of activities, a fixed resource availability over the complete scheduling horizon and the absence of project and resource calendars.

In many practical cases, these assumptions can be relaxed to more general settings, and hence, over-allocations of renewable resources can be eliminated by using other methods. In the next subsections, a number of extensions are discussed that can influence the resource feasibility of the schedule.

7.5.1   Variable Resource Availability

In the previous sections, it is assumed that the availability of the renewable resources is a predefined constant over the entire project horizon. More precisely, a_k was used to denote the amount of available resources for resource type k. Alternatively, the total availability of the resource availability may vary over the total time horizon of the project, denoted by a_{kt} (the amount of available resources of resource type k at time instance t).

Table 7.6 All possible (duration, resource demand) combinations for the example project of Fig. 7.1 under a fixed work mode

Activity	Predecessors	Work content	(Duration, Resource use)
1	–	0	**(0,0)**
2	1	42	~~(1,42)~~, ~~(2,21)~~, ~~(3,14)~~, (6,7), **(7,6)**, (14,3), (21,2), (42,1)
3	1	5	(1,5), **(5,1)**
4	1	15	~~(1,15)~~, (3,5), **(5,3)**, (15,1)
5	3	6	(1,6), **(2,3)**, (3,2), (6,1)
6	3	3	(1,3), **(3,1)**
7	3	4	**(1,4)**, (2,2), (4,1)
8	4	2	**(1,2)**, (2,1)
9	2	32	~~(1,32)~~, ~~(2,16)~~, (4,8), **(8,4)**, (16,2), (32,1)
10	5	18	~~(1,18)~~, (2,9), **(3,6)**, (6,3), (9,2), (18,1)
11	7	2	(1,2), **(2,1)**
12	6, 10, 11	18	~~(1,18)~~, (2,9), **(3,6)**, (6,3), (9,2), (18,1)
13	8, 12	40	~~(1,40)~~, ~~(2,20)~~, **(4,10)**, (5,8), (8,5), (10,4), (20,2), (40,1)
14	9, 13	0	**(0,0)**

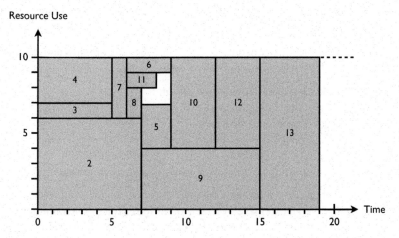

Fig. 7.11 Multi-mode resource-constrained project schedule

7.5.2 Multi-mode: A Time/Resource Trade-Off

In the previous sections, each activity duration and renewable resource demand are assumed to be fixed values which cannot be changed during the scheduling step. This so-called "fixed duration" mode can be extended to a "fixed work" mode by fixing the product of the two values to a fixed work content. In practical projects, the workload of project activities is often estimated by its work content (e.g. amount of man-days) such that several duration/resource demand combinations are possible for each individual project activity. Given an activity's work content, a set of possible duration/resource demand combinations can be specified during the project scheduling phase, each characterized by a fixed duration and a constant resource requirement.

Table 7.6 shows all possible combinations for the example project of Fig. 7.1. Combinations with renewable resource demand higher than its availability $a_1 = 10$ can be removed, leading to the remaining set of combinations among which one needs to be chosen. In case the scheduling objective is the minimization of time (i.e. the RCPSP), the selected combinations of duration and renewable resource use are indicated in bold, leading to an overall project duration of 19 time units. Figure 7.11 shows the resource graph for the solution of Table 7.6.

7.5.3 Others

In the previous sections, resource conflicts, i.e. over-allocations of renewable resources have been eliminated by using two possible methods, as follows:

• Shifting a task forwards or backwards.

- Reducing the duration of an activity within a fixed work content, known as multi-mode scheduling.

However, the project manager has access to a wide range of alternative methods, which will not be discussed in detail in this book, such as:

- Splitting a task, known as activity preemption.
- Adjusting the resources assigned to a task.
- Assigning more resources to a task.
- Replacing an over-allocated resource with an under-allocated one or removing a resource.
- Adjusting or contouring the amount of work assigned to a resource.

The interested reader is referred to two classification schemes of project scheduling, which both give an extensive overview of various project scheduling problems with and without renewable resources (Brucker et al. 1999; Herroelen et al. 1999). A further discussion on various extensions is outside the scope of this book. However, in Chap. 8, a number of extensions to realistic settings are discussed in detail.

7.6 Resource Cost

The calculation of costs is an important aspect of project scheduling and control. In this section, four main types of costs that should be linked to the project activities and their resources are discussed.

7.6.1 Types of Costs

The total cost of an activity is a sum of various cost factors that are classified in this subsection into four classes. Two are linked to the activity without the use of resources while the two others are due to the use of resources per activity. Obviously, more than one type of cost can be defined for a single resource. The various cost types operate in differing ways, depending upon whether the resource is a renewable or nonrenewable resource. In this section, the variable r_{ik} used in the previous section of this chapter is split up into a r_{ik}^r and r_{ik}^n variable to distinguish between the activity demand of renewable and nonrenewable resources. Both variables express the number of units required by activity i for the resource k. While the r_{ik}^r variable is always used to express the use per time unit, the total use r_{ik}^n of a nonrenewable resource can be a fixed value over the duration of the activity (*fixed use*) or can be a variable value to express the use per time (*variable use*) similar to the renewable resource use r_{ik}^r. Details on the four cost classes are given along the following lines.

Activity Cost

Fixed cost: A fixed cost can be assigned to an activity regardless of its use of renewable and nonrenewable resources. It is a fixed amount of money that is independent of the duration of the activity and the work content for one or more resources assigned to this activity.

Variable cost: A variable cost per time unit can be assigned to an activity regardless of its use of renewable and nonrenewable resources. It is a variable amount of money that is dependent on the activity duration and can be used to describe resource-independent costs such as activity overhead.

Resource Cost

Cost per use: The cost for the use of a resource can be considered as a one-time cost incurred every time that the resource is used by the activity. The per use cost for a nonrenewable resource is applied only once from the moment the resource is used. The per use cost for a renewable resource, however, depends on the resource demand of the activity (i.e. its resource requirement r_{ik}^r and *not* its total work content $r_{ik}^r * d_i$).

As an example, the cost per use for a nonrenewable resource like gallons of gasoline needed to feed excavators during a construction project is €250 per delivery, regardless of the amount of gallons brought per delivery per truck (obviously, this is cost of delivery and *not* the cost for the gasoline itself, which will be measured by the cost per unit discussed hereafter). The excavator itself, on the contrary, is a renewable resource and has a per use cost of €1,000. Working with three excavators in parallel to finish the activity makes the total per use cost equal to €3,000.

Cost per unit: Unlike the one-time cost per use, the cost per unit is a cost that typically depends on the amount of the resource demanded by the activity and its duration. The calculation of the total activity per unit cost differs along the resource type, renewable or nonrenewable, as explained along the following lines:

- Renewable resources: the costs per unit are cost rates calculated per time unit (hours, days, weeks, etc.) and per resource unit and hence are based on the total work content $r_{ik}^r * d_i$ of the activity i for the renewable resource k.
- Nonrenewable resources: Normally, the use of nonrenewable resources by project activities is expressed in units that are typically different from time units. Consequently, the costs per unit are monetary rates not calculated per hour but expressed in other units (per weight, per length, per pallet, etc.). However, there are examples where nonrenewable resource use is expressed as a time dimension. To that purpose, the assignment of a nonrenewable resource to an activity can be done in two alternative ways:

Table 7.7 The calculation of activity costs from their resource use

Cost	Renewable resource = *limited availability* *during scheduling*	Nonrenewable resource = *no limited availability* *during scheduling*
c_{use}	$c_{use} * r_{ik}^r$	c_{use}
c_{unit}	$c_{unit} * d_i * r_{ik}^r$	variable: $c_{unit} * d_i * r_{ik}^n$
		fixed: $c_{unit} * r_{ik}^n$

- Fixed use: the unit for the cost/unit calculation of a nonrenewable resource is anything but a time dimension. It is an indication that the quantity of the resource used by an activity is independent from its duration. A typical example is the cost per unit for materials, such as bricks needed to build a wall, which is equal to €100 per pallet, regardless how much time it takes to build that wall. The gasoline example for the excavator could also be considered as a nonrenewable resource with fixed use, since its cost completely depends on the amount used, expressed in gallons, to finish a certain activity.
- Variable use: the unit for the calculation of the cost/unit for a nonrenewable resource can be expressed in a time dimension (hours, days, ...). It is an indication that the quantity of resources used by an activity changes proportionally as its duration changes. In the gasoline example, the resource use could have been specified as the number of gallons needed per day. In this case, it is implicitly assumed that the daily occupation of the excavator is known and more or less stable, and the nonrenewable resource of gasoline then depends on the daily gasoline consumption of the excavator, and hence, on the number of days it takes to finish that activity with the help of that excavator.

The calculations of the costs for the two types of resources is summarized in Table 7.7, which gives a clear indication of the difference in total cost calculations depending on units of resource demands. The total activity cost is equal to the sum of these two resource type costs increased by the resource independent fixed and variable activity cost.

7.6.2 Cost Sensitivity

It has been mentioned in Chap. 5 that the sensitivity of project activities in a baseline schedule is of crucial importance and offers insight into the strengths and weaknesses of the baseline schedule and serves as a tool to trigger and control a project manager's corrective actions during project progress. However, Chap. 5 was restricted to a schedule risk analysis (SRA) where only the time sensitivity of project activities was analyzed. However, the sensitivity of the cost dimension of a project, and the influence of changes in the baseline schedule on the total cost of the project is of equal, if not more, importance. Table 7.7 shows that the SRA studies of Chap. 5 can also provide cost sensitivity information, since changes in activity durations have an effect on the total activity cost, which depends on the cost type (per unit versus per use) and the resource type (renewable versus nonrenewable). Consequently, variation in activity duration leads to variations in the total activity cost, and hence, a SRA study will also provide insight into the sensitivity of the activity and resource costs of the project.

7.7 Conclusions

This chapter gave an overview of resource-constrained project scheduling techniques under different scheduling objectives. It has been shown that the choice of an appropriate scheduling objective is one of the main decisions that needs to be made during the project scheduling phase, since it determines the look and shape of the project schedule, the critical chain and the efficiency of resource use.

Due to the inherent complexity of scheduling projects with renewable resources under a limited availability, many quick and easy heuristic methods have been developed. In the current chapter, priority based scheduling has been proposed as a heuristic method to schedule projects with a regular and nonregular scheduling objective. The obtained project scheduling objective values can be compared with lower bounds to validate and assess the quality of the schedule, and to determine room for possible improvement.

Extensions to more practically oriented project scheduling settings have been briefly described in the chapter. In practice, a never-ending list of undiscussed extensions is possibly leading to more relevant tools and techniques for certain projects. However, the general scheduling principles and lessons learned in this chapter will remain unchanged. More advanced resource-constrained scheduling topics will be discussed in the next chapter.

Chapter 8
Resource-Constrained Scheduling Extensions

Abstract Resource-constrained project scheduling has been a topic in both the research community and the practical oriented business magazines. This chapter presents some advanced results obtained by various research projects, extends the resource models of the previous chapter to other scheduling objectives, studies the effect of activity splitting and setup times and introduces learning effects in a resource-constrained project environment. Each part of this section can be considered as a special topic of resource-constrained project scheduling and can be easily skipped without losing overview on the general dynamic scheduling theme described throughout the book.

8.1 Introduction

The rich amount of research projects in resource-constrained project scheduling can be best illustrated by the classification schemes developed by Brucker et al. (1999) and Herroelen et al. (1999). Their intention was to classify all project scheduling related issues into a single scheme such that previous and future research efforts can be put into the right perspective, using a clear and unambiguous scheme. Both papers mention the use of the scheme as a dynamic instrument, indicating that new important issues related to project scheduling will pop up and need to get a place in the existing scheme. Up to today, the scheme is still widely used to classify new important aspects of project scheduling.

Although the scheme is not the topic of the current section, some parts of it will be outlined into more detail. This section has no intention whatsoever to give a complete overview of the state-of-the-art resource-constrained project scheduling research, but instead wants to highlight a number of resource-constrained scheduling related issues taken from literature that illustrate the importance of extending the basic project scheduling models to more realistic project settings.

M. Vanhoucke, *Project Management with Dynamic Scheduling*,
DOI 10.1007/978-3-642-40438-2_8, © Springer-Verlag Berlin Heidelberg 2013

The outline of this chapter can be summarized as follows. Section 8.2 presents three project scheduling objectives on top of the objectives presented in the previous chapter. While one extension is based on a problem from literature with a high relevance in practice, the two others are based on experience gained during consultancy projects. Section 8.3 briefly gives an overview of the literature regarding quantitative project descriptions to measure the structure of a project network and the scarceness of the resources used. Section 8.4 presents three extensions of project scheduling that have relevance in practice: the extension of the basic activity assumptions to more general settings, the use of setup times between parts of activities and the presence of learning when working with resources. Section 8.5 ends with conclusions and gives a brief sketch of future research needs.

8.2   Other Scheduling Objectives

8.2.1   Work Continuity Optimization

The previously discussed resource-constrained project scheduling techniques focused on resolving the resource conflicts by shifting activities in time. In doing so, these techniques guarantee that project activities do not use more renewable resources than available at each time period of the project life. However, these methods completely ignore the idle time of resources during the execution of the project as they do not try to schedule sets of activities that make use of a similar resource together. Though, there are numerous project examples where a subset of project activities (further referred to as an activity group) uses a common set of resources and where this set of resources is occupied from the first moment an activity from the group starts until the last activity. Therefore, so-called *work continuity constraints* (El-Rayes and Moselhi 1998) have been introduced in order to build a project schedule where the idle time of resources is minimized. A number of examples are given below:

- Spatial resources: A resource type that is not required by a single activity but rather by a group of activities. Examples are dry docks in a ship yard, shop floor space or pallets. Since the spatial resource unit is occupied from the first moment an activity from the group starts until the last activity of the group finishes, work continuity constraints can be of crucial importance (De Boer 1998).
- Time dependent cost resource: Time dependent costs (TDC) are the part of the project total cost that changes with the variation of activity times (Gong 1997). The TDC of a resource is the product of unit time cost and service time. Goto et al. (2000) have investigated the use of this concept and argue that the service time of a time dependent cost resource is the time duration starting from the first use and ending at the last. They refer to the use of a tower crane in the

construction industry and argue that the reduction of waiting times of TDC resources naturally reduces the time dependent cost.

- Repeating activities: Recognition of the drawbacks of traditional CPM network models in scheduling construction projects has led to the development of several alternative scheduling methodologies under different names, such as the Line of Balance (LOB) method or the Linear Scheduling Method (LSM). Harris and Ioannou (1998) give an excellent overview and integrate these methods into the so-called *repetitive scheduling method* (RSM), which is a practical scheduling methodology that ensures continuous resource utilization applicable to repetitive construction scheduling. A practical example of work continuity constraints in the repetitive construction industry will be discussed in Chap. 9.

Consequently, work continuity constraints are used to refer to the minimization of idle time of resources in a project. The introduction of work continuity constraints in the RCPSP leads to the *resource-constrained project scheduling problem with work continuity constraints* (RCPSPWC). This problem type involves the scheduling of project activities in order to minimize the total work continuity cost of the project subject to precedence relations and a predefined project deadline. The word 'constraint' is somewhat misleading and is only used to be in line with the terminology used in the literature. The resource idle time minimization is guaranteed by minimizing the total resource cost of the schedule that consists of the work continuity cost for each activity group g (which consists of the activity set $N^g \subset N$). This latter cost can be minimized by minimizing the time-span between the first and last activity of the activity group. Indeed, the resources are needed from the start of the first activity and will only be released at the completion of the last activity of the activity group. Consequently, the start times of all intermediate activities have no influence on the idle time of this resource and therefore do not influence the total work continuity cost. The following parameters are necessary to describe the scheduling problem formulation:

G	Set of activity groups, index g ($g = 1, \ldots, |G|$)
N^g	Set of activities of activity group g ($N^g \subset N$)
	(require a common set of resources (work continuity constraints))
SG^g	Earliest start of all activities of activity group g.
	(involves the start of the use of the resource)
FG^g	Earliest finish of all activities of activity group g
	(the resource can only be released after this time moment)
c_w^g	Work continuity cost of activity group g
	(cost per time unit for the set of resources of the activity group g)

A conceptual formulation for the RCPSPWC can be given as follows:

$$\text{Minimize} \sum_{g=1}^{|G|} c_w^g (FG^g - SG^g) \tag{8.1}$$

subject to

$$s_i + d_i \leq s_j \qquad\qquad \forall (i,j) \in A \qquad\qquad (8.2)$$

$$\sum_{i \in S(t)} r_{ik} \leq a_k \qquad\qquad k = 1,\ldots,K; t = 1,\ldots,T \qquad (8.3)$$

$$SG^g = \min_{i \in N^g} s_i \qquad\qquad g = 1,\ldots,|G| \qquad\qquad (8.4)$$

$$FG^g = \max_{i \in N^g}(s_i + d_i) \qquad g = 1,\ldots,|G| \qquad\qquad (8.5)$$

$$s_1 = 0 \qquad\qquad\qquad\qquad\qquad\qquad\qquad (8.6)$$

$$s_n \leq \delta_n \qquad\qquad\qquad\qquad\qquad\qquad\qquad (8.7)$$

$$s_i \in int^+ \qquad\qquad i = 1\ldots,n \qquad\qquad\qquad (8.8)$$

The objective in Eq. 8.1 minimizes the weighted time-span between the first and last activity of each activity group and hence, minimizes the total cost of work continuity. The constraint set given in Eq. 8.2 maintains the finish-start precedence relations among the activities. The limited availability of the renewable resources is modeled by Eq. 8.3. Equations 8.4 and 8.5 are introduced to model the start and finish time, respectively, for each activity group. These start and finish times determine the length of use of the resource and hence, the work continuity. Equation 8.6 forces the dummy start activity to start at time zero and Eq. 8.7 limits the project duration to a negotiated project deadline. Equations 8.8 ensure that the activity start times assume nonnegative integer values.

Figure 8.1 displays the optimal resource-feasible schedule for the RCPSPWC for the example project of Table 7.1. This project is subject to traditional renewable resources with a limited availability of ten units (see column resource use) as well as two resource groups (A and B). Some activities have been grouped to an activity group, since they rely on a common resource group (A or B) that is subject to work

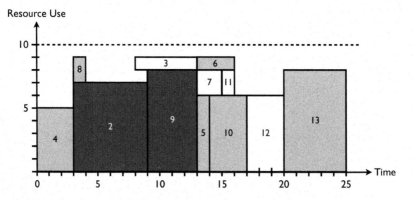

Fig. 8.1 Feasible resource graph with work continuity optimization

continuity constraints. More precisely, activities 2 and 9 have been grouped to an activity group since they use similar equipment tools of class A, while activities 3, 7, 11 and 12 need tools from group B during their execution, and hence, belong to a second activity group. The optimal resource graph with a minimal value for the resource idle time for resource groups A and B shows that activities 2 and 9 are grouped and activities 3, 7, 11 and 12 are grouped within the precedence and resource constraints. The time-span for the first activity group $N^1 = \{2, 9\}$ equals $\max(3 + 6, 9 + 4) - \min(3, 9) = 10$ while the time-span for the second activity group $N^2 = \{3, 7, 11, 12\}$ equals $\max(8 + 5, 13 + 2, 15 + 1, 17 + 3) - \min(8, 13, 15, 17) = 12$. Assume a cost of idle time of $c_w^1 = €10$ and $c_w^2 = €20$, then the total objective function cost equals $100 + 240 = €340$.

Work continuity constraints are particularly relevant in repetitive scheduling environments to minimize the idle time of various resources, which is discussed hereafter.

Repetitive Scheduling

Construction projects are often characterised by repeating activities that have to be performed from unit to unit. Highway projects, pipeline constructions and high-rise buildings, for example, commonly require resources to perform the work on similar activities that shift in stages. Indeed, construction crews perform the work in a sequence and move from one unit of the project to the next. This is mainly the result of the subdivision of a general activity (e.g. carpentry) into specific activities associated with particular units (e.g. carpentry at each floor of a high-rise building).

The repetitive processes of these construction projects can be classified according to the direction of successive work along the units. In *horizontal repetitive projects* the different processes are performed horizontally, as seen in pipeline construction or paving works. These construction projects are often referred to as continuous repetitive projects or linear projects due to the linear nature of the geometrical layout and work accomplishment. When progress is performed vertically, we refer to *vertical repetitive projects*, among which high-rise building construction is the classical example. Rather than a number of activities following each other linearly, these construction projects involve the repetition of a unit network throughout the project in discrete steps. It is therefore often referred to as discrete repetitive projects. Kang et al. (2001) argue that construction projects can consist of both horizontal and vertical repetitive processes among several multi-storey structures and refer to this type as *multiple repetitive projects*.

In the following two paragraphs, two fictitious project examples are used to illustrate the relevance of work continuity constraints in construction scheduling. The first example is taken from Harris and Ioannou (1998) to schedule a repetitive project to minimize crew idle time. In a second example, the complete trade-off between project duration and work continuity is illustrated. Chapter 9 describes a last example of a real-life project that aims at the construction of a tunnel at the Westerschelde in the Netherlands.

Fig. 8.2 An example project
with six repeating activities
(Source: Harris and Ioannou
(1998))

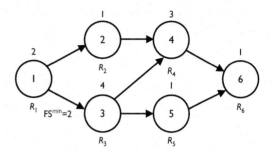

Example 1 (A six-unit repetitive project). Figure 8.2 displays an illustrative
activity-on-the-node project network for the activities in the first unit, as published
in Harris and Ioannou (1998). Each of these six activities has a duration, denoted
above the node and needs to use a certain resource R_i, denoted below the node. The
solid arcs are technological precedence relations between the activities. The default
value for each precedence relation is a finish-start relationship with a minimal
time-lag of zero (i.e. $FS^{min} = 0$), unless indicated otherwise. In this example, a
minimal time-lag of two time units between activity 1 and 3 is specified (this is
indicated as a 'lead time' in Harris and Ioannou (1998)). The construction of a
project schedule with repeating networks can be done by the so-called *Repetitive
Scheduling Method* (RSM).

Figure 8.3 displays the complete network for a project with six repeating units,
each having the six discrete activities of Fig. 8.2. The dashed arcs link similar
activities from unit to unit and are used to represent resource availability constraints.

Since it is assumed that the work to be done in units 3 and 4 for activity 1 is
twice the work to be done in unit 1, the durations of activities 13 and 19 have
been doubled. Moreover, a minimal time-lag of five is added between units 3 and 4
(i.e. $FS^{min}_{14,20} = 5$). This planned interruption in resource continuity is to meet
some known or predicted circumstance. Harris and Ioannou (1998) mention that the
delivery of materials by a subcontractor's truck is sufficient to completing only three
units, and consequently, a work break period is needed after unit 3. Remark that this
repetitive project does not have an activity 3 in unit 5, which is a characteristic of
an atypical project. To that purpose, the duration of activity 27 is set to zero, which
is similar to the deletion of this activity from the project network.

The purpose is to construct a feasible project schedule with a minimal value
for the resource idle time for all resources R_1 to R_6. The algorithm developed by
Vanhoucke (2006b) reports an idle time value of 5 with a total project duration
of 30. This project duration is in this case equal to the critical path length. The
start times reported by the algorithm are equal to $s_0 = 0$, $s_1 = 0$, $s_2 = 6$, $s_3 = 4$,
$s_4 = 11$, $s_5 = 19$, $s_6 = 24$, $s_7 = 2$, $s_8 = 7$, $s_9 = 8$, $s_{10} = 14$, $s_{11} = 20$, $s_{12} = 25$,
$s_{13} = 4$, $s_{14} = 8$, $s_{15} = 12$, $s_{16} = 17$, $s_{17} = 21$, $s_{18} = 26$, $s_{19} = 8$, $s_{20} = 14$, $s_{21} = 16$,
$s_{22} = 20$, $s_{23} = 22$, $s_{24} = 27$, $s_{25} = 12$, $s_{26} = 15$, $s_{27} = 20$, $s_{28} = 23$, $s_{29} = 23$,
$s_{30} = 28$, $s_{31} = 14$, $s_{32} = 16$, $s_{33} = 20$, $s_{34} = 26$, $s_{35} = 24$, $s_{36} = 29$ and $s_{37} = 30$. In
Fig. 8.4, an RSM diagram based on these start times is shown, which is similar to the
diagram given by Harris and Ioannou (1998). The vertical axis shows the work to be

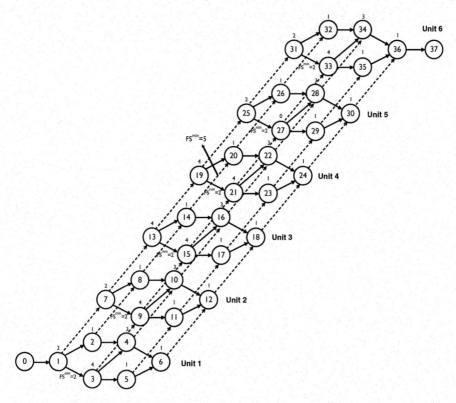

Fig. 8.3 The repetitive project network of Fig. 8.2 with six units

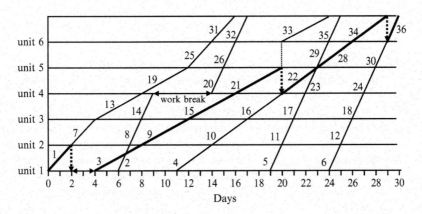

Fig. 8.4 RSM diagram for a six units project of Fig. 8.2

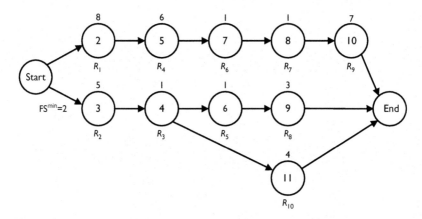

Fig. 8.5 An example project with ten repeating activities

done in the different units, the horizontal axis denotes the time line and the numbers next to the lines refer to the activity numbers of the project network of Fig. 8.3. The slope of each line is equal to the unit production rate, i.e. the number of repetitive units that can be accomplished by a resource during a unit of time. Consequently, it can be calculated as the inverse of the duration of that activity at that unit. Total project duration equals 30 days and the resource idle time amounts to 5 days (i.e. equal to the work break between activity 14 and 20 in the network of Fig. 8.2). The minimal time-lags between activities 1 and 3 at all units do not affect the resource idle time. The line in bold is the so-called *controlling sequence* and determines the length of the project duration. Obviously, this controlled sequence is similar to the critical path and critical chain concepts discussed in the previous chapters. This example illustrates that the general project scheduling approach can be easily applied and translated to more specific sectors (in this case, the RSM method is mainly used in the construction sector) without changing the general techniques and principles discussed earlier. More details on the repetitive scheduling method are outside the scope of this book.

Example 2 (Trade-off between work continuity and project duration). In the first example, the schedule with the best work continuity cost, expressed as the solution with the minimal idle time for all resources shifting between units, has a length equal to the critical path length. However, in reality, there is often a trade-off between idle time reduction and project duration, leading to a project schedule that can exceed its minimal critical path (or critical chain) duration. Indeed, thanks to a longer project duration, there are more degrees of freedom to group certain activities that require the same set of resources.[1] In this section, the use of the so-called horizon-varying scheduling approach (Vanhoucke, 2006b) is illustrated on the project example of Fig. 8.5. In this figure, a unit network is displayed with ten nondummy activities.

---

[1]In Chap. 9, it will be shown that there is a trade-off between the project duration and the idle time of expensive freezing machines for the construction of a tunnel under the Westerschelde.

In Table 8.1, the activity durations from units 1 to 5 are displayed. In this example, it is assumed that the crew productivity increases along the units, known as the learning effect of crews.

Figure 8.6 displays the complete trade-off profile between the total project duration and work continuity by means of the black bars. This is the result of a horizon-varying approach starting from the critical path length of 43 to a project duration of 55. A critical path length of 43 corresponds to a resource idle time of 32 time units due to waiting times of resources between units. Increasing the project deadline results in a lower resource idle time thanks to lower waiting times between units. A project duration of 55 time units corresponds to a minimal resource idle time between units. Note that the minimal resource idle time equals zero since only zero time-lags are involved. This trade-off profile can be used as a decision tool to determine an optimal level of resource idle time in the schedule. By assigning costs to both resource idle time and project duration, the optimal point in the complete profile with an associated project duration and idle time level can be determined. Assume that c_r is used to denote the cost per unit resource idle time and c_d is used to denote the cost per time unit that has to be paid during each day of the project duration. Consequently, the total cost of a schedule with total planned project duration PD and corresponding resource idle time (*idle*) equals $c_t = c_r * idle + c_d * PD$. Figure 8.6 reports the total cost c_t by four lines depending on the values for c_r and c_d.

Table 8.1 Activity durations of the activities of Fig. 8.5 for five units

Unit/activity	2	3	4	5	6	7	8	9	10	11
Unit 1	8	5	1	6	10	1	1	3	7	4
Unit 2	7	4	1	5	8	1	1	2	6	3
Unit 3	6	3	1	4	7	1	1	1	5	2
Unit 4	5	2	1	3	6	1	1	1	4	1
Unit 5	4	1	1	2	5	1	1	1	3	1

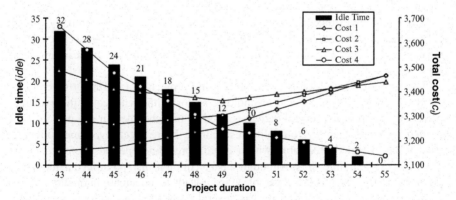

Fig. 8.6 Trade-off between work continuity and project deadline

The optimal project duration and the corresponding level of idle time depend on both the values for c_r and c_d. Each unit increase in the project duration involves an extra cost c_d while the total cost will be decreased by c_r times the idle time reduction due to the project duration increase. Consequently, a project duration increase is only beneficial as long as c_d/c_r is smaller than the (negative) slope of the crew idle time curve as displayed in Fig. 8.6. As an example, the black bars of Fig. 8.6 have 3 different values for the slope, i.e. 4 between 43 and 45, 3 between 45 and 49 and 2 from 49 onwards. Consequently, four different solutions can be optimal, depending on the cost values c_d and c_r:

- $\frac{c_d}{c_r} > 4$: It is never beneficial to increase the project duration, and the optimal solution equals the critical path length 43. This is displayed in Fig. 8.6 by the curve labelled 'Cost 1' with $c_d = 63$ and $c_r = 14$ which has its lowest point at project duration 43.
- $3 < \frac{c_d}{c_r} \leq 4$: It is beneficial to increase the project duration up to 45. This is displayed by the curve labelled 'Cost 2' with $c_d = 63$ and $c_r = 18$.
- $2 < \frac{c_d}{c_r} \leq 3$: It is beneficial to increase the project duration up to 49. This is displayed by the curve labelled 'Cost 3' with $c_d = 62.5$ and $c_r = 25$.
- $\frac{c_d}{c_r} \leq 2$: A maximal increase in the project duration leads to the lowest cost. This is displayed by the curve labelled 'Cost 4' with $c_d = 57$ and $c_r = 38$ with a minimal cost for a project duration of 55.

As a summary, the optimal project duration always coincides with a slope breakpoint in the trade-off curve between idle time and project duration, i.e. the optimal project duration will lie at the points with project durations equal to 43, 45, 49 or 55, depending on the costs c_d and c_r.

8.2.2 Quality Dependent Time Slots

Quality-dependent time slots refer to predefined time windows where certain activities can be executed under ideal circumstances (optimal level of quality) while outside these time windows, there is a loss of quality due to detrimental effects. The purpose is to select a quality-dependent time slot for each activity, resulting in a minimal loss of quality.

The topic of this section is based on real-life project data aiming at scheduling an R&D project from the bio-technology sector with genetically manipulated plants. In this project, several activities need to be scheduled in the presence of limited resources and severe quality restrictions. More precisely, some activities need to be executed preferably within certain predefined periods, referred to as quality-dependent time slots. Although the execution is also possible outside these predefined intervals, it is less desirable since it leads to a decrease in quality.

It is assumed that each activity has several predefined quality-dependent time slots, from which one has to be selected. The selection of a time slot must be done before the start of the project (i.e. during the scheduling phase). Given a fixed set of time slots per activity, the target is then to select a time slot and to schedule the project such that the loss in quality will be minimized. Each activity has a duration $d_i (1 \leq i \leq n)$ and a number of quality-dependent time windows $nr(i)$. Each window l of activity i ($1 \leq i \leq n$ and $1 \leq l \leq nr(i)$) is characterized by a time-interval $[q_{il}^-, q_{il}^+]$ of equal quality, while deviations outside that interval result in a loss of quality. Note that the time slot $[q_{il}^-, q_{il}^+]$ is used to refer to a window with optimal quality and can be either an interval or a single point in time. The quality deviation of each activity i can be computed as $Q_i^{loss} = \max(q_{il}^- - s_i; s_i - q_{il}^+; 0)$ and depends on the selection of the time window l, with s_i the start time of activity i.

To that purpose, a binary decision variable needs to be introduced in the conceptual model, which determines the selection of a specific time interval for each activity i, as follows:

$$y_{il} \qquad = 1, \text{ if time interval } l \text{ has been selected for activity } i,$$
$$= 0, \text{ otherwise}$$

q_{il}^{opt} is used to denote the minimal activity cost associated with a fixed and optimal level of quality for each time window l of activity i. q_{il}^{extra} is used to denote the loss in quality per time unit deviation from the time interval and consequently, the total cost of quality equals $\sum_{i=1}^{n} \sum_{l=1}^{nr(i)} (q_{il}^{opt} + q_{il}^{extra} Q_i^{loss}) y_{il}$. Note that $nr(1) = nr(n) = 1$, since nodes 1 and n are dummy activities with $q_{11}^- = q_{11}^+$ and $q_{n1}^- = q_{n1}^+$. Moreover, the dummy start activity must be forced to start at time instance zero. The project needs to be finished before a negotiated project deadline δ_n, i.e. $q_{n1}^- = q_{n1}^+ = \delta_n$. Consequently, setting $q_{n1}^{extra} = \infty$ denotes that the project deadline can not be exceeded (a hard constraint), while $q_{n1}^{extra} < \infty$ means that the project deadline can be exceeded at a certain penalty cost (soft constraint). The *resource-constrained project scheduling problem with quality-dependent time slots* (RCPSPQTS) can be conceptually formulated as follows:

$$\text{Minimize} \sum_{i=1}^{n} \sum_{l=1}^{nr(i)} (q_{il}^{opt} + q_{il}^{extra} Q_i^{loss}) y_{il} \qquad (8.9)$$

subject to

$$s_i + d_i \leq s_j \qquad\qquad \forall (i, j) \in A \qquad\qquad (8.10)$$

$$\sum_{i \in S(t)} r_{ik} \leq a_k \qquad\qquad k = 1, \ldots, K; t = 1, \ldots, T \qquad (8.11)$$

$$Q_i^{loss} \geq \sum_{l=1}^{nr(i)} q_{il}^- y_{il} - s_i \qquad i = 1 \ldots, n \qquad\qquad (8.12)$$

$$Q_i^{loss} \geq s_i - \sum_{l=1}^{nr(i)} q_{il}^+ y_{il} \qquad i = 1 \ldots, n \qquad\qquad (8.13)$$

$$\sum_{l=1}^{nr(i)} y_{il} = 1 \qquad\qquad i = 1\ldots,n \qquad\qquad (8.14)$$

$$s_1 = 0 \qquad\qquad\qquad\qquad\qquad\qquad (8.15)$$

$$s_i, Q_i^{loss} \in int^+ \qquad\qquad i = 1\ldots,n \qquad\qquad (8.16)$$

$$y_{il} \in 0, 1 \qquad\qquad i = 1\ldots,n; l = 1,\ldots,nr(i) \qquad (8.17)$$

where $S(t)$ denotes the set of activities in progress in period $]t - 1, t]$. The objective in Eq. 8.9 minimizes the total quality cost of the project (i.e. the fixed cost within the selected time window plus the extra cost of quality loss due to deviations from that interval). The constraint set given in Eq. 8.10 maintains the finish-start precedence relations among the activities. Equations 8.11 represent the renewable resource constraints and the constraint sets in Eq. 8.12 and 8.13 compute the deviation between the activity start time and the selected time window. Equations 8.14 represent the time window selection and forces the model to select a single time window for each activity. Equation 8.15 forces the dummy start activity to start at time zero and Eq. 8.16 ensure that the activity start times as well as the time window deviations assume nonnegative integer values. Equations 8.17 ensure that the time window selection variable is a binary (0/1) variable. Remark that the quality loss function measuring the quality decrease due to a deviation from the ideal time window l can be of any form (such as stepwise functions, convex functions, etc). However, Eqs. 8.9–8.17 assume, without loss of generality, a linear quality deviation function.

Although the first real-life application of this scheduling problem type was the scheduling of a genetically manipulated plants project, there are numerous other examples where predefined time-windows need to be selected before the execution of the project. The following four examples illustrate the possible generalization of multiple quality-dependent time windows to other project environments:

- Perishable items. The project scheduling problem with quality dependent time slots is a typical example of a scheduling environment where items (e.g. plants) are perishable. Many project activities consist of tests on growing plants where the quality is time-dependent since there is an optimal time interval of consumption. Earlier consumption is possible, at a cost of a loss in quality, since the plants are still in their ripening process. Later consumption results in loss of quality due to detrimental effects.
- State-of-nature dependencies. In many projects, the performance of some activities might depend on the state of nature. In this case, a predefined set of possible start times depending on the state of nature are linked with possible execution times of the activity and the deviation from these time windows is less desirable (resulting in higher costs or quality loss) or even completely intolerable. A spectacular example, where six different quality-dependent time slots due to an external state of nature reason, occurred in the Rosetta mission. In early

January 2003, an Ariane-5 rocket carrying the ESAs Rosetta Spacecraft was launched from Kourou, French Guiana. The main objective of the Rosetta mission was a rendez-vous with a Comet called Wirtanen. Therefore, the spacecraft had to gather momentum three times in the gravity fields of Mars (26/08/2005) and the Earth (28/11/2005 and 28/11/2007) in order to get into the outer regions of the planetary system. The planet constellation required for that purpose could only last for a short period. As a consequence, the launch window was only open for 6 specific days between January 13 and 31, 2003 (i.e. six different time slots). Afterwards, the comet Wirtanen could no longer be reached. Besides the restricted span of launch dates, there was also a tight limit on the time of day at which Rosetta could leave earth. Because the earth rotates, Kourou had to be correctly positioned in relation to the direction in which the spacecraft had to head off, on the first part of its interplanetary journey. The daily time span was about 20 min. So the ultimate deadline was the date of the first possible constellation.

- Multiple activity milestones. The project scheduling literature with activity due dates (milestones) has been restricted to considering projects with predefined due dates. In reality, milestones are the results of negotiations, rather than simply dictated by the client of the project. Indeed, due dates, including earliness and tardiness penalty costs for possible deviations, are agreed upon by the client and the contractor (and possibly some subcontractors). This results in a set of possible due dates for each activity, rather than a single predefined due date. The objective is then to select a due date for each activity such that the total earliness/tardiness penalty costs will be minimized.

- Time-dependent resource cost. In many projects, the cost of (renewable) resources heavily depends on the time of usage. The aforementioned time-switch constraints (see Chap. 2) are a typical and extreme example of time-dependent resource costs, since they restrict the execution of activities to predefined time intervals (work periods) without any possibility to deviate. However, when activities are allowed to deviate from their original work periods, these time slots can be considered as quality-dependent time slots (in this case, the cost of overtime). Indeed, it is often possible to deviate from an activity pattern by adding more (expensive) resources to an activity in the predefined rest period. The work periods can be considered as the time slots while the rest periods are periods outside these slots in which the activity can be executed at an additional cost.

This project scheduling type with limited resources and quality-dependent time slots can be easily illustrated by means of an example project in Fig. 8.7. The number above each node is used to denote the activity duration d_i while the number below the node represents its requirement r_{i1} for a single renewable resource with availability $a_1 = 10$. Table 8.2 shows the $(q_{il}^{opt}, q_{il}^- = q_{il}^+, q_{il}^{extra})$ data for each quality-dependent time slot l. For the sake of clarity, it is assumed that $q_{il}^- = q_{il}^+$, i.e. the quality-dependent time slots are a single point in time. Moreover, q_{il}^{extra} is assumed to be equal for each interval l. Each activity of the example project

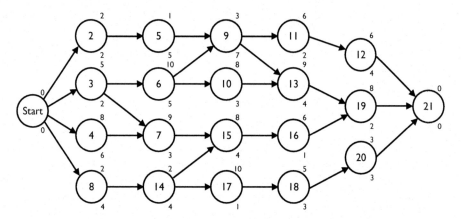

Fig. 8.7 An example project with quality-dependent time slots

Table 8.2 The quality dependent time slot data for Fig. 8.7

	q_{i1}^{opt}	$q_{i1}^{-} = q_{i1}^{+}$	q_{i1}^{extra}	q_{i2}^{opt}	$q_{i2}^{-} = q_{i2}^{+}$	q_{i2}^{extra}
1	–	–	–	–	–	–
2	0	0	4	–	–	–
3	0	1	19	2	4	19
4	0	0	6	–	–	–
5	0	9	2	2	19	2
6	0	5	1	–	–	–
7	0	8	8	–	–	–
8	0	8	16	2	18	16
9	0	15	1	–	–	–
10	3	15	6	–	–	–
11	0	18	6	–	–	–
12	0	37	8	–	–	–
13	0	23	2	–	–	–
14	0	20	2	–	–	–
15	0	22	6	–	–	–
16	0	30	1	–	–	–
17	0	23	4	–	–	–
18	0	23	3	2	33	3
19	0	36	7	–	–	–
20	0	19	6	2	39	6
21	–	–	–	–	–	–

belongs to one of the following categories. An activity can be subject to single
(activities 12 and 17) or multiple quality-dependent time slots (activities 3, 5, 8,
18 and 20). Activities can also have the requirement to be scheduled as-soon-
as-possible (ASAP; activities 2, 4, 6, 7, 9, 10, 11 and 13) or as-late-as-possible
(ALAP; activities 14, 15, 16 and 19). This can be incorporated in the network by

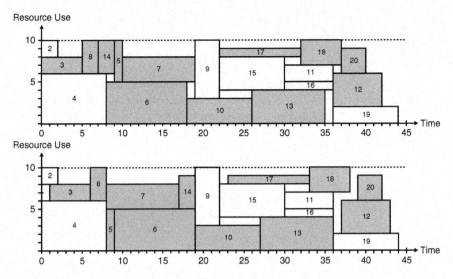

Fig. 8.8 The RCPSP schedule with minimal time (*top*) and quality-dependent time slots (*bottom*)

adding a single quality-dependent time slot with $q_{il}^- = q_{il}^+ = es_i$ (earliest start time of activity i) or $q_{il}^- = q_{il}^+ = ls_i$ (latest start time of activity i) to force an ASAP or ALAP constraint, respectively. Deviations from these requirements will be penalized by per time unit. The project deadline δ_n equals 44 time units.

Figure 8.8 displays the schedules found by solving the RCPSP without (i.e. minimization of project time) and with the quality-dependent time slots. The activities highlighted in dark grey are the activities that are scheduled at a different time instance between the two schedules. Activities 3, 6, 8, 10, 12, 13, 14, 17, 18 and 20 have been scheduled later than the classical RCPSP schedule, while activities 5 and 7 have been scheduled earlier.

8.2.3 Resource Availability Cost Problem

The *Resource Availability Cost Problem* (RACP) is a special case of the project scheduling problem, which can be considered as a combination of scheduling features discussed in the previous chapter. It is very much related to the resource leveling problem of Sect. 7.3.4 since it considers the use of resources in the objective and contains the time minimization problem of Sect. 7.3.2 as a subproblem. Despite its practical relevance, the scheduling problem has received relatively less attention than other scheduling problems, which might be attributed to its inherent scheduling complexity. The resource availability cost problem involves the construction of a project schedule within a predefined project deadline δ_n such that the total cost of the resources is found. It is assumed that the total cost $c_k(a_k)$ of a resource k depends on its availability a_k, regardless whether the resource is used by activities or not, with $c_k(a_k^1) < c_k(a_k^2)$ if $a_k^1 < a_k^2$. Consequently, the cheapest resource availability cost $c_k(a_k)$ is determined by the assigned availability a_k for each resource type k. The problem implicitly assumes that a resource is assigned to a project for the complete duration, leading to an overall cost, which depends on the amount of units assigned to the project. The RACP can be formulated as follows:

$$\text{Minimize} \sum_{k=1}^{K} c_k(a_k) \tag{8.18}$$

subject to

$$s_i + d_i \leq s_j \qquad\qquad \forall (i, j) \in A \tag{8.19}$$

$$\sum_{i \in S(t)} r_{ik} \leq a_k \qquad\qquad k = 1, \ldots, K; t = 1, \ldots, T \tag{8.20}$$

$$s_1 = 0 \tag{8.21}$$

$$s_n \leq \delta_n \tag{8.22}$$

$$s_i \in int^+ \qquad\qquad i = 1 \ldots, n \tag{8.23}$$

The objective in Eq. 8.18 is a discrete nondecreasing resource cost function that minimizes the total cost of the necessary resources, specified by their availability. All other constraints are similar to the resource-constrained project scheduling problems of Sect. 7.3.2 of the previous chapter. The difference, however, is that the resource availability a_k of Eq. 8.20 is now a decision variable instead of a predefined input parameter.

The construction of an RACP schedule consists of two steps: an availability assignment step followed by a project scheduling step. Indeed, once the availability a_k is determined for each resource type k, leading to a total cost as specified in the objective function, a resource-constrained project schedule needs to be constructed as discussed in Sect. 7.3.2. When the total duration of this schedule is lower than or equal to the predefined project deadline δ_n, the schedule is feasible, otherwise not. The feasible schedule with the lowest total cost, as a result of the weighted sum of resource costs with their availabilities, is the best possible schedule that can be found.

It has been mentioned that the use of resources often increases the complexity of a scheduling problem. It goes without saying that the RACP is also a complex problem since it consists of an iterative solution approach for the RCPSP. In order to reduce the computational effort when finding a feasible project schedule, the lower bound calculations of Sect. 7.4.2 can be easily applied as alternatives for the computational burdensome algorithms to construct a schedule with a minimal project duration. When the lower bound gives a minimal project duration that exceeds the project deadline δ_n, there is no need to construct a project schedule with the current combination of resource availabilities a_k. In doing so, the often time consuming RCPSP step can be avoided and another a_k value for at least one resource k is necessary. Further details on search procedures for the RACP are outside the scope of this book and can be found in Möhring (1984) and Demeulemeester (1995).

The RACP can be best illustrated by means of a project example using the activity-on-the-node network of Fig. 7.1. It is assumed that the project uses two resource types, i.e. resource type 1 and 2 of Table 7.2. It is assumed that the total resource cost $c_k(a_k)$ is a linear nondecreasing function of a_k with a per unit cost of $c_1(a_k = 1) = 3$ and $c_2(a_k = 1) = 2$ for resource types 1 and 2 and the project deadline is set to $\delta_n = 25$. The maximum resource demand is equal to 8 and 17 for resource types 1 and 2, respectively, requested by activities 9 and 10. Moreover, it can be shown that the minimum required resource availability is equal to 8 units for resource type 1 in order to be able to construct a resource feasible project schedule within the deadline of 25. This can be obtained by constructing an optimal resource-constrained project schedule (see Sect. 7.3.2) with a project deadline $\delta_n = 25$ only taking the first resource into account (the availability of resource type 2 is set to infinity). Likewise, resource type 2 needs at least 23 units within the given project deadline. Consequently, the search for the optimal combination between a_1 and a_2 starts at 8 and 23 units.

Table 8.3 enumerates eight possible combinations using the approach of Demeulemeester (1995). This approach stipulates that only efficient cost points needs to be evaluated in a strict order, starting from a low cost combination (denoted by START with a cost of 70) in increasing steps until the project duration is smaller than or equal to the project deadline (denoted by STOP). The exact sequence can be found by following the iso-cost curves denoted by the dashed lines with a cost slope equal to $\frac{c_1}{c_2} = \frac{3}{2} = 1.5$. Figure 8.9 illustrates the principle on the project example, starting with the minimal resource requirements $a_1 = 8$ and $a_2 = 23$ with a total resource cost of 41 and finishing at the best possible solution with $a_1 = 9$ and $a_2 = 25$. The dots represent a_1 and a_2 combinations and the dashed lines represent the iso-cost curves that determine the order in which the dots will be evaluated.

Table 8.3 Iterative search for the best possible resource availability combination

	a_1	a_2	Cost	Time	Feasible?
START →	8	23	70	28	no
	8	24	72	27	no
	9	23	73	28	no
	8	25	74	27	no
	9	24	75	27	no
	10	23	76	27	no
	8	26	76	27	no
	9	25	77	25	yes → STOP

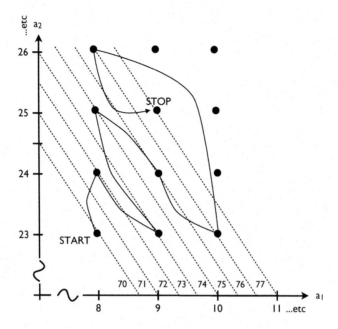

Fig. 8.9 The efficient cost curves for two resource types and the search for the best resource availabilities

8.3   Quantitative Project Descriptions

Quite a number of measures have been proposed in the literature to describe the characteristics of a project. A clear distinction can be made between measures capturing information about the size and the topological structure of the network and measures that are related to the different resources allocated to the project. In the following sections, the commonly used measures published in the project scheduling literature are briefly discussed, without going into mathematical details. Parts of it have already been discussed in a previous part of the book (Sect. 5.5.2). The reader is free to skip this section without running the risk to lose grip on the overall dynamic scheduling picture discussed throughout the various chapters of this book.

8.3.1   Network Topology

Numerous measures to indicate a network's topology have been presented in the literature. This section gives a brief overview of (some of) these measures used in the literature and/or software tools. A complete overview and mathematical details are outside the scope of this chapter. For a more detailed discussion of the network characteristics, the reader is referred to the references mentioned in this section.

In Demeulemeester et al. (2003), three well-known complexity measures to describe the topological structure of a network are used in a project network generator in order to test and validate project scheduling algorithms. These network measures are briefly described along the following lines:

- The *Coefficient of Network Complexity* (CNC) is probably the easiest measure to describe the topology of a project network and is calculated as the total number of precedence relations (arcs) over the total number of project activities (nodes) in the network (Davies, 1974; Davis, 1975; Kaimann, 1974, 1975; Pascoe, 1966).
- The *Order Strength* (OS) is defined as the number of precedence relations (not only the direct relations but also including the transitive ones) divided by the theoretical maximum number of precedence relations (Dar-El, 1973; Herroelen and De Reyck, 1999; Kao and Queyranne, 1982; Mastor, 1970; Tavares, 1999; Thesen, 1977). The maximum number of possible precedence relations in a project network is equal to $\frac{n(n-1)}{2}$ with n the number of nondummy activities. This is the most widely used measure in the literature and has been used in phase transition studies to show regions where resource-constrained project scheduling problems are very complex (Herroelen and De Reyck, 1999).
- The *Complexity Index* (CI) was originally defined for activity-on-the-arc networks as the so-called reduction complexity and basically measures the closeness of a network to a series-parallel directed graph. More precisely, it calculates the minimum number of node reductions that, along with series and parallel reductions, allow to reduce a two-terminal acyclic network to a single edge (Bein et al., 1992). Further details are outside the scope of this book.

Tavares et al. (1999) have proposed six network topology measures to describe the design and structure of an activity-on-the-node project network and they have been redefined by Vanhoucke et al. (2008) to use them in a comparative network study. Four of these indicators have been used in a dynamic project scheduling study of Vanhoucke and Vandevoorde (2007b). These four indicators have been rescaled and lie between 0 and 1, inclusive, denoting the two extreme structures. The logic behind each indicator is straightforward, as follows:

- The *Serial/Parallel* (SP) indicator measures the closeness of a network to a serial or parallel network. More precisely, when SP = 0, all activities are in parallel, and when SP = 1, the project is represented by a complete serial network. Between these two extreme values, networks can be generated close to a serial or parallel network. The SP indicator determines the maximal number of levels of the network, defined as the longest chain (in terms of the number of serial activities) in the network. This indicator has already been mentioned in Sect. 5.5.2 of the schedule risk analysis chapter.
- The *Activity Distribution* (AD) indicator measures the distribution of project activities along the levels of the project, and hence, the width of the network. When AD = 0, all levels contain a similar number of activities, and the number

of activities are uniformly distributed over all levels. When AD = 1, there is one level with a maximal number of activities, and all other levels contain a single activity.

- The *Length of Arcs* (LA) indicator measures the length of each precedence relation (i, j) in the network as the difference between the level of the end activity j and the level of the start activity i. When LA equals 0, the network has many precedence relations between two activities on levels far from each other such that the activity can be shifted further in the network. When LA equals 1, many precedence relations have a length of one, resulting in activities with immediate successors on the next level of the network and with little freedom to shift.

- The *Topological Float* (TF) indicator measures the topological float of a precedence relation as the number of levels each activity can shift without violating the maximal level of the network (as defined by SP). TF = 0 when the network structure is 100% dense and no activities can be shifted within its structure with a given SP value. A network with TF = 1 consists of one chain of activities without topological float (they define the maximal level and, consequently, the SP value) while the remaining activities have a maximal float value (which equals the maximal level, defined by SP, minus 1).

A more extensive discussion of the topology measures falls outside the scope of this book. Further mathematical details can be found in Vanhoucke et al. (2008), and illustrative examples are given by Vanhoucke (2010a).

8.3.2 *Resource Scarceness*

Several measures to describe the resource scarceness have been introduced in the literature. The scarceness of project resources can be measured along two dimensions. A first dimension is related to the number of resources used by the project activities and is measured as the density of the resource demand matrix r_{ik} (demand of activity i for resource k) in order to specify whether an activity uses a particular resource or not. This is done by computing the resource factor RF or the resource use RU. Secondly, the quantity in which these resources are used, measured by the amount of resource demand relative to its availability for each activity, plays an important role in the resource scarceness. This second dimension is measured by the resource strength RS or the resource-constrainedness RC. These two sets of resource scarceness indicators are briefly described along the following lines:

Average number of project resources used:

- The *Resource Factor* (RF) reflects the average portion of resource types requested per activity and consequently measures the density of the matrix r_{ik}. It simply scans for each activity/resource combination whether the resource is requested by the activity or not and calculates the average portion for all resources requested by all activities, which obviously results in a percentage of resource use (Pascoe, 1966; Cooper, 1976; Alvarez-Valdes and Tamarit, 1989). It is used in studies by Kolisch et al. (1995) and Schwindt (1995), among others.

- The *Resource Use* (RU) is a similar measure. However, it does not calculate the use of resources as a percentage for all resources used in the project, but instead, varies between zero and the number of resource types available and measures for each activity the number of resource types used for the project. It is used in a study by Demeulemeester et al. (2003).

Average amount of resource use:

- The *Resource Strength* (RS) can be calculated for a resource type k as $\frac{a_k - r_k^{\min}}{r_k^{\max} - r_k^{\min}}$ where a_k denotes the total availability of renewable resource type k, $r_k^{\min}$ is equal to the maximum requested amount for resource type k for all activities and $r_k^{\max}$ denotes the peak demand of resource type k in the resource-unconstrained earliest start schedule. The resource strength RS was first introduced by Cooper (1976), then later used by Alvarez-Valdes and Tamarit (1989) and finally redefined by Kolisch et al. (1995). The measure is criticized by various authors (Elmaghraby and Herroelen, 1980; Herroelen and De Reyck, 1999) since it cannot be considered as a pure resource measure due to the incorporation of network topology information (during the calculation of $r_k^{\max}$, an earliest start schedule is built).
- The *Resource Constrainedness* (RC) measures the average quantity of each resource type k required by all project activities, divided by its availability. The measure has been introduced by Patterson (1976) and is used in several resource complexity studies.

8.3.3 Relevance

The interest in project topology and resource measures dates back to Elmaghraby and Herroelen (1980) who draw attention to the need for project datasets that span the full range of problem complexity. Ever since, many researchers have followed this advice, leading to project network generators with resource generation capabilities using one or more of the measures described earlier (Demeulemeester et al., 1993; Kolisch et al., 1995; Schwindt, 1995; Agrawal et al., 1996; Tavares, 1999; Drexl et al., 2000; Demeulemeester et al., 2003; Akkan et al., 2005; Vanhoucke et al., 2008). Varying network topology structures and resource measures during the generation of fictitious project data is necessary due to the complexity of resource-constrained project scheduling. This is also illustrated by the complexity dimension of the project mapping Fig. 1.4 where it is said that the introduction of resources increases the project scheduling complexity. The incorporation of these measures in software tools can be interesting for the user and/or project manager for several reasons, for example:

- Quantitative description of the project: Having (quantitative) knowledge about the characteristics of the project (network and resources) can be helpful in selecting tools and techniques for project scheduling, risk analysis and project control purposes. In Chap. 5, it has been briefly shown that the reliability of sensitivity measures obtained by a schedule risk analysis depends on the use of network topology measures. Chapter 13 gives empirical evidence based on a simulation study that the efficiency of project control depends on the network topology of the project and that these quantitative measures can be used to select the most appropriate tracking method for the project under study.
- Automatic generation of project data: When using a software tool, many users initially try to use the functionalities of the tool without having real data. The generation of fictitious project data is an easy and powerful tool to let the user start immediately with the software to gain experience with all its features even before entering real project data. The generation of fictitious data can be best done under a user-defined design, having control over the network structure and the scarceness of project resources.
- Resource scarceness in multi-project environments: Knowledge about the scarceness of resources is particularly interesting in a multi-project environment. As an example, in Chap. 10, it will be briefly discussed that the size of project and feeding buffers should not only depend on the risk of the activities in the critical chain or feeding chains, but also on the scarceness of the project resources. The higher the resource scarceness, the more likely the project duration will increase when more projects enter the project portfolio.

8.4   Extra Scheduling Features

In Sect. 7.5 of Chap. 7, some commonly used extensions to the basic resource-constrained project scheduling techniques have been briefly discussed. However, the range of possible extensions to the basic resource-constrained project scheduling problems is wide and diverse and depends on the needs and wishes from industry as well as the state-of-the-art developments in research. This section gives an overview of three extensions that have an important impact on real-life project scheduling and is far from complete. Results are based on research projects done at Ghent University in collaboration with various companies.

8.4.1   Activity Assumptions

Most, if not all, project scheduling software tools aim at the construction of resource feasible schedules in order to minimize the total lead time of the project, known as the RCPSP as presented in Chap. 7. Hence, an activity-on-the-node project network with a list of activities with their corresponding precedence relations and resource requirements needs to be given as an input. However, various activity assumptions need to be made by the user in order to construct a feasible schedule. In a research project done by Vanhoucke and Debels (2008), the impact of the work content option, the possibility of activity preemption and the presence of fast tracking is studied on the resource utilization and project duration of a project. Figure 8.10 gives an overview of the three activity assumptions tested in the experimental study for a project activity with a total work content of 9 man-days (for example, the duration $d_i = 3$ and a single renewable resource requirement $r_{i1} = 3$), which will be briefly described along the following lines.

- Fixed duration or fixed work: The basic *resource-constrained project scheduling problem* RCPSP assumes that each activity i consists of a deterministic work content W_{ik} for each resource type k, and imposes a fixed duration d_i and a fixed renewable resource requirement r_{ik} on its execution. The extension to the *discrete time/resource trade-off problem* (DTRTP) still assumes a fixed work content but allows variable activity durations. As an example, the activity of Fig. 8.10 still has a fixed work content W_{i1} of 9 for the single resource type 1, but can now be executed under different scenarios. Note that many commercial software tools pay a lot of attention to this activity assumption and call for the well-considered use of this activity option before the construction of a schedule (see e.g Uyttewaal 2005 for examples). The choice between fixed durations or fixed work has been discussed previously in Sect. 7.5.2.
- The presence of activity preemption: The basic RCPSP assumes that each activity, once started, will be executed until its completion. The extension to the *preemptive resource-constrained project scheduling problem* (PRCPSP) allows activities to be preempted at any integer time instant and restarted later on at no additional cost, and has been investigated in the literature as an option to

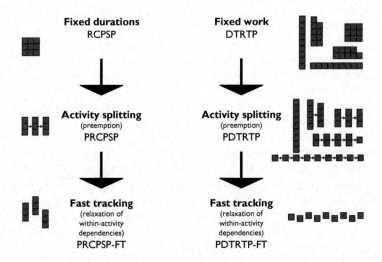

Fig. 8.10 Resource-constrained project scheduling under various activity assumptions

further reduce the total project lead time. In many project scheduling software tools, the option of activity splitting can be made before the construction of a resource-feasible schedule and has an effect on the number of execution scenarios, as displayed in Fig. 8.10. In theory, the DTRTP can also be extended to its preempted version (the *preemptive discrete time/resource trade-off problem* (PDTRTP)), but no results are available on this problem type in the literature.

• The effect of fast tracking: Fast tracking is a scheduling technique used to reduce the total project lead time during project execution even further. When projects are fast-tracked, it usually indicates the compression of a project schedule by doing certain activities in parallel that would normally be done in a sequence. Hence, it violates the precedence relations between activities, which implies activity execution at incomplete information. In the study, the impact of within-activity fast tracking is investigated, which allows the execution of preemptive subparts of an activity in parallel. The fast tracking option removes precedence relations between subparts of preempted activities and increases the number of execution scenarios. The within-activity fast tracking option is inspired by the idea that activities are often executed by groups of resources (with a fixed availability), but the total work can often be done by multiple groups (in parallel). The *preemptive resource-constrained project scheduling problem with fast tracking* (PRCPSP-FT) assumes preemptive activities with fixed durations, which results in d_i parallel subactivities for each original activity, each with a resource requirement r_{ik}. The *preemptive discrete time/resource trade-off problem with fast tracking* (PDTRTP-FT) assumes variable activity durations (under a fixed work content) and allows the preemptive and parallel execution of each subactivity with a duration and resource requirement equal to 1, as shown in the bottom part of Fig. 8.10.

The results of the study can be summarized as follows. First, allowing preemption in the RCPSP has almost no effect on both the lead time and the resource utilization when the resource availability a_k is fixed over the complete project life time horizon. Hence, the task splitting option of project scheduling software, which results in preemptive and often less clear schedules, is no good alternative to improve the schedule quality. Second, the shift from fixed duration activities to fixed work content activities (DTRTP), however, has a major effect on both the lead time (an improvement with approximately 21%) and the resource utilization (from approximately 75% to 94% or more). Hence, the fixed work option should be carefully considered as a default option, since it has a major beneficial effect on the schedule quality. Third, within-activity fast tracking turns out to have a beneficial effect on the fixed duration activities (PRCPSP-FT), leading to approximately 15% lead time improvement and an 88% resource utilization, but the extra benefits when using fixed work activities (PDTRTP-FT) are relatively small compared to the very efficient schedules found by the DTRTP. Hence, allowing fixed work activities already results in a very efficient schedule, making the within-activity fast tracking a redundant alternative to improve schedule quality.

8.4.2 Setup Times

In the previous section, it has been shown that activity preemption seldom has a significant impact on the total project duration compared to the RCPSP duration, but, on the contrary, activity preemption in combination with activity fast-tracking of these preempted subparts of activities can lead to large project duration reductions. However, preemptions in activities often come at a certain price. Indeed, the study of the previous section did not take preparation or setup work into account and simply assumed that activities can be started, preempted and/or fast-tracked at no extra time or cost. However, in daily scheduling activities, it is noticed that most project planners make a distinction in an activity duration between the actual work (in days) and the time needed to prepare the actual work (currently called setup time) such as installation time, releasing resources from other sites, etc. Figure 8.11a displays details about a fictitious activity with a total duration d_i of 6 days (horizontal direction of the activity), consisting of 1 setup day and 5 remaining days of actual work. The project activity needs to be executed by teams of two people working together (vertical axis of the activity). Part b of the figure shows that activity preemption results in a renewed setup time due to the interruption in time. Consequently, the total setup time amounts to 2 days while the actual work remains 5 days (which is known in the literature as preemption-resume). The activity fast-tracking option of part c is the result of assigning two teams (each containing two people working in parallel) on the interruptive parts of the activity, and hence, the two preemptive parts can now be executed in parallel. Consequently, this fast tracking option removes precedence relations between subparts of preempted activities and increases the number of execution scenarios for each activity of the project.

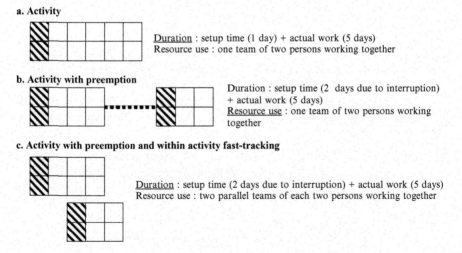

a. Activity

Duration : setup time (1 day) + actual work (5 days)
Resource use : one team of two persons working together

b. Activity with preemption

Duration : setup time (2 days due to interruption) + actual work (5 days)
Resource use : one team of two persons working together

c. Activity with preemption and within activity fast-tracking

Duration : setup time (2 days due to interruption) + actual work (5 days)
Resource use : two parallel teams of each two persons working together

Fig. 8.11 Resource-constrained project scheduling with setup times

Vanhoucke (2008c) has studied the impact of these setup times on the PRCPSP-FT as option c of Fig. 8.11 where activity preemptions and/or within-activity fast trackings are only allowed at the expense of an extra setup cost. Hence, the original defined activity durations d_i consist of both a single setup time t_i for starting the activity and a remaining processing time. The setup time component includes activity preparations such as equipping, resetting, changing, positioning, cleaning and warming up (Mika 2006). This setup time is added to the total duration each time the activity is interrupted. This problem formulation is highly relevant for projects where multiple resource units (e.g. teams of people or a combination of machines) are assigned to project activities. In this case, activity resource requirements are often defined as the minimal amount of resource units required to perform the activity, and hence, the duplication of this minimal amount of resource units allows the fast tracking of subparts of activities. Obviously, the duplication and corresponding fast tracking decision often involve extra setup time, as discussed before.

The author has performed an experimental study on randomly generated project data with up to 30 project activities and showed the relative decrease in the project duration when allowing activity preemption and fast tracking. The project networks have been generated such that they have different values for the network topology and resource scarceness. The network topology is determined by the amount of precedence relations between activities and leads to project networks with a lot of parallel to a lot of serial activities. The resource scarceness is measured by the average resource demand of the activities relative to its availability and has an influence on the scheduling complexity (vertical axis of Fig. 1.4). Each project requires four renewable resource types. In order to compare the resulting schedules with the optimal RCPSP schedules, it was assumed that part of the activity durations can be considered as the unavoidable setup time before the initial subactivity. Activity setup times have been generated under five settings as 0%, 25%, 50%, 75% or 100% of the original activity duration minus one. Consequently, the activity setup times and remaining activity durations have been calculated as follows: the author subtracted the generated setup time from the original activity duration to calculate the remaining activity duration. Hence, the sum of the activity setup time and its remaining duration was always equal to the original duration of the project network instance and the remaining duration is minimum one. This approach allows to measure the impact of preemptive fast tracking with setup times on the schedule quality by comparing it with the RCPSP project duration. The test set leads to three different scenarios, as follows:

1. If the setup time of each activity is set at $t_i = 0\%$, then the remaining duration for each activity is equal to the duration of the RCPSP instances. Since there are no setup times, the problem boils down to the PRCPSP-FT described in the previous section.
2. If the setup times for the activities are set at a value t_i from 25% to 75%, then the remaining durations of the activities are greater than 1 and lower than their

original duration. The minimal project duration will lie between the RCPSP-FT
and the PRCPSP minimal project duration.

3. If the setup time of each activity is set at $t_i = 100\%$, then each remaining activity
duration is equal to 1. In this case, activity preemption is impossible, and hence,
the problem boils down to the basic RCPSP.

The author has investigated the impact of the different settings for the setup
time, each split up to projects with a different network topology and resource
scarceness, and have measured the average relative project duration improvement
when introducing activity preemption and fast tracking with setup times, relatively
compared to the minimal RCPSP solution as described in Chap. 7. A detailed
analysis of the results of the experiment is outside the scope of this book. However,
the main results and conclusions can be summarized as follows:

- Effect of the size of the setup times: The higher the value for the setup times,
  the less beneficial it is to preempt activities and hence, the closer the problem
  resembles the basic RCPSP. It is worth mentioning that the option to fast track
  has a major effect on the project duration, even with high values for the setup
  times. As an example, the PRCPSP-FT with setup times up to 75% of the original
  duration still leads to average improvements varying from 0.11% to 1.53% on
  average (depending on the scarceness of resources). For smaller setup times, this
  percentage can go up to 6.40%. This illustrates that the presence of relatively
  high setup times does not prevent project duration reductions when allowing
  activity preemption and/or fast tracking. Hence, if technical restrictions allow a
  within-activity fast tracking, even within the presence of relatively high setup
  costs, it is still beneficial to allow activity preemption as a technique to reduce
  the project duration.
- Effect of the network topology: The topology of the project network has a clear
  effect on the impact of setup times on the project duration. A network with higher
  Serial/Parallel (SP) value (measured by a higher amount of precedence relations
  in the project network resulting in a more serial network, see Sect. 8.3.1) benefits
  more from activity preemption and fast tracking than less dense networks that
  already allow a high degree of flexibility thanks to the high degree of potential
  parallelism between project activities.
- Effect of the resource scarceness: The scarceness of resources has a negative
  effect on the total project duration. Obviously, higher resource scarceness results
  in a highly complex scheduling problem due to the relatively little room to
  schedule the projects, which prevents further project duration improvements by
  preempting or fast tracking project activities.

8.4.3   Learning

Minimizing the total project duration during project scheduling is an important goal
in today's competitive industrial environment (see Sect. 7.3.2 where the objective is
the minimization of time). In project management, the project baseline schedule is

used as a benchmark and point of reference during the project's progress. Activity start and finish times are often seen as milestones and are used to follow up the progress of the project. However, the presence of learning effects can dramatically change the project baseline schedule, leading to changes in the activity durations, their start and finish times and consequently the total project duration.

The presence and importance of learning in project management is based on the observation that in most projects, human resources are a critical factor in the scheduling process. Not only their availability, but also their productivity will influence the project duration. One of the main reasons why the productivity of a human resource varies over time is because of the effect of learning, which indicates the process of acquiring experience while performing similar activities leading to an improvement of the worker's skill. As a measurable result of learning, the time required to perform the next activities decreases. The mathematical modeling of learning effects is outside the scope of this chapter, and the reader is referred to papers written by Wright (1936), Yelle (1979) and Nembhard and Uzumeri (2000) for general learning concepts, and to Shtub et al. (1996), Amor and Teplitz (1998), Ash and Smith-Daniels (1999) and Heimerl and Kolisch (2010) for learning in a project scheduling setting.

In a study by Van Peteghem and Vanhoucke (2010b), three different project baseline schedules are compared to each other in order to investigate the effect of activity learning on the project duration. Each schedule has a specific purpose and is constructed under different assumptions. The construction and interpretation of the three schedules will be explained by the use of a fictitious illustrative example project. The example project contains eight nondummy activities and two dummy activities to represent the start and end of the project. Moreover, it is assumed that all activities can be scheduled according to the fixed work option, where each activity's work content is displayed above each node of the activity-on-the-node network of Fig. 8.12a. These numbers are expressed in man-hours, and do not contain any learning effects. Consequently, the scheduling problem is assumed to be a *discrete time/resource trade-off problem* (DTRTP) as discussed in Sect. 8.4.1 where the work content W_{ik} for each resource type k implies the choice of an activity duration d_i and a fixed renewable resource requirement r_{ik} for its execution. The availability of the single renewable resource is equal to 10. Table 8.5 gives for each activity an overview of the allowable duration/resource pairs, the best duration/resource combination selected for each of the three schedules S^O, S^L and S^R and the activity start time of the activity.[2]

Activity Learning: The incorporation of learning in the allowable activity combinations has an effect on the total work content of the activities which may vary along the choice of the activity (d_i, r_{ik}) combination. The general idea is that

---

[2]The activity durations, their start times and the corresponding project duration for each schedule depend on the degree of learning for each activity. The calculations and construction of the schedule are outside the scope of this section and are determined by an algorithm developed by Van Peteghem and Vanhoucke (2010a).

teams with a lot of people (low d_i values and high r_{ik} values) have little time to learn while teams with only few people (high d_i values and low r_{ik} values) have much more time to learn. This general principle is illustrated in Table 8.4 for the six duration/resource combinations of activity 7 displayed in Table 8.5. The table shows that the incorporation of learning effects leads to longer durations for teams with a lot of people (ten people) and smaller durations for teams with only few people (below ten people). Obviously, the specific values for the durations and work content of the activity with learning depend on the learning rate and initial efficiency of the team, but these calculations are outside the scope of this chapter. In the remainder of this section, it is assumed that the time estimates without learning are artificial estimates made by the project manager, and the learning durations are the real durations that occur in reality. A comparison between three schedules will analyze the impact of incorporating the learning effects during the construction of the baseline schedule and the impact on the project duration when this is not done.

Three Baseline Schedules: The three project baseline schedules can be described along the following lines.

- S^O: The optimal schedule without incorporation of the learning effects. Figure 8.12b shows the optimal solution found by solving the DTRTP without activity learning effects, resulting in a project duration of 48 time units.

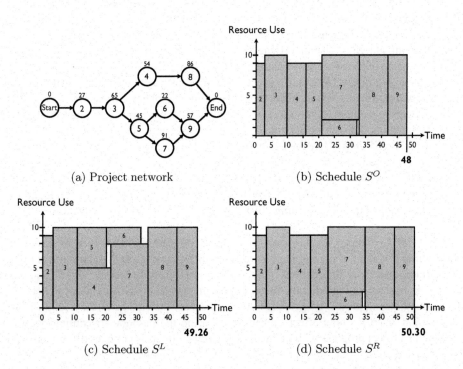

(a) Project network   (b) Schedule S^O

(c) Schedule S^L (d) Schedule S^R

Fig. 8.12 Different schedules for an example project (Source: Van Peteghem and Vanhoucke (2010b))

Table 8.4 Illustrative learning effects on activity/resource combinations of activity 7 of Table 8.5

Team	No learning		Learning	
	d_7	W_{71}	d_7	W_{71}
Team 1: 10 people	10	100	10.06	100.60
Team 2: 9 people	11	99	10.93	98.37
Team 3: 8 people	12	96	11.78	94.24
Team 4: 7 people	13	91	12.63	88.41
Team 5: 6 people	16	96	15.13	90.78
Team 6: 5 people	19	95	17.56	87.80
Average	5.67	28.33		

- S^L: The optimal schedule with the incorporation of the learning effects. Figure 8.12c shows the optimal schedule solved by the DTRTP where each activity was subject to activity learning, leading to a total project duration of 49.26 time units. Consequently, the introduction of learning effects has led to a project duration increase of 2% which means that ignoring learning during the construction of a baseline schedule would lead to an underestimate of the project duration by 2%.

- S^R: The optimal schedule without learning effect using activity duration with learning. Figure 8.12d displays the so-called *realistic schedule* where the activity sequence in the schedule has been found by solving the DTRTP without activity learning, but where the activity durations have afterwards been replaced by their learning duration. The underlying assumption made is that the project manager is not aware of the existence of learning effects during the construction of a baseline schedule and therefore starts executing the project as shown in S^O. However, activities will take more or less time than originally planned due to the existence of learning effects. Therefore, S^R is the schedule where the sequence of the activities is defined by the start times of the different activities in the optimal schedule S^O, but where the activity durations are changed to the durations where a learning effect is considered. In the example, this results in a project schedule with a project duration of 50.30 time units. Obviously, this project duration should always be equal to or larger than the project duration of the S^L schedule, since in the latter, the learning effects have been incorporated in advance.

Effect of Learning: In the study, the impact of learning effects on the project baseline schedule is investigated from three different angles. First, the impact of learning effects on the optimal project duration is measured to test the relevance and importance of predicting these effects in advance. Second, the impact of learning during project progress is tested to measure the change in the total project duration when learning effects are ignored during the baseline scheduling phase. Finally, project progress with and without learning effects is compared to reveal the beneficial effect of incorporating learning effects during the early project stages.

Table 8.5 Activity durations, resource requirements and schedule information for the example project

ID	Allowable (d_i, r_{ik}) combinations	Selected (d_i, r_{ik}) combinations			Start time		
		S^O	S^L	S^R	S^O	S^L	S^R
Start	(0,0)	(0,0)	(0,0)	(0,0)	0	0	0
2	(3,9), (4,7), (5,6), (6,5), (7,4), (9,3)	(3,9)	(3.54,9)	(3.54,9)	0	0	0
3	(7,10), (8,9), (9,8), (10,7), (11,6), (13,5)	(7,10)	(7.38,10)	(7.38,10)	3	3.54	3.54
4	(6,9), (7,8), (8,7), (9,6), (11,5), (14,4)	(6,9)	(10.93,5)	(6.46,9)	10	10.92	10.92
5	(5,9), (6,8), (7,7), (8,6), (9,5), (12,4)	(5,9)	(9.18,5)	(5.51,9)	16	10.92	17.37
6	(3,8), (4,6), (5,5), (6,4), (8,3), (11,2)	(11,2)	(10.93,2)	(10.93,2)	21	20.10	22.88
7	(10,10), (11,9), (12,8), (13,7), (16,6), (19,5)	(12,8)	(11.78,8)	(11.78,8)	21	21.84	22.88
8	(9,10), (10,9), (11,8), (13,7), (15,6), (18,5)	(9,10)	(9.19,10)	(9.19,10)	33	33.63	34.67
9	(6,10), (7,9), (8,8), (9,7), (10,6), (12,5)	(6,10)	(6.46,10)	(6.46,10)	42	42.81	43.85
End	(0,0)	(0,0)	(0,0)	(0,0)	48	49.26	50.30

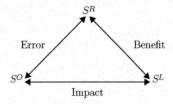

Fig. 8.13 Comparison of three project baseline schedules to measure the influence of activity learning

In order to analyze these three research questions, the authors have compared the three schedules S^O, S^L and S^R to each other, as graphically displayed in Fig. 8.13. The underlying idea of each comparison is briefly outlined along the following lines.

1. Impact of learning: The project baseline schedule without learning effects S^O and the baseline schedule with learning effects S^L are compared in order to investigate the *impact* of the introduction of learning effects during the project scheduling phase and to determine the driving variables of the differences between the project durations of both schedules.
2. Margin of error: The proposed schedule S^O is compared to the realistic schedule S^R in order to discover the potential *margin of error* made during project progress (S^R) when the learning effects have been ignored during the project scheduling phase (S^O) but observed afterwards during project progress. The smaller the deviation between both solutions is, the less important it is to spend time and effort to predict the learning effects in advance in order to incorporate them in the project schedule during baseline schedule construction.
3. Benefits of early knowledge of learning effects: The realistic schedule S^R is compared to the learning schedule S^L in order to measure the *benefits* that can possibly be made when learning effects are detected in early stages of the project progress. Indeed, the S^L takes all the learning effects into account when constructing a baseline schedule, and optimally assigns the teams to the activities. The S^R schedule, however, follows the timetable proposed by the S^O but observes longer or shorter activity durations due to learning. When learning is observed (S^R), the remaining part of the work yet to be done could be rescheduled taking learning into account (i.e. the remaining work is scheduled

according to the S^L scheduling approach). This rescheduling can be done under two scenarios. In a first scenario, it is implied that teams cannot be changed and hence only learning can be taken into account on the fixed activity durations. In a second scenario, it is assumed that teams can also be changed for the remaining work, leading to new duration/resource combinations with learning.

Research Results: The main results and conclusions of the study can be summarized as follows:

- Impact of learning on the project baseline schedule: In this computational experiment, the authors have investigated the impact of learning effects on the project schedule and its corresponding duration and searched for drivers of differences between baseline schedules with and without activity learning. The results can be briefly summarized as follows:

  - Learning rate: The degree of activity learning has a significant impact on the project duration. The faster the resources learn, the higher the project duration reductions in the S^L schedule relative to the S^O schedule. The experiments have also shown that low initial efficiencies of resources when starting to work on an activity can be quickly recuperated by the learning effects, leading to improvements up to 35% compared to the S^O schedule.
  - Network topology: Results have shown that activity learning has especially beneficial effects when many activities can be executed in parallel. In these cases, many activities are performed in parallel and have therefore more degrees of freedom to be scheduled with a relatively longer duration within the predefined project deadline. Obviously, when working longer on an activity, the benefits of learning can be fully exploited. The inverse is true for more serial networks where activities have on average shorter durations to guarantee a similar project duration, which prevents the resources to learn a lot within each activity execution.
  - Team assignment flexibility: When more duration/resource combinations can be chosen for each activity (see Table 8.5), there is more flexibility and room for project duration improvement when learning effects are incorporated. Consequently, the higher the number of allowable duration/resource combinations for the activities, the larger the differences are between the S^O and the S^L schedules.

- Margin of error during project progress: The S^O project schedule is assumed to be the baseline schedule proposed to the client and/or is used to set milestones without being aware that the learning effect will occur during project execution. However, efficiency improvements or deficiencies (i.e. learning) might occur during project progress, which affect the activity durations and the total project duration. This leads to a project progress captured by the S^R schedule, which might deviate from the original S^O baseline schedule. The test experiments have shown that prior information about the learning effects during the scheduling phase will often generate a competitive advantage in terms of the accuracy of the project schedule and the promised project duration towards the client. As an illustration, tests have shown that only 7.53% of the project schedules has an absolute deviation smaller than 1%. Most projects (approximately 78%) have a deviation of more than 10%. These tests clearly have shown that the original baseline schedule S^O is often not an accurate prediction of the real project progress since learning effects will often lead to high deviations between the proposed project duration of S^O and the observed project duration given by the S^R schedule.

- Benefits of early knowledge of learning effects: The computational experiments have shown that a timely incorporation of learning effects leads to significant project duration reductions. It could be shown that the project duration reductions after rescheduling are significantly larger when changes in the duration/resource combinations are allowed, illustrating that changes in the team member assignments largely affect the efficiency gain which can be obtained. As an example, incorporating learning effects after a quarter of the project progress can lead to 55% of the maximum improvement when team member assignments are allowed to be modified. This value drops to approximately 37% and 13% of the maximum improvement, in case the incorporation of learning is done at respectively 50% and 75% of the project progress. The maximum improvement is calculated as the project duration reduction when learning effects are incorporated in advance (i.e. at 0% of the project progress).

8.5 Conclusions

This chapter extends the lessons learned from the resource-constrained project scheduling methods discussed in Chap. 7 to more advanced methods and model formulations in order to be used in more practical oriented settings.

First, three different scheduling objectives have been discussed in detail based on features taken from literature or detected in real-life projects. The presence of work continuity aims at the minimization of idle time of bottleneck resources and can often be used in projects with repeating activities. The use of quality dependent time slots is based on a real-life project in the biotechnology sector and assumes that activities can ideally be scheduled in certain time-slots and are subject to penalties (costs, detrimental effects, etc. . . .) outside these time slots. The resource availability cost problem is a well-known extension of the basic resource-constrained project scheduling problem (RCPSP, see Sect. 7.3.2) but assumes that the availability of resources is not fixed but can be set based on the cost of the resources.

In a second part of this chapter, some basic quantitative project descriptions have been presented to measure the topology of a project network and the scarceness of the resources used in the project and their relevance in practice is briefly shown.

Finally, three extra scheduling features have been described that allow to make the project schedule more realistic. The relaxation of the often strict activity assumptions has led to the formulation of various but related resource-constrained project scheduling problems. The presence of setup times between activities and learning effects of the resources working on these activities has been investigated and their impact on the project duration has been shown based on different research studies.

In the next chapter, the resource-constrained project scheduling problem with work continuity constraints will be illustrated on a real-life tunnel construction project performed in the Netherlands.

Chapter 9
The Westerschelde Tunnel Project

Abstract This chapter presents a real-life project example where the minimization of a bottleneck resource's idle time is the scheduling objective. The project is an illustration of a project scheduling problem with a work continuity scheduling objective as discussed in Sect. 8.2.1. The chapter illustrates that the use of dedicated scheduling algorithms can lead to improvements in the cost outline of the schedule. Various parts of this chapter have been published in Vanhoucke (2006b, 2007).

9.1 Introduction

This chapter describes the use of an optimization procedure on a real-life application aiming at minimizing the idle time of (capital intensive) resources in a project environment. More precisely, the focus is on a huge project with a groundbreaking boring technique at the Netherlands: the construction of the Westerschelde tunnel. This tunnel provides a fixed link between Zeeuws-Vlaanderen and Zuid-Beveland, both situated in the Netherlands with a length of 6.6 km. There are two tunnel tubes and in each tube, there are two road lanes.

It will be shown that the development of a case-specific scheduling algorithm has a beneficial effect on the total idle time of resources, which cannot be optimized by using the well-known standard project scheduling software tools. This will be illustrated by results for a subproject of the construction project where an improved schedule results in significant cost savings.

The construction of the schedule has been done by carefully analyzing the overwhelming amount of data, by gradually learning the specific characteristics and needs of the construction project and by adapting existing algorithms from literature to specific project needs. The focus lies on the necessary steps needed during the construction of the project schedule, rather than explaining all technical details of the algorithm. Details on the project scheduling objective have been explained earlier in Sect. 8.2.1.

M. Vanhoucke, *Project Management with Dynamic Scheduling*,
DOI 10.1007/978-3-642-40438-2_9, © Springer-Verlag Berlin Heidelberg 2013

The outline of the chapter is as follows. In Sect. 9.2, the characteristics of the Westerschelde tunnel project are described. Section 9.3 analyses the various characteristics of the project necessary to improve the total resource idle time. Different project schedules are proposed under various scenarios to compare their results. Section 9.4 ends with overall conclusions and highlights important future research avenues.

9.2   The Project

In 1996, the national and the provincial government of the Netherlands assigned the construction of the tunnel by public tender to Kombinatie Middelplaat Westerschelde (KMW), a combination of six companies (Bam infrabouw, Heijmans, Voormolen bouw, Franki construct, Philipp Holzmann and Wayss & Freytag). The total project (the main tunnel, 22 km service roads, several entry roads and viaducts, toll square, etc.) took 5 years to complete. The construction started at the end of 1997 and the completion date was March 14, 2003. The cost of the project was €750 million. The construction of the tunnel was a technically unique project. Most tunnels in Europe are built in hard, rocky material. Never before in Western Europe has a tunnel so long or so deep been bored through relatively soft substrates such as sand and clay. The deepest point lies 60 m below sea level. The construction logistics were extremely complex because many different actions had to take place simultaneously and so they had to be very well planned. The degree of difficulty of the work was high, especially due to the depth of the tunnel and building activities. At the deepest point, the pressure was seven bar. For more general information, the reader can visit www.westerscheldetunnel.nl. In the next section, a subpart of the project, i.e. the construction of the transverse links, is briefly described.

9.2.1   The Project Network

Every 250 m the tunnel tubes are connected by transverse links (sometimes referred to as cross passages), as displayed in Fig. 9.1. Under normal circumstances, the doors to the transverse links are locked. In case of an emergency, they are unlocked automatically and one can walk to the other tunnel tube. Consequently, the emergency services can use this road to reach the site in case of an accident. The transverse links account for 10% of the construction budget. Construction is done by means of a freezing technique. This guarantees watertight transverse links and does not harm the environment. The freezing technique is used for the first time on such a large scale during the construction of the Westerscheldetunnel.

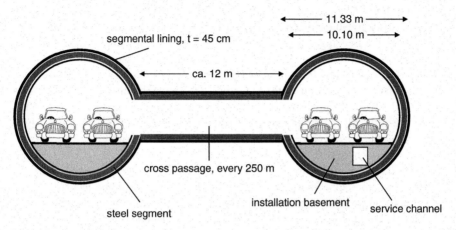

Fig. 9.1 The transverse link subproject: section in the area of a cross passage (Source: KMW)

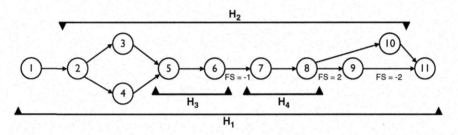

Fig. 9.2 The unit project network of the "Transverse Links" subproject

First, 26 pipes fitted with drill heads are bored from the eastern tube to the western tube (activity 1 of Fig. 9.2) and a refrigeration unit is built in the eastern tube (activity 2). After that, a brine solution that has been cooled to −35°C by the refrigeration unit is pumped into 22 of these steel pipes (activity 3 or 4, dependent on whether it is sand or clay that has to be frozen). Two of the pipes are used to monitor the progress of the freezing activity and one pipe is for drainage. When the ice around the future transverse link is sufficiently thick, the installation of the link can begin.

In the western tube, the future entrance to the link is opened and the frozen ground is excavated step by step with a cutting machine (activity 5). To prevent the ice capsule from deforming under the great pressure, a layer of gunite concrete is immediately sprayed under high pressure against the exposed ground. In this way, meter by meter, a concrete outer wall is created. Subsequently, watertight foil, which prevents the mixing of thawing water and concrete, is applied (activity 6). After that, shuttering is laid for the spraying of concrete for the inner casing that will form the floor (activity 7) and also the wall and the roof (activity 8) of the transverse link.

Then the shuttering is removed (activity 9) but the surrounding ground is still being frozen to discharge the concrete (activity 10). Only when this concrete has hardened sufficiently the freezing process can be discontinued. Finally, the refrigeration unit can be drawn off (activity 11). The links are completed at a later stage.

Figure 9.2 displays the activity-on-the-node network of the construction of a single transverse link unit with 11 activities. Although this unit network is a simplified and an adapted version of the real network, it is useful to illustrate the overall results. All technological precedence relations are of the finish-start type with a time-lag of zero (FS = 0), except where indicated otherwise.

Activities denoted by the black bars are so-called hammock activities. These activities have a variable duration that is equal to the time-span between the start and end of this hammock activity. Hammock 1 denotes the total subproject (transverse links) per unit and has a duration that equals the total duration of the subproject. Hammock 2 refers to the time span that the freezing machine is necessary during the execution of the subproject. Figure 9.2 reveals that this freezing machine is needed between the start of activity 2 and the finish of activity 10. The freezing activities are split into two subactivities: hammock 3 refers to all freezing activities on the gunite concrete, while hammock 4 refers to freezing activities during the construction of concrete.

Although the freezing machine is an important resource that is necessary during the construction of a transverse link at each unit, the crews that pass along the units (i.e. along the transverse links) are also considered as an important resource type. The network incorporates five different crews (referred to, for the sake of simplicity, as crew 1, crew 2, crew 3, crew 4 and crew 5), i.e. activity 1 needs crew 1, activity 2 needs crew 2, activity 5 needs crew 3, activity 7 needs crew 4 and activity 8 needs crew 5. The crews mainly consist of employees and specialists.

The network displayed in Fig. 9.2 is a unit network, which means that this is a graphical representation of the subproject for only one unit. For the sake of completeness, the original Dutch activity names are given in Table 9.1 and will be used in the Gantt chart of Fig. 9.3. As mentioned before, a transverse link has to be built every 250 m, resulting in 26 cross passages in the tunnel (i.e. 26 units). The unit network will, therefore, be repeated 26 times, as will be explained in the next section. Each unit makes use of the freezing machine while the different crews pass along the units.

9.2.2 The Project Characteristics

The construction project under study involves the scheduling of project activities subject to resource constraints. The main resources are the crews performing the work along the units and a large freezing machine needed during the construction process. Similar construction scheduling problems have been discussed in the

Table 9.1 Original activity description of the unit network activities (in Dutch)

ID	Activity description (Dutch)
1	Boren Lanzen
	Hammock 2: Opbouw vriessteiger
2	Opbouwen vriessteiger
3	Bevriezen klei
4	Bevriezen zand
	Hammock 3: Vriezen tijdens spuitbeton
5	Openen/ontgraven/spuitbeton
6	Aanbrengen folie
	Hammock 4: Vriezen tijdens betonwerk
7	Betonwerk vloer
8	Betonwerk wanden + Dak
9	Ontkisten
10	Vriezen ter ontlasting beton
11	Demontage vriessteiger

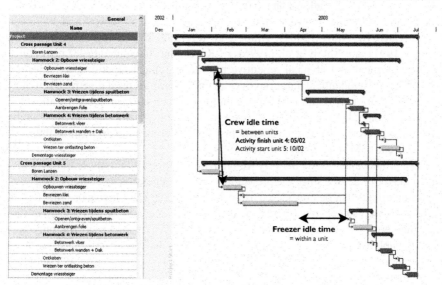

Fig. 9.3 Gantt chart obtained by the ESS of the project (units 4 and 5)

previous chapter under a work continuity scheduling objective and focus on two main characteristics:

1. Construction projects are often characterized by repeating activities that have to be performed from unit to unit.
2. It may be necessary to incorporate the learning effects into activity time estimates in order to improve the accuracy of schedules.

Characteristic (1) has been described in literature for the scheduling of highway projects, pipeline constructions and high-rise buildings in which the crews perform the work in a sequence and move from one unit of the project to the next. The repetitive processes of these construction projects can be classified according to the direction of successive work along the units. In horizontal repetitive projects, the different processes are performed horizontally, as seen in pipeline construction or paving works. These construction projects are often referred to as continuous repetitive projects or linear projects due to the linear nature of the geometrical layout and work accomplishment. When progress is performed vertically, it is referred to as vertical repetitive projects, among which high-rise building construction is the classical example. Rather than a number of activities following each other linearly, these construction projects involve the repetition of a unit network throughout the project in discrete steps. They are therefore often referred to as discrete repetitive projects. When both horizontal and vertical repetitive processes among several multi-storey structures in construction projects occur, they are referred to as multiple repetitive projects (Kang et al. 2001).

Characteristic (2) allows the incorporation of crew productivity, differences in amounts of work between units or learning effects of crews and has been investigated by Amor (2002), Amor and Teplitz (1993, 1998), Badiru (1995), Shtub (1991) and Shtub et al. (1996). El-Rayes and Moselhi (1998) distinguish between typical and atypical repetitive activities. Typical repetitive activities are characterized by identical durations over all units, while atypical repetitive activities assume variation of duration from one unit to another and consequently, allow the incorporation of learning effects. This variation can be attributed to variations in the quantities of work encountered or crew productivity attained in performing the work of these units (Moselhi and El-Rayes 1993).

The project under study fits very well into this framework. Firstly, learning effects are a matter of degree since the project involves the repetition of 26 units. Note that learning effects can be considered as positive (experience of crews or reduction of errors), as well as negative (increasing complexity). Secondly, it is crucial to ensure the uninterrupted usage of resources of similar activities between different units, as to enable timely movement of resources (crews and a freezing machine) from one unit to the other, avoiding idle time. This feature is known as work continuity constraints and has been previously discussed in Sect. 8.2.1.

9.3 Project Scheduling

In this section, a project schedule is constructed taking various objectives into account. Section 9.3.1 constructs a straightforward project schedule with a minimum project duration with any commercial software tool. Section 9.3.2 introduces the work continuity constraints into the schedule. Section 9.3.3 presents various alternative scenarios and discusses their financial implications.

9.3.1   An Earliest Start Schedule

In this section the project is scheduled with commonly used software tools using the well-known CPM technique. A Gantt chart is constructed in which all activities are performed as soon as possible (i.e. an earliest start schedule (ESS)), using the activity time estimates as shown in Table 9.2. For the sake of clarity, the analysis is restricted to units 4–26 since the networks of units 1–3 have a different topological structure than the one depicted in Fig. 9.2. This does, however, not harm the overall results presented in this chapter.

Clearly, the ESS does not take the work continuity constraints into account and consequently, it does not assure the minimization of idle time of resources. Although work continuity constraints are often linked with crew idle time, in the sequel of this section, the more general term resource idle time is used, since the minimization of idle time of resources may not be restricted to crews only. Figure 9.3 displays the Gantt chart (units 4 and 5) obtained by the ESS schedule, assuming that the project starts at the beginning of January, 2003. This schedule clearly results in a lot of resource idle time, both for the freezing machine (within each unit) and for the crews (along the units). The idle time of crews, on the one hand, results from time-lags

Table 9.2   The activity time estimates for the Westerschelde tunnel project (in weeks)

	Activity ID										
	1	2	3	4	5	6	7	8	9	10	11
Unit 4	17	9	0	51	25	8	1	9	2	12	2
Unit 5	11	12	0	33	1	12	1	8	2	8	7
Unit 6	14	10	0	41	10	8	3	4	2	5	1
Unit 7	7	4	39	0	7	10	3	10	5	9	3
Unit 8	9	9	38	0	15	11	3	6	2	10	2
Unit 9	9	8	38	0	9	8	3	5	4	5	4
Unit 10	11	4	42	0	10	9	4	4	2	11	5
Unit 11	9	5	47	0	12	10	7	7	2	10	4
Unit 12	9	4	50	0	6	8	5	5	2	23	3
Unit 13	12	6	47	0	9	9	4	10	2	19	3
Unit 14	14	4	47	0	8	10	5	6	2	10	4
Unit 15	11	7	40	0	10	11	5	10	2	11	5
Unit 16	12	5	42	0	9	9	5	7	2	10	3
Unit 17	12	5	40	0	7	9	3	5	3	4	4
Unit 18	13	5	0	39	10	4	4	3	2	11	4
Unit 19	10	5	57	0	8	9	4	6	3	8	5
Unit 20	7	4	0	48	19	9	2	4	2	9	2
Unit 21	7	5	0	44	12	9	3	5	2	11	4
Unit 22	9	4	0	38	17	4	4	4	2	10	4
Unit 23	8	5	0	45	12	8	6	4	2	5	5
Unit 24	9	5	0	53	8	10	5	7	2	10	3
Unit 25	9	4	0	31	10	6	3	9	2	4	4
Unit 26	12	4	0	42	12	9	4	4	2	7	4

between the finish of work at one unit and the start at the next unit. The idle time of the freezer, on the other hand, appears within units, due to the earliest start time of all activities. As an example, the idle time between units 4 and 5 of crew 2 and the idle time of the freezer at unit 5 have been indicated in Fig. 9.3. The total crew idle time in the ESS schedule amounts to 165 days while the set of freezing machines is idle for 343 days in total. The total scheduled project duration of the transverse link subproject equals 380 days (for the sake of simplicity, weekends and holidays are ignored). Note that it is assumed that there is access to an unlimited number of freezing machines, such that parts of the projects at different units can be performed in parallel. If this is not the case, the total idle time of the freezing machines will change dramatically. This is the subject of Sect. 9.3.3, in which different scenarios are analyzed.

9.3.2 Minimizing Resource Idle Time

As stated earlier, it is assumed that a project is represented by an activity-on-the-node network (see Fig. 9.2) where the set of nodes, N, represents activities and the set of arcs, A, represents the precedence constraints. Since progress is performed in discrete steps (as in vertical repetitive projects), it is assumed that this network is repeated in K units ($K = 26$). The duration of each activity i at unit k is denoted by d_{ik} ($1 \leq i \leq n$ and $1 \leq k \leq K$ with $n = |N|$). In a similar way, the start time of activity i at unit k is given by s_{ik}. Consequently, the original unit network of Fig. 9.2 is extended to a large network consisting of n repeating activities between K units. This network is extended with a dummy start activity 0 at the first unit and a dummy end node $n + 1$ at the last unit, denoting the start and finish of the project.

The project scheduling problem with work continuity constraints can be formulated as follows:

$$\text{Minimize} \sum_{i \in N'} (s_{ik} - s_{i1}) \tag{9.1}$$

subject to

$$s_{ik} + l_{ijkk} \leq s_{jk} \qquad k = 1, \ldots, K; \forall (i, j) \in A \tag{9.2}$$

$$s_{ik} + l_{iikk+1} \leq s_{ik+1} \qquad k = 1, \ldots, K - 1; \forall i \in N \tag{9.3}$$

$$s_{01} = 0 \tag{9.4}$$

$$s_{n+1K} \leq \delta_{n+1} \tag{9.5}$$

$$s_i \in int^+ \qquad k = 1, \ldots, K; \forall i \in N \tag{9.6}$$

where l_{ijkl} denotes the time-lag between activity i on unit level k and activity j on unit level l. These time-lags denoting the different types of generalized precedence relations can be represented in a standardized form by reducing them to minimal start-start precedence relations as shown by the transformation rules shown in

Sect. 2.2.3. As an example, l_{ijkl} has to be replaced by d_{ik} in Eq. 9.2 to model the simple CPM case where only minimal precedence relations with zero time-lags are involved. More details can be found in Sect. 2.2.3.

The objective in Eq. 9.1 denotes the work continuity constraints and minimizes the resource idle time between similar activities at different units. The set N' is used to denote the set of activities that make use of the resource type that is subject to resource idle time minimization (i.e. freezing machines or crews in this case) with $N' \subset N$. Note that the word constraint is somewhat confusing since the work continuity of the schedule is guaranteed in the objective function of the model. Since the resource idle time is measured for resources that shift between units, it is sufficient to minimize the timespan of activities between the first and last unit. Indeed, these resources are needed at the start of the activity at the first unit and will only be released at the completion of this activity at the last unit K. Consequently, the start times of all intermediate activities have no influence on the idle time of this resource and are therefore not included in the objective function. The constraint set given in Eq. 9.2 maintains the (generalized) precedence relations among the activities of the project network at each unit. The constraint set in Eq. 9.3 maintains the (generalized) precedence relations among similar activities between consecutive units. Equation 9.4 forces the dummy start activity 0 to start at time zero and Eq. 9.5 forces the dummy end activity $n + 1$ (and consequently the project) to end on or before a negotiated deadline. Equations 9.6 ensure that the activity start times assume nonnegative integer values.

This scheduling problem can be solved efficiently by the procedure of Vanhoucke (2006b) that carefully shifts activities further in time in order to reduce the total resource idle time. Technical details of this algorithm are outside the scope of this chapter. In doing so, it takes the minimization of resource idle time into account and new results compared to the traditional CPM schedules will be obtained. More precisely, total idle time can be reduced from 165 to 107 days for crews and from 343 to 5 days for the freezing machine. The total project duration still remains 380 days.

The new schedule has positive implications on the outline of costs of the project. The costs of the crew are generally as follows: An ordinary employee has a cost of, on average, €40/man hour while a specialist has an average cost of €60/man hour. Consequently, the average cost of 1 man-hour amounts to €50. Each crew consists of 3 people that work for 8 h/day, resulting in a total cost of 50 * 3 * 8 = €1,200/day. The freezing machine has a cost of €3,000/day and is needed at each unit from the start of activity 2 until the completion of activity 10.

Taking these cost figures into account, the following outline of costs for the earliest start schedule can be derived. The crew idle time takes 165 days, resulting in 165 * €1,200 = €198,000 while the idle time of all the freezing machines results in a cost of 343 days * €3,000 = €1,029,000. The new schedule minimizes the resource idle time and results in the following outline of costs. The crew idle time cost amounts to 107 days * €1,200 = €128,400 and the idle time off all the freezing machines has a cost of 5 days * €3,000 = €15,000. The difference in idle time cost between the two schedules amounts to €1,083,600.

9.3.3 Various Other Scenarios

In the previous section, it is assumed that there is access to an unlimited amount
of freezing machines. In doing so, a lot of the activities of different units can be
performed in parallel. Due to the expensive nature of these machines, it is almost
impossible to rely on a large amount of freezing machines. Table 9.3 displays
the results for a limited amount of freezing machines. Since a decrease in the
number of freezing machines prevents the parallel execution of consecutive units,
the total project duration will automatically increase (similar to resolving resource
conflicts in a resource-constrained project scheduling problem). In the table, the
label 'deadline' is used to refer to the total project duration, 'CIT' to refer to the crew
idle time and 'FIT' to refer to the freezing machine idle time. The column 'Min-
CPM' has been created to display the results of the schedules with the commonly
used CPM tools, while the column 'Min-WC' displays the results with the approach
described in this chapter. This table reveals, on the one hand, that more freezing
machines result in slightly more idle time of this resource but a shorter project
deadline. Indeed, the freezing machine is used within each unit, and consequently,
the more freezing machines available, the more the units can be performed in
parallel. Moreover, the larger the total project duration, the more degrees of freedom
to schedule all the activities and the lower the idle time of the freezing machine. The
idle time of crews, on the other hand, reveals an opposite behavior: the larger the
increase in the project deadline, the larger the idle time of crews. This is mainly
because of the limited amount of resources (the freezing machine in this case).
Indeed, due to a limited amount of freezing machines, work at one unit can only
start after the finish of the previous unit. In doing so, the crews are idle for quite
some time since the freezing machine is then the bottleneck resource that determines
the progress of the project. The trade-off between idle time of resources (freezing
machines) and the total project duration has also been discussed in Sect. 8.2.1.

Table 9.3 The idle time
calculations for various
scenarios

Freezers	Deadline	Min-CPM		Min-WC	
		CIT	FIT	CIT	FIT
1	2,101	3,641	0	3,641	0
2	1,124	1,687	39	1,687	0
3	788	1,015	82	1,015	0
4	629	696	161	696	1
5	527	493	161	493	0
6	462	363	180	363	2
7	436	310	353	310	1
8	405	204	342	204	1
9	380	167	305	162	1
10	380	165	347	129	3
11	380	165	343	117	5
12	380	165	343	107	5
13	380	165	343	107	5

In the previous section, the cost difference between the two schedules is outlined under the assumption of an unlimited amount of freezing machines (i.e. for the rows with 12 or 13 freezing machines in Table 9.3). A similar analysis could have been done for all other rows of this table, making it able to assign the optimal number of machines leading to the lowest overall cost. This example illustrates the advantages of incorporating resource idle time minimization in a project scheduling environment.

9.4 Conclusions

In this chapter, real-life data of a construction project of a tunnel in the Netherlands are used to show the relevance of work continuity constraints in project scheduling. In analyzing the data, some shortcomings in the commonly used software tools were detected. While the vast amount of software tools focus on resource leveling and time minimization, they do not take the work continuity constraints into account. This chapter has shown that the incorporation of work continuity constraints takes the minimization of resource idle time into account.

The incorporation of work continuity constraints in the schedule has revealed two important insights. Firstly, the minimization of resource idle time results in a dramatic decrease in the cost of the resource use. Indeed, resource idle time results from the fact that one has to pay for this resource while it is not really necessary. This chapter referred to crews that have to wait to pass along units and a freezing machine that might be in operation while no real work is done during that time. Secondly, the minimization of resource idle time involves a trade-off between cost of idle time and project deadline increase. Indeed, the larger the project deadline, the more degrees of freedom in scheduling the activities and, consequently, the lower the resource idle time. An opposite effect was revealed for the crew idle time, but this was mainly due to a limited amount of the bottleneck resource (i.e. the freezing machine) that prevented progress of the project.

The problem under study is of crucial importance in projects which are characterized by repeating activities that have to be performed from unit to unit, such as highway projects, pipeline constructions and high-rise buildings. Resources that move along the units can be the subject of idle time between these units. Work continuity constraints can also be of importance for the minimization of within-unit idle time, as is the case for the freezing machine. Consequently, the problem under study can also be crucial in projects without repeating activities but with important, capital-intensive resources such as machines, specialized consultants, etc.

Chapter 10
Critical Chain/Buffer Management

Abstract Resource-constrained project scheduling is often a complex task due to the presence of dependencies between activities and the limited availability of renewable resources. The previous two chapters gave an extensive overview of different techniques to construct such a schedule, taking various scheduling objectives into account. This chapter extends this resource-constrained scheduling approach to a more flexible baseline schedule in order to be protected against unexpected events. The Critical Chain/Buffer Management approach assumes the construction of a resource feasible schedule as discussed in the previous chapters, but incorporates a certain degree of flexibility in the activity start times in order to easily monitor schedule deviations and quickly respond by taking corrective actions to keep the whole project on schedule.

10.1 Introduction

There have been a significant number of international high profile projects failing to be delivered on-time and on-budget. The Channel Tunnel project to provide an undersea connection between France and the UK is probably the most well-known example, but undoubtedly, most readers can also think back of smaller scale projects closer to their work environment that failed miserably. A number of undesirable characteristics are associated with many failing projects: budget overruns, compromised project specifications, and missed milestones. Consequently, the three basic dimensions of project success (time, cost and quality) are often in jeopardy. In his successful business novel, "Critical Chain", Goldratt reasoned that time was more important than cost for project managers (Goldratt 1997). Support for this idea can be found in numerous articles. As an example, a McKinsey study reported in Business Week (Port et al. 1990) that a project that is on-time but over-budget by 50% will earn 4% less than an on-budget project. In contrast, the study predicted that a project that is on-budget but 6 months late will earn 33% less than an on-time project. Both sources support the strategic importance of reducing project time.

Quality or scope of project output (meeting the required specifications) is very much sector and environment dependent and will not be studied separately in this chapter. As usual, the focus lies on a dynamic scheduling perspective and more precisely on the inability of project management to stick to the initially proposed schedule. Budget overruns are clearly visible and attributable. They are often an explicit choice of management to speed up the project (overtime, purchase of extra resources, ...) or rather the implicit consequences of the project taking more time than initially anticipated, reflecting the financial implications of occupying resources longer than projected. Multiple other sources for budget overruns exist, e.g. the necessity of acquiring new equipment because the present turns out to be insufficient for the project needs, but such risks are either completely unforeseeable, or they are predictable and consequently they should be included in the initial budget development. Such project features are often out of management control, or else need only careful attention but not a lot of management action.

Unlike these unforeseeable events, the main topic of this chapter deals with the presence of variability in the project schedule that can be foreseen to a certain extent. This chapter takes a similar view on project variation as has been taken in Chap. 5, but also takes the renewable resources into account. Consequently, the projects need to be scheduled under high complexity and within the presence of uncertainty and can therefore be classified in the fourth quadrant of Fig. 1.4. Throughout the chapter, it is implicitly assumed that the reader bears in mind at all times that actions to influence project schedule performance often risk to have direct implications on the budget as well as on the quality of the project. It is surprising to see that, given the large amount of projects that have finished late during the last decades, management still fails to quote accurate project deadlines. This is problematic, because virtually all organizations use their project plans not only as tools with which to manage the projects, but also as a basis on which to make delivery commitments to clients. Therefore, a vitally important purpose of project plans and of effective scheduling methods is to enable organizations to estimate the completion dates of the corresponding projects. This is particularly true for organizations that serve industrial clients, because such clients regularly have projects of their own, which require the outputs that the supplier organizations agree to deliver.

The outline of this chapter can be summarized as follows. Section 10.2 gives an overview of different sources of uncertainty in project management and scheduling. In Sect. 10.3, the main components of the Critical Chain/Buffer Management (CC/BM) scheduling technique is highlighted in detail. Section 10.4 gives a fictitious illustrative example using a six step CC/BM approach. Section 10.5 illustrates how a so-called buffered CC/BM project schedule can be used during the project execution phase to monitor and control the project performance and to trigger corrective actions in case the project deadline is in danger. Section 10.6 gives an overview of the main criticism on the CC/BM approach, highlighting clear merits and showing weaknesses and potential pitfalls. Section 10.7 draws overall chapter conclusions.

10.2 Sources of Uncertainty

In a manufacturing environment, machines regularly break down and need to be repaired. This is a random process that can be observed and for which the parameters can be estimated, such that a rather accurate picture of the availability of this machine can be obtained. In most manufacturing settings, such as job shop environments, job routings and machine utilizations are fairly predictable. Since the daily operation is one in which a certain degree of routine reigns, the manager in charge can invoke logic and calculus to estimate average lead times and average system load. A routine project is not like a job submitted to a job shop, but one that is important enough to deserve to be managed separately. As a consequence, averages are not so much important to a project manager as is variability. Unfortunately, because of the unique nature of each project, estimates based on previous experience are often unreliable, if ever previous experience has already been accumulated (compare the rather routine activities involved in the construction of a building with the scheduling effort required for an R&D project). On top of that, people plan and execute projects, not machines or computer programs. Therefore, some insight into human nature is crucial in project management. Every good project manager is equipped with a toolset of human resources management skills.

The required input to obtain a deterministic schedule is a single duration estimate for each activity of the project. Nevertheless, this duration is a stochastic variable, which is assumed to be independent of the other activities. Most often, such durations have a probability density function that is skewed to the right, for instance as pictured in Fig. 10.1.[1]

If one asks a programmer in a software development project how much time the development of the component he/she is working on will take, he/she will never select the expected value $E(d_i)$ or the median (50%-percentile). Rather he/she will mention something in the neighbourhood of the 90%-percentile, such that the duration estimate can be made with a certain amount of safety. Otherwise, in approximately 1 out of 2 cases, his/her programming will finish late (see Fig. 10.2), and this is not at all beneficial to his/her performance appraisal. Of course, the real

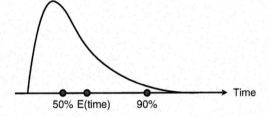

Fig. 10.1 A typical right skewed probability density function

50% E(time) 90% Time

---

[1]The PERT technique discussed in Chap. 2 also assumes that the duration of a project activity is distributed according to a right-skewed beta distribution.

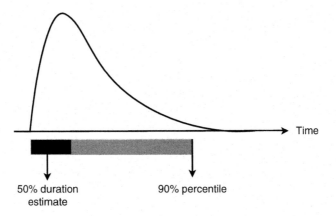

50% duration   90% percentile
estimate

Fig. 10.2 50% time estimate and 90%-percentile

density curve is never known beforehand, so to protect himself/herself even more, the programmer will pad the time estimate even more. As a result, in many project environments, individual activity duration estimates all include a reasonable amount of safety.

Furthermore, setting completion dates is often seen as a negotiation process. In negotiation it is common practice to make an opening bid that allows for cuts later on. Should planners foresee an overall schedule cut, they could be expected to add additional reserve in order to protect their schedules from such a cut. Also, managers at each level of the organizational hierarchy tend to add their own precautionary measures on top of the estimates of managers or coordinators reporting to them. In such a system of arbitrary safety insertion and schedule cuts along the different levels of organizational hierarchy, final projected activity durations will have very little, if any, real value.

10.2.1   Parkinson's Law

When a project schedule is to be developed based on the estimated single moment durations, some deterministic scheduling algorithm can be invoked, for instance by using the critical path and resource leveling options of standard project management software as discussed in the previous chapters. But what will happen when the software component the programmer is developing is finished in 70% of the estimated time? Most project schedules have milestones associated with activity finish times, meaning that an early finish will not be especially rewarded, but a late finish is undesirable. The worker will probably not pass on the output of his/her programming to the resources assigned to successor activities, but rather start streamlining his/her code, adding extra nice graphical features or so (gold plating or adding unnecessary bells and whistles). This is an illustration of what is called "Parkinson's law".

Work expands to fill the allotted time (Parkinson's law)

The programmer is not rewarded for early finishes, but rather he/she risks seeing future time estimates reduced by a certain factor, because he/she appears to be over-estimating his/her time needs. Also, if he/she hands in his/her outputs early, he/she will probably be assigned new work immediately, and it is more pleasant and less stressful to remain on the initial activity for some time longer. In other cases, people will simply adjust the level of effort to keep busy for the entire activity schedule. As was already mentioned, traditional project environments stress not being late, but they do not promote being early. This environment encourages Parkinson's law. In many environments, there are still other disincentives to report an activity completion early: work performed on time and material contracts for instance results in less revenue if the work is completed early. If the functional organization completes the work in less time than estimated, they cannot continue to charge the project.

10.2.2   The Student Syndrome

A second type of undesirable effect that can come into play in standard project management environments, can be nicely described in an academic setting. Consider a course for which the students enrolled have to write a paper and they have a deadline within 3 months from now. The paper itself however would, if worked at full effort and with a reasonable degree of safety included, require no more than 4 weeks. What would be the work planning of any 'regular' student? He or she will mostly postpone the real start of research and preparation to only some 4 weeks before the deadline. Undoubtedly, similar behavior can be observed in project management practice. This effect is known as the "student syndrome": many people have a tendency to wait until activities get really urgent before they work on them.

Wait until activities get really urgent (student syndrome)

Both scenarios, Parkinson's law and the student syndrome, will occur in projects with deterministic schedules with ample safety time built in and where milestones are used to evaluate workers. They will cause the initial duration estimates to become *self-fulfilling prophecies*, at least when activities could hypothetically be completed faster. This implies that although unforeseen disruptions induce delays, there will be no positive schedule variations to compensate for the negative ones. Such delays will also regularly occur exactly because of the student syndrome: when an unexpected problem is encountered when the work is halfway done, all safety is gone already and the estimate will be overrun. This makes it feel like the activity was underestimated to begin with, possibly leading to even higher future estimates.

10.2.3 Multiple Parallel Paths

If the project network does not simply consist of one simple path of activities, but rather has multiple parallel paths that diverge and join at different places in the network, there is another reason why favorable activity finishes cannot always be exploited, whereas delays often have immediate repercussions on the entire project. This is caused by the predominant use of finish-start precedence relations to model activity networks, which imply that a successor activity can only be started when the latest of its predecessors finishes. This effect is unavoidable, as the type of precedence relation is the most logical choice and models reality in the most natural way. Usually, the path merges tend to concentrate near the end of the project: indeed, "assembly", "integration" or "test" operations mostly occur close to project completion, requiring many elements to come together. This is one reason why project managers state that "many projects complete 90% the first year, and complete the final 10% in the second year". Consider Fig. 10.3, in which activity A has an undetermined number of m immediate predecessors $P_i, i = 1, \ldots, m$.

If each of the merging paths has a 50% probability of being done by the estimated time, the probability of at least one being late is already almost 88% when three activities merge together. Even if each individual activity had an 85% probability of on-time completion, the probability that at least one is late still approaches 40%. These observations are related to the disadvantages of the application of the classical PERT model and justify the need for more sophisticated simulation or analytical tools when the activity durations can indeed be modeled as independent random variables. The occurrence of multiple parallel paths and the influence on their successor activities is also discussed in Sect. 5.5.2 as the "merge bias".

10.2.4 Multitasking

A last project management practice that requires attention in this section is that of *multitasking*, which is not that much related to human behavior itself as it is to work organization. Multitasking is the performance of multiple project activities at the same time. In reality, time is divided between multiple activities, for instance by working on one project in the morning and one in the afternoon. Most people

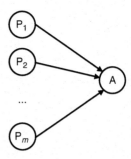

Fig. 10.3 An assembly activity can only start when multiple predecessors are finished

Fig. 10.4 Multitasking
versus no multitasking

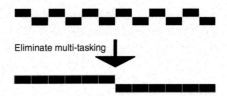

Eliminate multi-tasking

think of multitasking as a good way to improve efficiency: it ensures everyone is busy all the time. However, it has a detrimental effect on activity durations, which is illustrated in Fig. 10.4. Assume two activities that have to be performed by a single resource. The top picture of Fig. 10.4 displays a Gantt chart that represents the case of multitasking: both activities only finish at the end of the scheduling horizon. The bottom part of Fig. 10.4 illustrates the benefits that can be achieved by eliminating multitasking: there is no change in the finish time of activity 2, but activity 1 will be finished in half the time if it is worked on at full effort. Nevertheless, towards management, the worker will at least be able to present progress on all activities. In this example, the influence of set-up times is ignored: each time a worker changes from one activity to another, he/she will need a certain amount of time to handle this change-over, both in case of physical and of intellectual labor.

Single moment time estimates in an environment of multitasking become very much dependent upon the degree of multitasking that will be adhered to during activity execution. If experience from the past is used to develop estimates, those estimates are only meaningful if the same degree of multitasking was present at the time of reference. In most cases, the actually achievable activity duration (at full effort) remains concealed. This reasoning is very similar to the estimation of the lead times of product batches in a manufacturing company: if one looks at lead times achieved in the past to produce a value, he/she should only consider those observations where the company was working under a comparable system load.

Multitasking need not only occur within one project: most of project work is executed on a multi-project basis (as opposed to the use of entirely dedicated resources). Multitasking or jumping between projects could result in a number of negative effects, especially in the case of bottleneck resources. A multi-project environment will pose particular difficulties, because the workers probably report to multiple project managers and will have to comply with the desires of each of them. There is clearly a need for prioritization of projects and reduction of multitasking to an acceptable level. Otherwise, considerable competition for resources among the projects will be created.

10.3   Critical Chain/Buffer Management

This section presents an integrated project management methodology that is especially focused on controlling uncertainty during project execution and its undesirable effects discussed in the previous section. The Critical Chain/Buffer

Management (CC/BM) methodology is an application of the Theory of Constraints (TOC). In the end of the 1970s, dr. Eli Goldratt developed a planning methodology and corresponding software under the name OPT (Optimized Production Technology). In the midst of the 1980s, the term OPT was replaced by TOC. TOC offers a structured logic approach to problem solving and applies its brainstorming efforts mainly to the manufacturing environment. The TOC has a management focus on bottlenecks, or constraints, that keep the production process from increasing its output. Once managers identify the bottlenecks, overall operation is planned entirely as a function of the bottleneck schedule. When the whole is as effective as it can be at a given capacity, managers can elevate the constraint by investing extra capacity at the bottlenecks. Once a constraint has been lifted, these steps need to be repeated to identify other emerging constraints. A full overview of TOC is outside the scope of this book. The reader is referred to a brief introduction in Sect. 2.3.2.

10.3.1   Theory of Constraints in Project Management

Of course, project management texts have long told managers to focus on constraints. For projects, the constraint is perceived to be the critical path, which is the series of activities that determines the minimum time needed for the project to complete (see Part I of this book). Goldratt adds an important second ingredient to this framework that management often overlooks: scarce resources needed by activities both on and off the critical path and possibly also by other projects. In the case of developing a new product, for example, a manager may schedule the different activities according to the pace of the critical path but still face delays because the computer-aided design console is held up by other jobs. The critical chain (CC) is defined as that set of activities that determines the overall duration of the project, taking into account both resource and precedence dependencies. To prevent this critical chain from delays, CC/BM advises managers to build multiple types of safety (time) buffers into the schedule, similar to the inventory buffers used in production lines to make sure that bottleneck machines always have material to work on.

10.3.2   Working Backwards in Time

A CC/BM schedule is developed backwards in time from a target end date for the project. In the previous chapters of this book, activities have been scheduled as-soon-as-possible (ASAP) from the project start date, as usually done in traditional project scheduling. This scheduling places work as close as possible to the front of the schedule. In CC/BM planning, work is placed as close as possible to the end of the schedule, in an as-late-as-possible (ALAP) fashion. This approach provides advantages similar to those the just in time (JIT) approach offers in a production environment. These benefits include minimizing work-in-progress

(WIP), and not incurring costs earlier than necessary, thus improving project cash flow (under the assumption that only cash outflows are associated with intermediate project activities). Also, possible changes in the scope of the activity (altered client specifications or changes to subsystems interfacing with the activity), imply a higher risk of rework of activities that are started ASAP. Less rework will also result from the fact that workers simply have better information about their assignments. The main drawback directly related to scheduling in an ALAP fashion is that, in traditional critical path terminology, all activities will become critical. Any increase in duration of any activity will result in an equal increase in project end date. As will be explained in detail below, buffers will be inserted at key points in the project plan that will act as shock absorbers to protect the project end date against variations in activity duration. In this way, the benefits of ALAP scheduling are fully exploited with adequate protection against uncertainty.

Consider a project consisting of six activities in series, as shown in Fig. 10.5. The duration of each activity can be modeled as a stochastic variable, for instance with a univariate density function as pictured in Fig. 10.1 (where the variance will vary between the activities). Clearly, an organization's reputation as a reliable supplier is at stake when it quotes unreliable deadlines to customers, so its project schedules should protect the customers against the variability inherent in the activity durations. However, an overly large protection on the contrary will result in uncompetitive proposals and the loss of business opportunities. In order to cope with this complex task of project deadline estimation, one method of shielding its customers from the effects of the duration variability might be to ensure the timely completion of every individual activity. In fact, the widely accepted method of tracking progress relative to a schedule of milestones is an example of this approach. Choosing a safe time estimate for each activity separately will result in the choice of an approximation of the 90%-percentile estimate of each activity duration separately, resulting in the Gantt chart displayed at the bottom of Fig. 10.5. As discussed earlier, these milestones are self-fulfilling prophecies, so the project will most probably end no sooner than the quoted deadline.

10.3.3   The Project Buffer

It is very doubtful that any organization could be competitive in today's business environment if the organization's managers attempted to manage variability in this manner. Most managers know this, of course. This is why they struggle with a

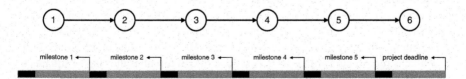

Fig. 10.5 A serial project network with safety time for each individual activity

conflict, between being able to present a competitive proposal to a customer and protecting the same customer from the adverse effects of the inevitable variability in project duration. The basic problem is that, as already mentioned, early finishes are wasted while late finishes are accumulated as the project progresses. In the TOC approach to project management, the seemingly logical protection of the scheduled completion of individual activities is not the goal. Rather, in the spirit of speed-to-market driven project performance, management only desires the rapid and successful completion of the project as a whole. Thus, CC/BM eliminates safety time for individual activities, and aggregates this protection at the end of the project under the form of a project buffer (PB). This implies a review of all activity duration estimates, such that protection against variability is excluded. One could quote the average duration of comparable activities, when they are worked on at full effort, or alternatively, choose a duration that will only be exceeded approximately one out of every two times (the median). The CC/BM approach constructs a project schedule based on so-called *aggressive duration estimates* (average, median, or any other value) that are not (individually at least) padded with safety. The reduction in the activity time estimates to aggressive time estimates also implies that it is essential to execute the project according to the *roadrunner mentality* or the *relay race approach*. This approach forces an activity to start as soon as the predecessor activities are finished. Exactly as in a relay race, the goal is to capitalize on the early finishes of preceding activities. The resulting project schedule based on aggressive time estimates is only an aid to come up with a project deadline, and not to check on individual activity schedule performance (or in other words: there are no milestones for the individual activities).

The removal of the protection from the individual activities must be aggregated into a project buffer PB with an appropriate size. However, since both positive and negative activity finishes will be attained (e.g. 50% estimates), these fluctuations will (partially) compensate for one another along the chain. Consequently, the aggregate protection to be provided at the end of the schedule needs not to be as large as the sum of the removed safety time of the individual activities. This is an intuitive result, but it can also easily be demonstrated mathematically. Assume that all n activities on a chain have equal variance σ^2. If the safety time of each individual activity is assumed to be equal to two standard deviations, the cumulative safety time will be $n(2\sigma)$. The variance of the sum of the durations on the other hand is the sum of variances, so to protect the chain executed according to the roadrunner mentality, the required safety time is $2\sigma\sqrt{n}$. The sum of a number of independent random variables tends to a normal distribution (according to the central limit theorem), which implies that the percentage protection provided for the individual strongly skewed distributions is actually even less than for the more normal chain of activities by selecting the same number of standard deviations. The less statistically inclined reader needs not to worry about these details: a valid rough cut approach would be to paste 50% of the removed safety time of each activity into the PB, which is also the method Goldratt proposed in his novel. This 50%-rule results in the reduced PB-size that is represented in Fig. 10.6. A second rule of thumb is the sum of squares or root square error method: the required PB size is set equal to the square root of the

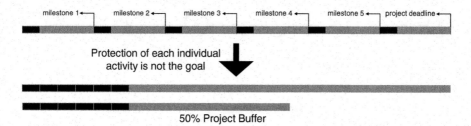

Fig. 10.6 Inserting a project buffer

sum of squares of the removed safety in the individual activities. This second rule is preferable for projects with a large number of activities, because the 50%-rule will tend to overestimate the required protection in such case. This is because it is a purely linear procedure: a 12-month project could end up with a 6-month PB, a 2-year project could end up with a year-long PB.

10.3.4   Feeding Buffers

The previous section explained how to properly handle individual activities and chains of activities. However, no project consists of a single chain of activities. All projects will have multiple chains in parallel, although mostly, only one will be the longest. The effects of these parallel chains on the variability in the overall duration of a project have been discussed in Fig. 10.3 and should be incorporated in the CC/BM approach. Figure 10.7 shows a fictitious project network with nine activities. The second but last activity of the longest chain (critical chain) with ID = 5 is an assembly activity: its start requires the output generated by the first four activities of the longest chain, and also the outputs generated by the so-called feeding chain. The absence of any of these outputs precludes the start of the assembly activity. For the moment, it is assumed that no resource conflicts occur between the different chains, such that they can indeed be executed in parallel, independently of one another. The bottom part of Fig. 10.7 displays a Gantt chart where the feeding chain has been scheduled ALAP, as the CC/BM theory prescribes.

From the discussion of Fig. 10.3, it is known that establishing your project baseline duration projections based on the critical chain alone will yield strongly downwards biased results, and this effect is only increased by our ALAP scheduling. Assume that chain 1–4 has a probability of 50% of finishing at the aggressive schedule duration forecast, and similarly for the feeding chain, then activity 5 will only start on time in one out of every 4 (=0.50^2) cases. One mathematically correct way to handle the complication of parallel chains would be to use either simulation or statistical calculations to adapt the size of the PB accordingly, as explained in the schedule risk analysis Chap. 5 without the presence of resources. However, this is where the elegance and simplicity of CC/BM comes in. The PB serves only to

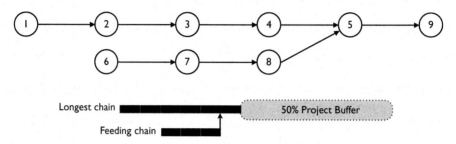

Fig. 10.7   A project with a feeding chain

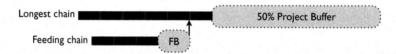

Fig. 10.8   Inserting a feeding buffer

protect the CC itself and the CC is decoupled from all outside (noncritical chain) feeding chains by means of so-called feeding buffers (FB). More precisely, a FB is inserted wherever a nonCC activity feeds into a CC activity. If the 50% rule is used to size the PB and a somewhat smaller (than 50%) FB is inserted, the buffered schedule of Fig. 10.8 will be obtained. Usual practice when multiple chains are interconnected, is to protect only for the longest of all those feeding chains, disregarding the other ones.

10.3.5   The Critical Chain

Up to now, the limited availability of renewable resources has been largely ignored. However, the presence of resources often leads to situations where resource conflicts are involved, as shown in Chaps. 7 and 8. Consider the simple project network of Fig. 10.9. Activities 1 and 3 and activities 2 and 4 must be performed in series due to the finish-start precedence relation defined to hold between them. Activity 1 and activity 2 must be performed by the same (renewable) resource X, of which only 1 unit is available. The activity durations are assumed to be aggressive 50% estimates. CC/BM starts by deriving a resource-feasible schedule in which all activities start ALAP (this can be achieved by the "resource leveling" function in standard project management software tools or by the backwards use of the priority rule based scheduling techniques of Sect. 7.4.1). Such an (unbuffered) schedule is depicted in Fig. 10.9. Based on such a schedule, it is easy to identify the CC, defined as the longest chain of activities that considers both technological and resource dependencies: it will be a chain of activities for which the end of each activity equals

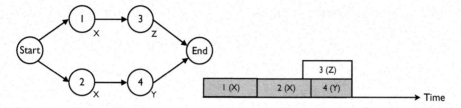

Fig. 10.9   An unbuffered resource feasible schedule (CC = 1-2-4)

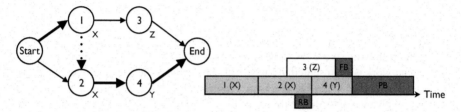

Fig. 10.10   A buffered resource feasible schedule

the start of the next. In the example, the CC is the chain "start-1-2-4-end". The resource conflict is resolved by forcing activities 1 and 2 to be performed in series, as indicated by the dotted arc in the network in Fig. 10.10. The buffered schedule is shown in the same figure. The resource buffer RB is discussed below.

10.3.6   Resource Buffers

One of the leading causes of late projects is that resources are not available or not available in sufficient quantity when they are needed. CC/BM requires a mechanism to prevent the CC activities from starting late or taking longer due to resource unavailabilities (other activities are less important). The selected method is to use a resource buffer (RB) to provide information to the CC resources about when they will be needed. This RB is different from the PB and FBs in that it does not normally occupy time in the project baseline schedule. It is an information tool to alert the project manager and performing resources of the impending necessity to work on a CC activity. RBs are placed whenever a resource has an activity on the CC, and the previous CC activity is done by a different resource. Resource buffers should make sure that resources will be available when needed and CC activities can start on time or (if possible) early. RBs usually take the form of an advance warning, i.e. a wake-up call for every new instance of a resource on the CC. Alternatively, space (idle time) can be created on the resource to provide a kind of protective capacity. An illustration of the placement of a RB is provided in Fig. 10.10: it warns resource Y some time before it is to start working on the CC, that it should be ready.

10.4   An Illustrative Example

Having covered all the basic scheduling aspects of CC/BM, a brief summary of the scheduling methodology of CC/BM for deriving the buffered baseline schedule can be outlined as follows:

1. Come up with aggressive estimates.
2. Construct an ALAP schedule.
3. Identify the Critical Chain.
4. Determine appropriate buffer positions.
5. Determine appropriate buffer sizes.
6. Insert the buffers into the schedule.

In the following, these six steps will be applied to a larger example project. The project network is represented in Fig. 10.11. The activity duration is indicated above each activity node while the resource requirements for three renewable resource types are given below the node. Activities 0 and 12 are dummies, representing project start and finish, respectively.

Step 1.   It is assumed that the activity durations represented in the network are already aggressive 50% time estimates (see Fig. 10.1).

Step 2.   To construct a resource feasible project schedule, information is needed about the resource requirements of the different activities. In the project, three resource types are used, named A, B and C, with availability of 3, 1 and 2 units, respectively. The resource requirements of each activity are pictured in the Table 10.1. By use of a commercial software tool or scheduling techniques discussed in Sect. 7.4.1, the schedule of Fig. 10.12 can be obtained. In this schedule, all activities are scheduled ALAP.

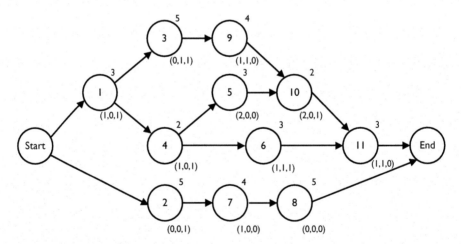

Fig. 10.11 An example project network with 11 nondummy activities

Table 10.1 Resource requirements for each activity i

i	d_i	r_{i1}	r_{i2}	r_{i3}
0	0	0	0	0
1	3	1	0	1
2	5	0	0	1
3	5	0	1	1
4	2	1	0	1
5	3	2	0	0
6	3	1	1	1
7	4	1	0	0
8	5	0	0	0
9	4	1	1	0
10	2	2	0	1
11	3	1	1	0
12	0	0	0	0

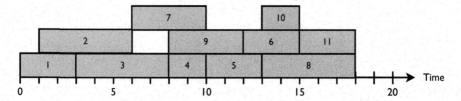

Fig. 10.12 A resource feasible latest start schedule

Step 3. Based on the above schedule, there are three choices for the CC: either "1-3-4-5-8", "1-3-4-5-10-11" or "1-3-9-6-11".[2] Based on a project manager's knowledge of the project environment (subjective!), it can for example be concluded that the third of the three candidate chains is the most constraining: there is only one resource link, and resources are amply available in the company, while the technological precedences are strict. Also, the activities on the second chain are perceived more as "standard" activities, that are better manageable.

Step 4. Appropriate buffer positions are indicated in Fig. 10.13, together with the chosen CC.

Three feeding buffers will be inserted, the first between activities 4 and 6, to protect the CC in activity 6 from variability in the noncritical feeding chain consisting only of activity 4 (subsequently referred to as FB_{4-6}). A second feeding buffer (FB_{10-11}) is inserted before activity 11, to protect it from variability on the feeding chain 4-5-10. Finally, FB_{8-12} is present to protect the project end from variability in feeding chain 2-7-8. A project buffer will of course

---

[2]It has been extensively shown in Chap. 7 that the critical chain depends on the algorithm used to construct a resource feasible schedule, and on the scheduling objective, which is assumed to be the minimization of time throughout this chapter.

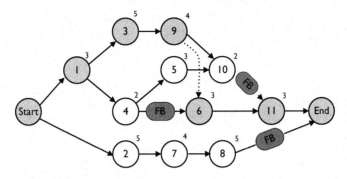

Fig. 10.13 The buffered network of Fig. 10.11

also be inserted, after activity 12. Resource buffers should be placed whenever resources are transferred from nonCC to CC-activities. It is left up to the reader to determine the position of these buffers. As RBs will only be implemented as a wake-up call, they will not be further considered in this exercise. In practical settings, it may be wise to wait with the identification of these RBs until the final buffered baseline schedule has been developed, as resources may be planned to be transferred differently in this final schedule.

Step 5.   Based on studies of similar activity durations of previous comparable projects, the company has estimated that the standard deviation σ of each activity duration is about 0.4 times the duration. Corresponding standard deviation estimates for all activity durations are provided in Table 10.2. Management has decided that a time protection of two standard deviations suffices for buffer sizing. Hence, the following buffer sizes can be calculated: $FB_{4-6} = 1.6$ time periods $\rightarrow$ choose 2; $FB_{8-12} = 2 * \sqrt{2^2 + 1.6^2 + 2^2} = 6.5 \rightarrow$ choose 7; $FB_{10-11} = 2 * \sqrt{0.8^2 + 1.2^2 + 0.8^2} = 3.3 \rightarrow$ choose 4. In a similar way, the size of the project buffer is equal to $PB = 2 * \sqrt{1.2^2 + 2^2 + 1.6^2 + 1.2^2 + 1.2^2} = 6.6$ $\rightarrow$ take 7.

Step 6.   The FBs and PB can now be inserted into the baseline schedule, as shown in Fig. 10.14.

10.5   Project Execution and Buffer Management

The construction of a buffered baseline schedule as explained in the previous sections serves as an ideal tool during the project execution phase to monitor the project's performance and to take corrective actions when necessary. Once the project is set off, the execution of project activities should be done according to the roadrunner mentality. As explained above, this implies that individual activity finish times are not seen as individual milestones or deadlines to guarantee that early

Table 10.2 Estimated standard deviations for each activity i

i	d_i	σ_i
0	0	0
1	3	1.2
2	5	2
3	5	2
4	2	0.8
5	3	1.2
6	3	1.2
7	4	1.6
8	5	2
9	4	1.6
10	2	0.8
11	3	1.2
12	0	0

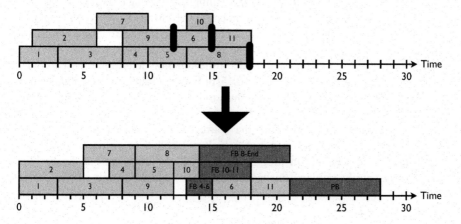

Fig. 10.14 Insertion of the buffers into the baseline schedule

finishes of activity predecessors have an immediate effect on the start of the activity. This mentality also implies that during project execution, contrary to initial baseline scheduling, all activities start ASAP. The key to reducing system-wide work-in-process and other disadvantages of starting activities ASAP is to control the flow of work into the system: activities without (nondummy) predecessors, the so-called gating activities, should not start before the scheduled start time, while nongating activities, especially those on the CC, should be started as soon as they can when work becomes available.

The execution of the project is managed by the use of buffers: in addition to providing aggregated protection against statistical variation, buffers are supposed to act as vital warning mechanisms. Buffer management is the key to tracking project performance in CC/BM (notice the distinct but related essential functions of buffers during baseline development and project execution). The CC is the sequence of dependent events that prevents the project from being planned with a shorter estimate of overall duration. In this way, the CC highlights where additional resources can cause the project to be completed in a shorter interval. Given the goal of completing the project as quickly as possible, the CC is the constraint that prevents the project from making greater progress towards this goal. At the same time, the buffers are the instruments that can be utilized during project execution to determine whether the total project duration in the baseline schedule is still achievable with an appropriate degree of certainty. By comparing the current ASAP schedule with the buffer positions in the baseline, the project manager gets an idea of how many buffers have been used versus how much of the processing of its feeding chains has been completed. If the project's progress is at the start of a chain and the entire buffer has already been consumed, the project is in danger. If the progress is at the end and no buffer has been consumed, the project will probably be early. This buffer management process can be formalized. As long as there is some predetermined proportion of the buffer remaining, everything is assumed to go well (the green OK zone). If activity variation consumes buffers by a certain amount, a warning is raised to determine what needs to be done if the situation continues to worsen (the yellow watch out zone). These actions (expediting, working overtime, subcontract, etc.) are to be put into effect if the situation deteriorates past a critical point (the red action zone). Figure 10.15 provides possible buffer management thresholds. Obviously, the threshold values to trigger actions vary as a function of project or path completion.

One advantage of the FBs and the entire CC/BM method is that the need to re-schedule the project is reduced (which is labelled as *proactive scheduling* in Chap. 1). The schedule in progress is updated continuously, but the baseline schedule ordinarily remains unchanged. CC/BM states that only if the project

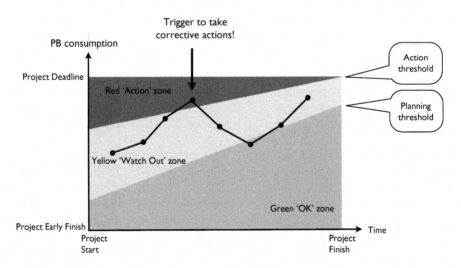

Fig. 10.15 Buffer management thresholds as a function of proportion of project completed

is in real trouble, meaning the PB is in real trouble, it will make sense to reschedule. Such circumstances will occur when it is impossible to restore the schedule in progress to the safe zone by routine actions as a response to buffer monitoring. At that moment, a new CC is identified, and a new baseline schedule needs to be developed that provides the project manager with a new assessment of the date at which he/she can anticipate the project to be completed with a convenient amount of certainty. Most CC/BM sources say that more often than not, recomputing a baseline is a final recourse that should be avoided whenever possible, to avoid system nervousness. Nevertheless, uncertain events during project execution (activity delays, the necessity to insert new activities, unavailability of resources, late deliveries by a subcontractor, etc.) may dramatically change the composition of the critical sequences. A CC may shift just as a bottleneck may shift, and although perhaps the project baseline duration is not in immediate danger, one should remain focused on a chain of activities that may have lost its criticality. This topic has been described in a number of critical review papers in which the authors state that CC/BM suffers from serious oversimplification. A few words on the main CC/BM critical points is the topic of the next section.

10.6   A Critical Note

Since its introduction in 1997, CC/BM is seen as an important eye opener to project management and dynamic project scheduling. The idea of protecting a deterministic baseline schedule in order to cope with uncertainties is sound and appeals to management (Herroelen and Leus 2001) and is one of the foundations of dynamic scheduling (see e.g. the topic of Chap. 5). However, shortcomings and oversimplifications are mentioned throughout various sources in the literature, which have resulted in an overwhelming amount of extensions, both research papers and books, on top of the original CC/BM philosophy. In what follows, the main points of criticism highlighted in research papers written by Herroelen and Leus (2001) and Herroelen et al. (2002) are briefly mentioned, without going into much detail.

10.6.1   Scheduling Objective

The CC/BM philosophy assumes that time is *the* number one scheduling objective, and ignores other regular and/or nonregular scheduling objectives as discussed throughout Chaps. 7 and 8. Consequently, it is implicitly assumed that each project is a resource-constrained project scheduling problem where the scheduling objective is the minimization of time, as discussed in Sect. 7.3.2. It should be noted, however, that a second important scheduling objective is implicitly taken into account, i.e. the minimization of the work in progress (WIP). As mentioned earlier, this scheduling objective is taken into account through the use of the as-late-as-possible scheduling approach, and is similar to the leveling objective discussed in Sect. 7.3.4. Moreover, by scheduling activities as-late-as-possible and assuming that these activities have a negative cash flow (i.e. cost), the net present value objective of Sect. 7.3.3 has also been taken into account. However, apart from the time, leveling and net present value objectives, no other objectives that might be relevant in practice are explicitly taken into account. Future research efforts should focus on the influence of incorporating these other scheduling objectives on the relevance and use of the CC/BM approach.

10.6.2   Scheduling Quality

Goldratt minimizes the effect of the use of high-quality scheduling algorithms and states that the impact of uncertainty is much larger than the impact of using proper scheduling methods. While it can hardly be denied that uncertainty is a crucial dimension of dynamic scheduling and often has a large effect on the project performance, the beneficiary effect of sound scheduling methods should be put into the right perspective. It has been shown extensively throughout previous chapters that the critical chain not only depends on the scheduling objective, but also on the quality of the algorithm used to construct a resource feasible schedule. Consequently, the use of high-quality scheduling methods is not only crucial for the quality of the project scheduling objective (time), but also determines which activities are critical and make part of the critical chain. Moreover, when time is considered as the main scheduling objective, it is a logical choice to focus on the best performing scheduling techniques that lead to the best optimized scheduling objective value.

10.6.3   Critical Chain

The CC/BM philosophy prescribes the use and presence of a single critical chain that can be best kept constant throughout the whole project life cycle. However, it can be easily verified that in a realistic project setting, more than one chain can be critical and the presence of single or multiple critical chains depends on the way the baseline schedule is constructed (scheduling objective and scheduling quality). Moreover, a dynamic setting results in a shift of the critical chain caused by changes in activity time estimates, precedence relations, etc. The combined effects of multiple dynamic critical chains, that furthermore depend on the scheduling objective and quality of the methods used, puts the buffering approach in a more complex perspective. The CC/BM approach does not properly address these issues.

10.6.4 Buffer Sizing

Sizing buffers can be done based on the length of the critical chain (project buffer) or feeding chains (feeding buffers) as initially proposed by Goldratt, or by taking risk information of the activities on the (feeding or critical) chain into account. However, potential delays in activities that lead to buffer consumption can also be caused by the unavailability of resources. Although the original CC/BM approach suggests to use resource buffers to guarantee timely availability of these resources, it is conjectured that they are not an ideal solution to solve unexpected delays. The impact of potential delays due to resource unavailability depends on the scarceness of these resources, and therefore, knowledge about the scarceness of resources should also be taken into account when sizing buffers. A way to measure resource scarceness has been proposed in Sect. 8.3.2.

10.6.5 Buffer Management

The use of time buffers to protect the project deadline can be questioned in highly complex projects where the efficient use of limited resources is the main driver of project progress performance. Both the static insertion of buffers in the baseline schedule (scheduling phase) and the dynamic penetration of buffers during project progress (execution phase) might and often will cause new resource conflicts. Resolving these new resource conflicts might result in a need to adapt the original baseline schedule, leading to changes in the critical chain(s) and feeding chains and in the corresponding buffer sizes. Although this anomaly can be considered as a technical scheduling detail, no rules-of-thumb on best-practices to repair the original baseline schedule are given.

10.7 Conclusions

The translation of the theory of constraints philosophy discussed in "The Goal" to a project environment, as described in "Critical Chain", was a major step forward in the development of project management theory. Indeed, Goldratt illustrates in his novel the applicability of the bottleneck focus to project management environments and defines the critical chain as the project bottleneck to focus on. Similar to the inventory buffers in production environments (The Goal), he introduces the use of time buffers to protect the bottleneck (Critical Chain) against variability.

Quite a number of studies have focused on the pitfalls of the critical chain philosophy. In these studies, the authors argue that the CC/BM theory is an important eye-opener. Indeed, the point that the interaction between activity durations, precedence relations, resource requirements and availabilities determines the project duration is well-taken but not at all a new idea (this idea was the central theme of Chaps. 7 and 8). Moreover, the protection of a deterministic baseline schedule through the insertion of buffers (project, feeding and resource buffers) is a pragmatic but sometimes a bit overly simplistic approach to the management of all forms of variability that might arise in project scheduling. Various studies stress the need for efficient algorithms for the creation of robust baseline schedules, powerful and effective warning mechanisms and mechanisms for dynamic evaluation of criticality of project activities. Nevertheless, most studies recognize that the breakthrough of project management was caused by the novel by a man who already claimed two decades ago that the identification and focus on the limiting factor (the bottleneck or the critical chain) is primordial in changing the behavior of the system under study.

Chapter 11
The Mutum-Paraná II Bridge Project (B)

Abstract The case description of this chapter is a follow-up exercise of the case of Chap. 6 and also acts as an integrated exercise to get acquainted with the scheduling principles discussed in Part II of this book. The primary goal of this fictitious case study is to get acquainted with project scheduling software and to construct a feasible resource-constrained project schedule, which is clearly understandable by all project stakeholders. The goal of the student is to go further than submitting software print-outs to the project team. Instead, the purpose is the integration of the resource-constrained scheduling principles of the previous chapters within the features of a project scheduling tool in order to provide an easy and understandable information sheet on the predicted project execution to the various members of a project team.
Similar to the first case study, the topic of this chapter can also be used to teach extended scheduling principles, such as the use of CC/BM scheduling principles, the incorporation of other scheduling objectives in a resource-constrained project setting, and many more. In this chapter, only the case description is given. The solution and the educational approach depend on the wishes and needs of the students who solve the case and the teacher who can act as the moderator during the case teaching session.

11.1 Introduction

The second longest river in South America after the Amazon, the Paraná River joins with the Paraguay and Uruguay Rivers before emptying into the Ro de la Plata estuary on its way to the Atlantic Ocean. The river begins its 3,032-mile (4,879-km) course in east-central Brazil. The Paraná flows mainly among high plateaus through Paraguay and Argentina.

The Brazilian company Curitiba Pontes Ltd. has been awarded for the construction of the Mutum-Paraná II bridge over the river Paraná. The river Paraná in Argentina was the last obstacle in the highway project. This highway was a promise

M. Vanhoucke, *Project Management with Dynamic Scheduling*,
DOI 10.1007/978-3-642-40438-2_11, © Springer-Verlag Berlin Heidelberg 2013

from the government to the poor people of the interior to link their region to Buenos Aires. Therefore large investments were made to stimulate the economy.

A team meeting was held last week in which initial estimates about the project activity duration have been reviewed and updated, resource requirements and risk numbers have been analyzed, proposed and evaluated. Exactly 1 week later, the team received a detailed outline of the different activities from Orlando Carvalheiro, in which all activities have been described into detail, with a more precise duration estimate and the nine most important resources. Management has instructed Orlando for a project finish at the earliest possible time. They have requested a complete plan.

11.2 The Project in Detail

José Silva Coelho opened the team meeting with the announcement that the executive committee of Curitiba Pontes Ltd. confirmed the starting date for the project of January 2nd, 2012 and asked Orlando to project a completion date with his submission of the plan. The committee's request implied that whatever date Orlando came up with was acceptable, but Orlando knew that he would be expected to keep the project lead-time under control.

Orlando noticed that the final project deadline proposed last week (February 25th, 2013) would be an unfair and unrealistic estimate. He was proud about the detailed analysis of the project and presented the detailed information in a long and monotone monologue about the various project activities and their need for resources. The major parts of this overwhelming monologue of Orlando were accompanied by a detailed description and tables with the technological precedence relations between the activities and the resource requirements (see Tables 11.2 and 11.3). Maria Mota Pereira was proud to tell the team that the resource problem at the beginning of the project was solved, and presented a detailed outline of the availability of all resources necessary to complete the project with success (Table 11.1).

During the previous meeting held last week, Carlos Garez expressed his concern regarding the possible unstable underground of the river banks. Today, he was proud

Table 11.1 The resource availability and cost for the highway bridge construction project

Description	Availability	Cost/h
Crane	1	150
Pile driver man	4; 2 (June, July and August)	60
Carpenter	7	60
Labourer	12	40
Iron worker	4; 2 (July and August)	60
Equipment operator	2	60
Oiler	1	60
Cement mason	2	100
Truck driver	2	60

Table 11.2 The resource use for the highway bridge construction project

	Activity description	Time (weeks)	CR	PD	CA	LA	IW	EO	OI	CM	TD	MDC
1	Preparatory work and move in	6			3	5		2			2	
2	Mobilize pile rig 1	1	1	2		1		2	1		1	350
3	Mobilize pile rig 2	1	1	2		2		1	1		2	350
4	Mobilize pile rig 3	1	1	2		1		1	1		2	350
5	Excavate abutment 1	1				5		1				
6	Excavate abutment 2	1				5		1				
7	Excavate abutment 3	1				5		1				
8	Drive piles abutment 1	3		4	1	2		1	1			350
9	Drive piles abutment 2	3		4	1	2		1	1			350
10	Drive piles abutment 3	1		4	1	2		1	1			350
11	Demobolize pile rig 1	1	1	2		2		1	1		1	350
12	Demobolize pile rig 2	4	1	2		2		2	1		2	350
13	Demobolize pile rig 3	4	1	2		2		1	1		1	350
14	Forms, pour and strip footing 1	1			3	5		1	1	1		1,850
15	Forms, pour and strip footing 2	8			4	5		1	1	1		1,850
16	Forms, pour and strip footing 3	1			3	5		1	1	1		350
17	Forms, pour and strip abutment 1	2			6	10		1	1	1		1,850
18	Forms, pour and strip abutment 2	1			7	12		1	1	1		1,850
19	Forms, pour and strip abutment 3	2			6	10		1	1	1		1,850
20	Backfill abutment 1	4			4	4		1	1			
21	Backfill abutment 2	2			4	4		1	1			
22	Backfill abutment 3	3			4	4		1	1			
23	Set girders and forms deck 1–2	2			3	4	4	1	1			2,350
24	Set girders and forms deck 2–3	2			3	4	4	1	1			5,350
25	Pour deck	1			2	5		1	1	2		3,350
26	Saw joints	2				1						
27	Strip deck and rub concrete	1				7						
28	Clean up and final inspection	1				6		1	1			350

to present his report consisting of a detailed engineering study concluding that the unstable river banks problem due to the swirling water was no longer a threat for this project.

In addition, Orlando points out that labor costs in Argentina are extremely low due to the economic crisis. The accounting department told Orlando that he could estimate a cost of €40 per hour per employee (laborer) and €60 for other employees. Moreover, it is assumed that a working day contains 8 working hours (between 8.00 and 17.00 with 1 h break between 12.00 and 13.00) from Monday till Friday, resulting in a 40 h workweek. This information would enable him to provide a cash flow forecast along with his plan, which the chief accountant said would be expected. José knew that it was customary at Curitiba Pontes Ltd. to provide the following as parts of a plan to be submitted to the executive committee:

- Work breakdown structure.
- Network diagram.
- A Gantt-chart with the earliest possible project completion time that can be achieved with unlimited resources.
- The critical activities and milestones.
- Resource loading charts and cumulative labor requirements, for every resource separately and in total.
- A feasible project schedule satisfying the existing resource constraints that minimizes the project duration.
- A cash flow requirements graph for the project when leveled.
- A personal opinion on the project and a proposal to the management committee.

In the new detailed information it is stated that the government is willing to pay a bonus of €15,000 per week that the project end date can be moved forward. Knowing this, you are asked to find the ideal number of laborers to employ.

11.2.1   The Resources

The resource use is shown in the Table 11.2. Each resource has been abbreviated as follows: crane (CR), pile driver man (PD), carpenter (CA), laborer (LA), ironworker (IW), equipment operator (EO), oiler (OI), cement mason (CM) and truck driver (TD). The cost for material and other direct charges (MDC) have been indicated in the last column.

11.2.2   The Relations

The precedence relations between all activities are shown in Table 11.3.

Table 11.3 The minimal time-lag precedence relations for the highway bridge construction project (in weeks)

		Minimal time lags		
		SS	FS	FF
1	2	2		
	3		5	
	4		5	
	5		0	
	6		8	
	7		8	
2	8		0	
3	9		0	
4	10		0	
5	8			3
6	9	6		
7	10	3		
8	11		0	
	14		0	
9	12		0	
	15		0	
10	13		0	
	16		0	
11	17		0	
12	18		0	
13	19		0	
14	17		0	
15	18		0	
16	19		0	
17	20		0	
	23		0	
18	21		0	
	23		0	
	24		0	
19	22		0	
	24		0	
20	28		0	
21	28		0	
22	28		0	
23	25	1		
24	25	1		
25	26		1	
	27		2	
26	28		0	
27	28			2

Part III
Project Control

Chapter 12
Earned Value Management

Abstract In the previous parts of this book, it was assumed that the project has not started yet, and hence, the project was still in the definition and scheduling phase of the project life cycle. From this chapter on, it is assumed that the project has started (execution phase) and that the project is in progress. Consequently, it is the task of the project manager to carefully control the performance of the project, using his/her knowledge of the schedule risk analyses and baseline scheduling steps discussed in the two previous parts. The project control dimension of dynamic scheduling can be done relying on a well-established technique known as *Earned Value Management*.

Earned Value Management (EVM) is a methodology used since the 1960s, when the USA department of defense proposed a standard method to measure a project's performance. The system relies on a set of often straightforward metrics to measure and evaluate the general health of a project. These metrics serve as early warning signals to timely detect project problems or to exploit project opportunities. The purpose of an EVM system is to provide answers to project managers on questions such as:

- What is the difference between budgeted and actual costs?
- What is the current project status? Ahead of schedule or schedule delay?
- Given the current project performance, what is the expected remaining time and cost of the project?

This chapter gives an overview of all EVM metrics and performance measures to monitor the time and cost dimension of a project's current progress to date, and shows how this information can be used to predict the expected remaining time and cost to finalize the project. This information serves as a trigger to take corrective actions to bring the project back on track when needed.

M. Vanhoucke, *Project Management with Dynamic Scheduling*,
DOI 10.1007/978-3-642-40438-2_12, © Springer-Verlag Berlin Heidelberg 2013

12.1   Introduction

Earned Value Management is a methodology used to measure and communicate the real physical progress of a project and to integrate the three critical elements of project management (scope, time and cost management). It takes into account the work completed, the time taken and the costs incurred to complete the project and it helps to evaluate and control project risks by measuring project progress in monetary terms. The basic principles and the use in practice have been comprehensively described in many sources (for an overview, see e.g. Anbari 2003 or Fleming and Koppelman 2005). Although EVM has been set up to follow up both time and cost, the majority of the research has been focused on the cost aspect (see e.g. the paper written by Fleming and Koppelman (2003) who discuss EVM from a price tag point of view). This chapter reviews the basic key metrics in earned value, elaborates on the recent research focused on the time aspect of EVM and compares a newly developed method, called earned schedule (Lipke 2003), with the more traditional approach of forecasting a project's duration.

The outline of the chapter is as follows. In Sect. 12.2, the different metrics of an EVM system will be reviewed (top layer of Fig. 12.1) and will later be used in Sects. 12.3 and 12.4. The three basic EVM metrics will be extended with a fourth more recently developed metric to measure the time progress of a project in time units. Section 12.3 reviews the existing performance measurement metrics (middle layer) to evaluate the current time and cost performance of a project in progress.

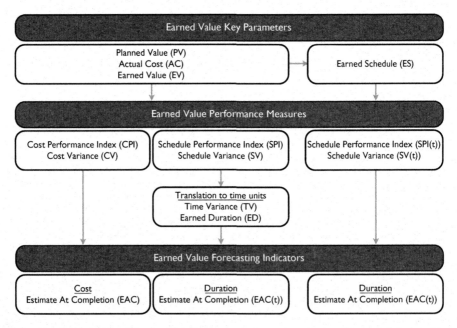

Fig. 12.1 Earned Value Management: key parameters, performance measures and forecasting indicators

Section 12.4 discusses the use of these performance measures to forecast the future time and cost performance of the project (bottom layer). Figure 12.1 serves as a guideline to Sects. 12.2–12.4. The different metrics presented in these sections will be illustrated on a fictitious project example in Sect. 12.5. Section 12.6 gives overall chapter conclusions on the relevance and use of EVM systems.

12.2 EVM Key Parameters

Measuring the performance of a project in progress requires a certain point of reference and knowledge about the basic metrics used in an EVM system. Since project performance should be measured throughout the entire life of the project at regular time intervals, the ideal point of reference is a fixed time frame known as the baseline schedule of the project. This project schedule can be constructed using the techniques discussed in the previous parts of the book and defines start times (and finish times) for each project activity. Having knowledge about activity costs, this baseline schedule can be translated into a time-phased planned value for each activity and for the total project. The planned duration PD equals the total project duration as a result of the constructed CPM schedule or its resource related extensions and is often referred to as schedule at completion (SAC, Anbari 2003). The actual time AT or actual duration AD defines the number of time periods (e.g. weeks) the project is in progress at the current time instance. Consequently, these measures are used to calculate the project progress and the number of time increments that the project is running and are used to define the reporting periods for performance measurement from the start to the finish of the project. The real duration RD defines the real final project duration known upon the project's finish. The budget at completion BAC is the sum of all budgeted costs for the individual activities. These variables can be summarized as follows:

PD   Planned Duration (often known as Schedule At Completion (SAC))
        → expected total duration known from the baseline schedule
RD   Real Duration
        → real project duration only known when the project is finished
BAC   Budget At Completion
        → expected total cost as a result of the baseline schedule
RAC   Real At Completion
        → real project cost only known when the project is finished
AD   Actual Duration (or Actual Time AT) at the current time
        → number of time periods the project is in progress

EVM requires three key parameters to measure the project performance, i.e. the Planned Value (PV), the Actual Cost (AC) and the Earned Value (EV). These three metrics will be discussed in the Sects. 12.2.1–12.2.3. A fourth indicator, known as the Earned Schedule (ES) indicator, is an extension of the three EVM key parameters, and is discussed in Sect. 12.2.4.

12.2.1 Planned Value

The *Planned Value* PV is the time-phased budget baseline as an immediate translation of the schedule constructed from the project network (without or with resources, as discussed in Parts I and II of this book). It is a cumulative increase in the total budgeted activity cost given the start and finish times stipulated in the baseline schedule. The planned value is often called *budgeted cost of work scheduled* (BCWS).

Figure 12.2 displays a straightforward project schedule of a project network with 5 activities in series. Each activity has a duration of 1 week and a budgeted cost of €20,000, leading to a schedule with a planned duration of PD = 5 weeks and a total expected cost of BAC = €100,000. The translation of the baseline schedule displayed at the top of Fig. 12.2 into monetary terms leads to the planned value curve as displayed in the figure.

12.2.2 Actual Cost

The *Actual Cost* AC is often referred to as the *actual cost of work performed* (ACWP) and is the cumulative actual cost spent at a given point AT in time.

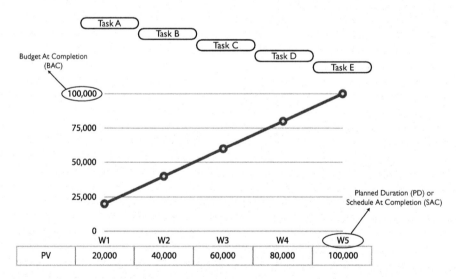

Fig. 12.2 Planned Value of a 5-activity project with BAC = €100,000 and PD = 5 weeks

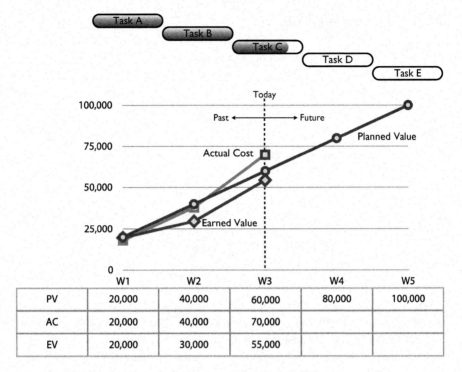

Fig. 12.3 The planned value, actual cost and earned value at week 3

	W1	W2	W3	W4	W5
PV	20,000	40,000	60,000	80,000	100,000
AC	20,000	40,000	70,000		
EV	20,000	30,000	55,000		

The fictitious actual cost line of the 5-activity project is given in Fig. 12.3. It shows that the actual costs are in line with the planned value curve for the first 2 weeks, but exceed the PV curve at the current time (week 3). Note that the PV curve is known for all 5 weeks of the project life cycle, as a result of the baseline schedule. Obviously, the actual costs are only known up to today, which is assumed to be week 3.

12.2.3   Earned Value

The *Earned Value* EV represents the amount budgeted for performing the work that was accomplished at a given point AT in time. It is often called the *budgeted cost of work performed* (BCWP) and equals the total activity (or project) budget at completion multiplied by the percentage activity (or project) completion (PC) at the particular point in time ($=$ PC $*$ BAC).

It is assumed that 55% of the work has been finished by the end of week 3 (this is the estimate of the project manager in collaboration with his/her team). The total EV $= 0.55*$BAC$= €55,000$.

12.2.4   Earned Schedule

Both the Planned Value (PV) and the Earned Value (EV) metrics show a (planned and earned) increase of a project in monetary terms, while EVM has been constructed to monitor both time and cost of a project. The Earned Schedule (ES) is an extended version of the EV and PV metrics and can be calculated as follows:

Find t such that $EV \geq PV_t$ and $EV < PV_{t+1}$

$$ES = t + \frac{EV - PV_t}{PV_{t+1} - PV_t}$$

with

ES	Earned Schedule
EV	Earned Value at the actual time
PV_t	Planned Value at time instance t

The cumulative value for the ES is found by using the EV to identify in which time increment t of PV the cost value for EV occurs. ES is then equal to the cumulative time t to the beginning of that time increment, plus a fraction $\frac{EV-PV_t}{PV_{t+1}-PV_t}$ of it. The fraction equals the portion of EV extending into the incomplete time increment divided by the total PV planned for that same time period, which is simply calculated as a linear interpolation between the time-span of time increment t and $t+1$. Note that the formula description is not completely mathematically correct in case $EV = PV_t = PV_{t+1}$. In this case, the ES is equal to the earliest period t for which $EV = PV_t$. Figure 12.4 shows a graphical fictitious example of the linear interpolation of the planned values between review period t and $t+1$.

The ES metric for the 5-activity example project at the current moment (week 3) is equal to $2 + \frac{55,000-40,000}{60,000-40,000} = 2.75$ weeks.

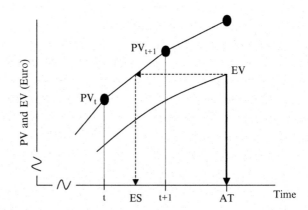

Fig. 12.4 Linear interpolation between PV_t and PV_{t+1}

12.3   Performance Measurement

The key parameters of the previous section can be used to measure the current and past performance of the project in progress. In the example, the values for the three key parameters are as follows:

Since

- The EV curve measures how much value has been earned at the current time (W3) given the work that has been done up to now, which is equal to €55,000,
- The PV curve measures how much value should have been earned according to the baseline schedule at W3, and is equal to €60,000,
- The AC curve measures the actual cost incurred up to the current time (W3) given the work that has been done and equals €70,000,

Consequently, the following conclusions can be made:

- Since the baseline schedule (PV) stipulates that there should have been earned €5,000 more than actually earned (EV) at week 3, the project is clearly late.
- Since the value of the work done up to now (AC) exceeds the value that should have been earned with that current work done as stipulated in the baseline schedule (EV), the project is clearly over budget.

These time and cost deviations (underruns and overruns) can be expressed by variances or unitless indicators, as discussed in the two following sections.

12.3.1   Variances

Project performance, both in terms of time and costs, is determined by comparing the three key parameters PV, AC and EV, resulting in two well-known performance variances:

SV   Schedule Variance ($SV = EV - PV$)
                          $= 0$: project on schedule
                          < 0: project delay
                          > 0: project ahead of schedule
CV   Cost Variance ($CV = EV - AC$)
                          $= 0$: project on budget
                          < 0: budget overrun
                          > 0: budget underrun

Given the two dimensions (time and cost) and their possible variances (zero, positive or negative), nine different project performance situations might occur. The 5-activity project example of Fig. 12.3 shows that the $SV = -€5,000$ and the $CV = -€15,000$, denoting a project being late and over budget. Figure 12.5 displays

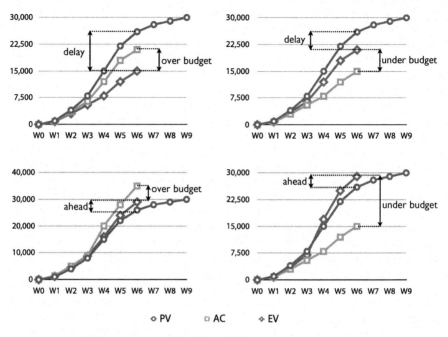

Fig. 12.5 The EVM key parameters PV, AC and EV for a project under four scenarios

the three EVM key parameters for a fictitious project under four different possible time/cost scenarios[1]:

> Scenario 1: late project, over budget
> Scenario 2: late project, under budget
> Scenario 3: early project, over budget
> Scenario 4: early project, under budget

Since time variances SV are expressed in monetary units, the ES metric can be used to translate this variance to time units, using the following performance variance:

SV(t)   Schedule Variance with earned schedule $(SV(t) = ES - AT)$
               $= 0$: project on schedule
               < 0: project delay
               > 0: project ahead of schedule

where (t) is used to make a distinction with the traditional SV time indicator. The SV(t) metric of the 5-activity project is equal to $2.75 - 3 = -0.25$ weeks, clearly denoting a project which is currently behind schedule.

---

[1]Excluding situations where projects are on time and/or on budget.

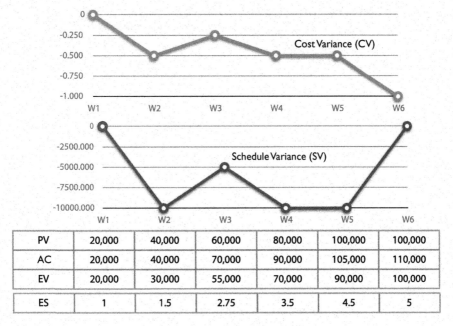

PV	20,000	40,000	60,000	80,000	100,000	100,000
AC	20,000	40,000	70,000	90,000	105,000	110,000
EV	20,000	30,000	55,000	70,000	90,000	100,000
ES	1	1.5	2.75	3.5	4.5	5

Fig. 12.6 The SV and CV graph for the 5-activity example project

Figure 12.6 shows a graph for the CV (top) and SV (bottom) indicators for the example project. The figure clearly shows that the SV metric ends at 0, which is an indication that the project finishes on time, although the project ends 1 week later than originally planned. Obviously, since PV = EV at the end of the project (always!), the SV metric will always end at zero, regardless of the real project performance. This strange behavior was one of the main reasons why the ES metric has been developed as an alternative, and more reliable metric to measure the time performance of a project. This unreliable effect does not occur, however, for the CV metric. The unreliability of the traditional time metrics will be further explained in the following Sect. 12.3.2.

Figure 12.7 illustrates the translation of the earned value into the ES metric for two possible scenarios to clearly show whether a project is behind (left) or ahead of (right) schedule.

12.3.2   Indicators

Variances are expressed in absolute terms (monetary (SV and CV) or time (SV(t)) and their values depend on the measurement unit (euro, dollar, days, weeks, ...). When performance is measured by a unitless metric, the time and cost metrics can be replaced by the schedule and cost performance indices, which express a project's

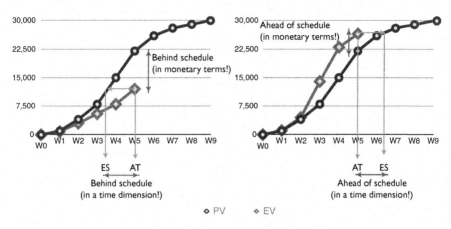

Fig. 12.7 The ES metric for a late (*left*) and early (*right*) project

performance as a percentage of the baseline performance (which is assumed to be equal to 100%). These performance measures can be calculated as follows:

SPI   Schedule Performance Index $\left(\text{SPI} = \frac{EV}{PV}\right)$
                 $= 1$: project on schedule
                 < 1: project delay
                 > 1: project ahead of schedule
CPI   Cost Performance Index $\left(\text{CPI} = \frac{EV}{AC}\right)$
                 $= 1$: project on budget
                 < 1: budget overrun
                 > 1: budget underrun

Using the ES concept, an alternative to the traditional SPI indicator can be defined as follows:

SPI(t)   Schedule Performance Index with earned schedule $\left(\text{SPI(t)} = \frac{ES}{AT}\right)$
                 $= 1$: project on schedule
                 < 1: project delay
                 > 1: project ahead of schedule

The 5-activity project example of Fig. 12.3 shows that the $\text{SPI} = \text{SPI(t)} = 0.92$ and the $\text{CPI} = 0.79$, still denoting that the project is late and over budget at week 3.

An advantage of the ES based performance indicator SV(t) is that, unlike the SV indicator, it can be expressed in a time dimension. However, the main advantage of using the SV(t) and SPI(t) indicators not only lies in the time dimension of a project's performance measurement. Lipke (2003) criticized the use of the classic SV and SPI metrics since they give false and unreliable time forecasts near the end of the project, as illustrated in Fig. 12.6 for the SV metric. For this reason, he provided a time-based measure to overcome the strange behavior of the SV and SPI indicators, known as the Earned Schedule metric, which provides time performance measures (SV(t) and SPI(t)) that do not suffer from this unreliable effect at the finish of the project.

The reasons why the SPI is unreliable at the end of the project are similar to the reasons why the SV metric fails to provide a reliable time deviation at the project finish. The Schedule Performance Index SPI is equal to EV/PV. Since the EV metric is equal to PC*BAC and, by definition, PC = 100% at the end of the project, the SPI is *always* equal to 1, regardless of the real project status (early, on time or late). Figure 12.8 shows the SPI and SPI(t) graph for the 5-activity example project under the assumption that the project status is known: 1 week project delay and a cost overrun of €10,000. It illustrates the unreliability of the SPI metric for the example project and shows that SPI = 1, although the project is late. The unreliability of the SV and SPI metrics at the end of a project results in an unreliable zone towards the project end where these metrics can not be trusted. In the figure, the SPI and SPI(t) metrics have similar values except at the project end. In more realistic settings, the SPI indicator shows a clear trend towards 1, regardless whether the project is early, on time or late, which results in a certain point in time where this performance measure provides unreliable results.

The Earned Schedule based performance measures (SV(t) and SPI(t)) do not suffer from this unreliable trend towards one at the project finish. The reason is similar to the previously mentioned reasons. The ES metric is always equal to the PD at the project finish (similar to EV = PV at the project end) and hence, the SPI(t) metric, calculated as ES/AT or ES/AD (with AD the actual duration of the project which can be bigger than, equal to or smaller than the PD at the project finish), can be different from one, reflecting the real time performance of the project from the

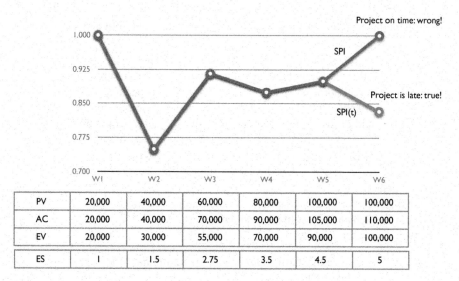

	W1	W2	W3	W4	W5	W6
PV	20,000	40,000	60,000	80,000	100,000	100,000
AC	20,000	40,000	70,000	90,000	105,000	110,000
EV	20,000	30,000	55,000	70,000	90,000	100,000

ES	1	1.5	2.75	3.5	4.5	5

Fig. 12.8 The SPI and SPI(t) graph for the 5-activity example project

Table 12.1 Comparison of possible SPI and SPI(t) values at the project finish

Performance index	End of project	Index value at project finish
SPI = EV/PV	EV = PV	SPI = 1 (always)
		SPI(t) > 1 (early project, i.e. ES = PD > AD)
SPI(t) = ES/AD	ES = PD	SPI(t) = 1 (on time project, i.e. ES = PD = AD)
		SPI(t) < 1 (late project, i.e. ES = PD < AD)

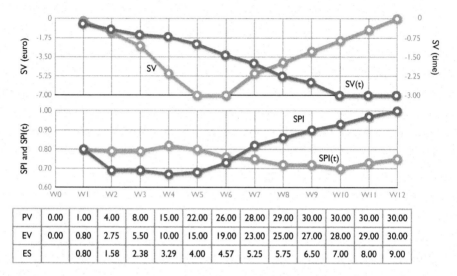

	W0	W1	W2	W3	W4	W5	W6	W7	W8	W9	W10	W11	W12
PV	0.00	1.00	4.00	8.00	15.00	22.00	26.00	28.00	29.00	30.00	30.00	30.00	30.00
EV	0.00	0.80	2.75	5.50	10.00	15.00	19.00	23.00	25.00	27.00	28.00	29.00	30.00
ES		0.80	1.58	2.38	3.29	4.00	4.57	5.25	5.75	6.50	7.00	8.00	9.00

Fig. 12.9 The SPI and SV versus SPI(t) and SV(t) performance measures

start till its finish. Table 12.1 gives an overview of the possible SPI and SPI(t) values at the project finish.

Figure 12.9 shows the unreliability of the SV and SPI metrics at the end of a project on another fictitious project example with a planned duration of 9 weeks (PD = 9) and a real duration of 12 weeks (RD = 12). The last review periods of the project are unreliable since both the SV and SPI metrics clearly show an improving trend. At the end of the project, both metrics give a signal that the project finishes within time (SV = 0 and SPI = 1 at the end of the project), although it is 3 weeks late. The SV(t) and SPI(t) metrics give a correct signal along the whole life of the project. The SV(t) equals −3 at the end of the project, which is a reflection of the 3 weeks delay.

In the remainder of this chapter, an additional performance index will be used, known as the Schedule Cost Index, and defined as:

SCI   Schedule Cost Index (using the traditional SPI)
       SPI * CPI
SCI(t)   Schedule Cost Index (using the SPI(t))
       SPI(t) * CPI

12.4 Forecasting

One of the primary tasks of a project manager is making decisions about the future. EVM systems are designed to follow up the performance of a project and to act as a warning signal to take corrective actions in the (near) future. Forecasting the total project cost and the time to completion is crucial to take corrective actions when problems or opportunities arise and hence, the performance measures will be mainly used as early warning signals to detect these project problems and/or opportunities. EVM metrics are designed to forecast these two important performance measures (time and cost) based on the actual performance up to date and the assumptions about future performance. In this section, some generally accepted and newly developed forecasting measures will be reviewed.

The general formula for predicting a project's total duration is given by the *Estimated duration At Completion* (EAC(t)), as follows:

$$EAC(t) = AD + PDWR$$

with

EAC(t)	Estimated duration at Completion
AD	Actual Duration (or Actual Time AT)
PDWR	Planned Duration of Work Remaining

The general and similar formula for predicting a project's final cost is given by the *Estimated cost At Completion* (EAC), as follows:

$$EAC = AC + PCWR$$

with

EAC	Estimated cost at Completion
AC	Actual Cost
PCWR	Planned Cost of Work Remaining

Note that the abbreviation EAC is used for cost forecasting and a t between brackets is added (i.e. EAC(t)) for time forecasting. Figure 12.10 shows the general idea of the time (EAC(t)) and cost (EAC) forecasting methods on a fictitious project. The time overrun EAC(t) − PD is often referred to as the project slippage and the estimated final cost overrun is equal to EAC − BAC. Mathematical details of both forecasting methods are given in the next two sections.

12.4.1 Time Forecasting

Table 12.2 summarizes the forecasting metrics used by EVM time forecasting. The PDWR metric is the component that has to be estimated, and heavily depends on the specific characteristics and the current status of the project (Anbari 2003).

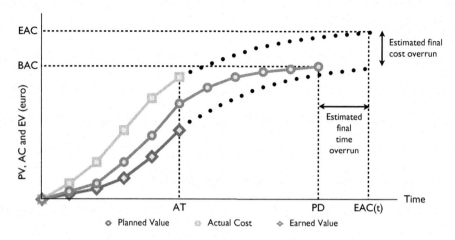

Fig. 12.10 Expected cost and time performance

Table 12.2 Time forecasting methods (EAC(t)) (Source: Vandevoorde and Vanhoucke (2006))

Expected future performance	Forecasting method		
	Anbari (2003)	Jacob (2003)	Lipke (2003)
According to plan	$EAC(t)_{PV1}$	$EAC(t)_{ED1}$	$EAC(t)_{ES1}$
Follows current SPI or SPI(t) trend	$EAC(t)_{PV2}$	$EAC(t)_{ED2}$	–
	–	–	$EAC(t)_{ES2}$
Follows current SCI or SCI(t) trend	$EAC(t)_{PV3}$	$EAC(t)_{ED3}$	–
	–	–	$EAC(t)_{ES3}$
	$=$	$=$	$=$
	Planned value	Earned duration	Earned schedule

The table makes a distinction between three different project situations based on the classification described in Anbari (2003). Each situation involves another assumption about the future performance of the work yet undone to finish the project.

The first project situation assumes that the remaining work PDWR will be done according to the baseline schedule, The second situation assumes the future work will follow the current SPI trend while the third situation assumes that the remaining work will follow the current SCI or SCI(t) trend. Moreover, for each of these three assumptions about future expected performance, three methods to forecast the final project duration can be used. These methods are referred to as the planned value method (Anbari 2003), the earned duration method (Jacob 2003) and the earned schedule method (Lipke 2003).

The Planned Value Method

The planned value method described by Anbari (2003) does not directly give an estimate for the PDWR but relies on the planned value rate, which is equal to the average planned value per time period, i.e. $PV_{rate} = \frac{BAC}{PD}$ where BAC is used to denote the budget at completion and PD to denote total planned project duration. This method assumes that the schedule variance can be translated into time units by dividing the schedule variance by the planned value rate, resulting in the time variance TV as follows:

$$TV = \frac{SV}{PV_{Rate}} = \frac{SV * PD}{BAC} = \frac{(EV - PV) * PD}{BAC} \tag{12.1}$$

According to the project characteristics (reflected by the three situations of Table 12.2), the following forecasting formulas have been derived:

• EAC(t) with the duration of remaining work as planned

$$EAC(t)_{PV1} = PD - TV$$

• EAC(t) with the duration of remaining work following the current SPI trend

$$EAC(t)_{PV2} = \frac{PD}{SPI}$$

• EAC(t) with the duration of remaining work following the current SCI trend

$$EAC(t)_{PV3} = \frac{PD}{SCI}$$

It can be easily verified that $EAC(t)_{PV1} = 5.25$, $EAC(t)_{PV2} = 5.45$ and $EAC(t)_{PV3} = 6.94$ for the 5-activity project example of Fig. 12.3 at week 3.

The Earned Duration Method

The earned duration method is described by Jacob (2003) and extended by Jacob and Kane (2004). The earned duration ED is the product of the actual duration AD and the schedule performance index SPI, i.e. $ED = AD * SPI$, and hence, the generic earned duration forecasting formula is:

$$EAC(t)_{ED} = AD + \frac{PD - ED}{PF} \tag{12.2}$$

The performance factor PF is used to adapt the future performance to the past performance (depending on the project characteristics) and reflects the three situations of Table 12.2. Indeed, a $PF = 1$ denotes a future performance at the efficiency rate of the original plan (100% efficiency). However, the future performance can be corrected towards the current SPI trend or the current SCI $=$ CPI $*$ SPI trend. Hence, the three forecasting methods to predict total project duration are:

- PF $= 1$: Duration of remaining work as planned

$$EAC(t)_{ED1} = AD + (PD - ED) = PD + AD * (1 - SPI)$$

- PF $=$ SPI: Duration of remaining work with SPI trend

$$EAC(t)_{ED2} = AD + \frac{PD - ED}{SPI} = \frac{PD}{SPI}$$

- PF $=$ SCI: Duration of remaining work with SCI trend

$$EAC(t)_{ED3} = AD + \frac{PD - ED}{SCI} = \frac{PD}{SCI} + AD * \left(1 - \frac{1}{CPI}\right)$$

In situations where the actual project duration exceeds the planned duration (i.e. AD $>$ PD), and the work is not yet completed, the PD will be substituted by the AD in the above mentioned formulas. In these cases, the formulas are:

$$EAC(t)_{ED1} = AD + (AD - ED) = AD * (2 - SPI)$$

$$EAC(t)_{ED2} = AD + \frac{AD - ED}{SPI} = \frac{AD}{SPI}$$

$$EAC(t)_{ED3} = AD + \frac{AD - ED}{SCI} = AD * \left(1 - \frac{1}{CPI} + \frac{1}{SCI}\right)$$

The alert reader has already noticed that EAC(t)$_{ED1}$=5.25, EAC(t)$_{ED2}$=5.45 and EAC(t)$_{ED3}$=6.12 for the 5-activity project example of Fig. 12.3 at week 3.

The Earned Schedule Method

The generic earned schedule duration forecasting formula is:

$$EAC(t)_{ES} = AD + \frac{PD - ES}{PF} \qquad (12.3)$$

The performance factor used depends on the project situation:

- PF $= 1$: Duration of remaining work as planned

$$EAC(t)_{ES1} = AD + (PD - ES)$$

- PF = SPI(t): Duration of remaining work with SPI(t) trend

$$EAC(t)_{ES2} = AD + \frac{PD - ES}{SPI(t)}$$

- PF = SCI(t): Duration of remaining work with SCI(t) trend

$$EAC(t)_{ES3} = AD + \frac{PD - ES}{CPI * SPI(t)} = AD + \frac{PD - ES}{SCI(t)}$$

The alert reader has already noticed that $EAC(t)_{ES1} = 5.25$, $EAC(t)_{ES2} = 5.45$ and $EAC(t)_{ES3} = 6.12$ for the 5-activity project example of Fig. 12.3 at week 3. The values are identical to the Earned Duration values, due to the simplicity of the project example. Obviously, this is not generally true.

12.4.2 Cost Forecasting

Cost performance and forecasting have been widely investigated by numerous researchers. For an overview, the reader is referred to Christensen (1993), who reviewed different EAC formulas and several studies that examine their accuracy. Predicting the final cost of the project during its progress can be easily done using a similar approach than the time prediction methods. Table 12.3 displays four main predefined methods, although many extensions are possible. Most of these methods have been validated in literature and make use of the following generic cost forecasting formula:

$$EAC = AC + \frac{BAC - EV}{PF} \qquad (12.4)$$

Similar to the time prediction methods, each method relies on another performance factor (PF) which refers to the assumption about the expected performance of the future work, as follows:

Table 12.3 Cost forecasting methods (EAC)

		SPI	SPI(t)
Version 1	According to plan	PF = 1	
Version 2	According to current cost performance	PF = CPI	
Version 3	According to current time performance	PF = SPI	PF = SPI(t)
Version 4	According to current time/cost performance	PF = SCI	PF = SCI(t)
Version 4'	According to weighted time/cost performance	PF = 0.8*CPI + 0.2*SPI	PF = 0.8*CPI + 0.2*SPI(t)

- PF $= 1$: Future performance is expected to follow the baseline schedule (version 1).
- PF $=$ CPI: Future performance is expected to follow the current cost performance (version 2).
- PF $=$ SPI or SPI(t): Future performance is expected to follow the current time performance (version 3).
- PF $=$ SCI or SCI(t): Future performance is expected to follow the current time and cost performance. This method can be used under two versions, i.e. PF is equal to the current SCI or SCI(t) performance (version 4) or to a weighted time and cost performance (version 4′).

Note that versions 3, 4 and 4′ can be used under the traditional Schedule Performance Index (SPI) assumptions, or with the new Earned Schedule based Schedule Performance Index (SPI(t)). All these methods provide an estimate for the total predicted cost at the end of the project, and offer a range of possibilities and hence a lower and upper bound on what the project manager expects to spend on the project. The choice of a specific forecasting method depends on the project, the project manager's expertise and many other often unknown factors.

Quick and easy calculations show the following cost forecasts for the 5-activity project example of Fig. 12.3 at week 3: $EAC_{V1} = €115,000.00$, $EAC_{V2} = €127,272.73$, $EAC_{V3-SPI} = EAC_{V3-SPI(t)} = €119,090.91$, $EAC_{V4-SCI} = EAC_{V4-SCI(t)} = €132,479.34$ and $EAC_{V4'-SCI} = EAC_{V4'-SCI(t)} = €125,425.22$.

12.5 A Fictitious Project Example

Consider the project network example in Fig. 12.11. Each activity has an estimated duration as denoted above each node in Fig. 12.11, with a corresponding budgeted cost denoted below the node. Activities 1 and 12 are dummies and are used to denote the start and end of the project (with a zero duration and a zero cost). A schedule is defined by a vector of start times, which implies a vector of finish times, as given in the Gantt chart of Fig. 12.12. This figure displays the baseline earliest start schedule with a total planned duration PD equal to 16. The budget at completion (BAC) is the sum of the individual activity costs, which is equals to €456.

In order to show the detailed calculations of all forecasting measures, it is assumed that the project execution is known and finishes with a two-periods delay as displayed in Fig. 12.13. This figure displays the (fictitious) real life execution (actual values for each activity duration and the corresponding actual costs) of all project activities with a real project duration RD equal to 18. The final (real) total project cost amounts to €643, which is higher than the BAC value due to the activity delays (see Table 12.4 for detailed calculations). The project tracking process assumes a reporting period per time unit, from AD $= 1, 2, \ldots, 18$.

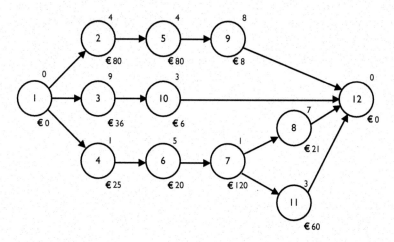

Fig. 12.11 The example project of Fig. 5.4 with activity cash flows

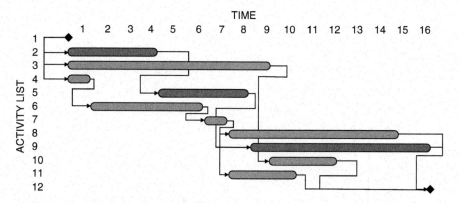

Fig. 12.12 The baseline schedule for the project of Fig. 12.11

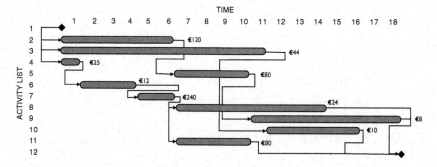

Fig. 12.13 The actual project execution Gantt chart of the example project

Table 12.4 The cumulative planned value PV, actual cost AC and earned value EV for each activity along the life of the example project and the performance measures on the project level

PV	1	2	3	4	5	6	7	8	9	10	11	12	13	14	15	16	17	18
2	20	40	60	80	80	80	80	80	80	80	80	80	80	80	80	80	—	—
3	4	8	12	16	20	24	28	32	36	36	36	36	36	36	36	36	—	—
4	25	25	25	25	25	25	25	25	25	25	25	25	25	25	25	25	—	—
5	0	0	0	0	20	40	60	80	80	80	80	80	80	80	80	80	—	—
6	0	4	8	12	16	20	20	20	20	20	20	20	20	20	20	20	—	—
7	0	0	0	0	0	0	120	120	120	120	120	120	120	120	120	120	—	—
8	0	0	0	0	0	0	0	3	6	9	12	15	18	21	21	21	—	—
9	0	0	0	0	0	0	0	0	1	2	3	4	5	6	7	8	—	—
10	0	0	0	0	0	0	0	0	0	2	4	6	6	6	6	6	—	—
11	0	0	0	0	0	0	0	20	40	60	60	60	60	60	60	60	—	—
Total	49	77	105	133	161	189	333	380	408	434	440	446	450	454	455	456	456	456

AC	1	2	3	4	5	6	7	8	9	10	11	12	13	14	15	16	17	18
2	20	40	60	80	100	120	120	120	120	120	120	120	120	120	120	120	120	120
3	4	8	12	16	20	24	28	32	36	40	44	44	44	44	44	44	44	44
4	25	25	25	25	25	25	25	25	25	25	25	25	25	25	25	25	25	25
5	0	0	0	0	0	0	20	40	60	80	80	80	80	80	80	80	80	80
6	0	4	8	12	12	12	12	12	12	12	12	12	12	12	12	12	12	12
7	0	0	0	0	120	240	240	240	240	240	240	240	240	240	240	240	240	240
8	0	0	0	0	0	0	3	6	9	12	15	18	21	24	24	24	24	24
9	0	0	0	0	0	0	0	0	0	0	1	2	3	4	5	6	7	8
10	0	0	0	0	0	0	0	0	0	0	0	2	4	6	8	10	10	10
11	0	0	0	0	0	0	20	40	60	80	80	80	80	80	80	80	80	80
Total	49	77	105	133	277	421	468	515	562	609	617	623	629	635	638	641	642	643

	1	2	3	4	5	6	7	8	9	10	11	12	13	14	15	16	17	18
EV	13.33	26.67	40	53.33	66.67	80	80	80	80	80	80	80	80	80	80	80	80	80
2	3.27	6.55	9.82	13.09	16.36	19.64	22.91	26.18	29.45	32.73	36	36	36	36	36	36	36	36
3	25	25	25	25	25	25	25	25	25	25	25	25	25	25	25	25	25	25
4	0	0	13.33	0	0	0	20	40	60	80	80	80	80	80	80	80	80	80
5	0	6.67	0	20	20	0	20	20	20	20	20	20	20	20	20	20	20	20
6	0	0	0	0	60	120	120	120	120	120	120	120	120	120	120	120	120	120
7	0	0	0	0	0	0	2.62	5.25	7.88	10.5	13.12	15.75	18.38	21	21	21	21	21
8	0	0	0	0	0	0	0	0	0	0	1	2	3	4	5	6	7	8
9	0	0	0	0	0	0	0	0	0	0	0	1.2	2.4	3.6	4.8	6	6	6
10	0	0	0	0	0	0	0	0	0	0	0	0	0	0	0	0	0	0
11	0	0	0	0	0	0	15	30	45	60	60	60	60	60	60	60	60	60
Total	41.6	64.89	88.15	111.42	188.03	264.64	305.53	346.43	387.33	428.23	435.12	439.95	444.78	449.6	451.8	454	455	456
SV	−7.39	−12.12	−16.85	−21.58	27.03	75.64	−27.47	−33.57	−20.67	−5.77	−4.88	−6.05	−5.23	−4.4	−3.2	−2	−1	0
CV	−7.39	−12.12	−16.85	−21.58	−88.97	−156.36	−162.47	−168.57	−174.67	−180.77	−181.88	−183.05	−184.23	−185.4	−186.2	−187	−187	−187
SPI	0.85	0.84	0.84	0.84	1.17	1.4	0.92	0.91	0.95	0.99	0.99	0.99	0.99	0.99	0.99	1	1	1
CPI	0.85	0.84	0.84	0.84	0.68	0.63	0.65	0.67	0.69	0.7	0.71	0.71	0.71	0.71	0.71	0.71	0.71	0.71
ES	0.85	1.57	2.4	3.23	5.97	6.53	6.81	7.29	8.26	9.78	10.19	10.99	11.8	12.9	13.45	14	15	16
SV(t)	−0.15	−0.43	−0.6	−0.77	0.97	0.53	−0.19	−0.71	−0.74	−0.22	−0.81	−1.01	−1.2	−1.1	−1.55	−2	−2	−2
SPI(t)	0.85	0.78	0.8	0.81	1.19	1.09	0.97	0.91	0.92	0.98	0.93	0.92	0.91	0.92	0.9	0.88	0.88	0.89

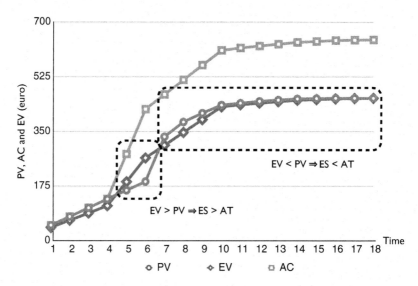

Fig. 12.14 The traditional S-curves for the example project

Table 12.4 reports the cumulative values for the three earned value key parameters on the level of an individual activity as well as the performance measures on the level of the project along the life of the example project. The top displays the planned value key parameter for each project activity for each period of the baseline schedule (i.e. PD = 1, 2, ..., 16). It is assumed that the cost increases linearly over the duration of the activity, but obviously, other increasing patterns can be assumed. As an example, the cumulative planned value for activity 2 increases with $\frac{80}{4} = €20$ per period. The second and the third parts of the table display the cumulative values for the two remaining key parameters for each project activity along the life of the project (i.e. AT = 1, 2, ..., 18). The actual cost for activity 2 amounts to €120 in total due to a 2 days delay. The cumulative earned value measures the amount that is earned per period during its execution time, and hence, equals $\frac{80}{6} = €13.33$ per period. The bottom of the table displays the performance metrics of the different methods described above, calculated on the level of the project. Figure 12.14 displays the traditional S-curve of the PV, EV and AC project metrics along the time horizon of the example project. This figure reveals a temporary project ahead of schedule situation at time instances 5, 6 and 7 (EV > PV), followed by a project delay (EV < PV) resulting in the final 2 days delay. This situation is reflected by the earned schedule metric of Table 12.4, which clearly shows that ES > AT at time instances 5–7 and ES < AT the periods afterwards. As an example, the ES at time period 6, denoted by ES_6, equals $6 + \frac{264.64-189}{333-189} = 6.53$, since $EV \geq PV_6$ (264.64 > 189) and $EV < PV_7$ (264.64 < 333).

Figure 12.15 shows the time forecasting values for each review period (from 1 to 18), grouped according to the performance factor PF (see Table 12.2). The top, middle and bottom graphs display the forecasts with a performance factor PF = 1,

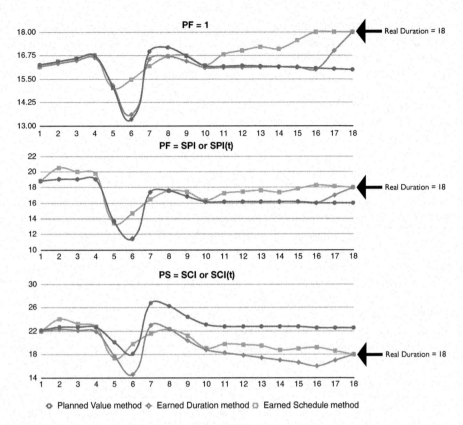

Fig. 12.15 The nine duration forecasts along the life of the project

PF = SPI and PF = SPI*CPI (or SPI(t)*CPI), respectively. The figures reveal that all forecasting methods report an underestimation for the final project duration when PF = 1, while both under- and overestimates occur for the PF = SPI and PF = SPI*CPI (or SPI(t)*CPI) forecasting methods. Obviously, these results are case-specific and only hold for the fictitious project example and hence, they cannot be generalized to any project setting. A similar figure could have been made for the cost performance and forecasting methods.

12.6 Conclusions

This chapter reviewed the key parameters and performance measures of earned value management systems and discussed various project duration and cost fore-casting methods that can be used based on these earned value parameters. A generic formula to forecast the total duration and cost of a project has been presented and has been further split into different submethods. More precisely, each method, both for time and cost forecasting, can be further subdivided into different forecasting submodels as a function of the current project situation and the assumption about future expected performance.

In this chapter, it is shown that the use of the Schedule Performance Index (SPI) as is done in the planned value method and the earned duration method might lead to biased and unreliable results when predicting the final duration of a project. The earned schedule, on the contrary, has been developed to overcome this unreliable behavior, possibly leading to more accurate forecasts thanks to the use of an adapted Schedule Performance Index SPI(t).

Throughout this chapter, the performance measures SPI, SPI(t) and CPI have always been calculated on the project level, to express the general 'health' of the project in terms of time and cost. It is recommended to use these schedule forecasting methods at least at the cost account level or at higher levels of the work breakdown structure. This is contradictory to the statements given by Jacob (2003), who argues that the schedule forecast metrics should only be used at the level of the activity. This concern has also been raised by other authors and has led to a discussion summarized in articles such as Book (2006a,b), Jacob (2006) and Lipke (2006). Although it is recognized that, at higher WBS levels, effects (delays) of nonperforming activities can be neutralized by well performing activities (ahead of schedule), which might result in masking potential problems, it is the only approach that can be taken by practitioners. Indeed, the earned value metrics are set up as early warning signals to detect problems and/or opportunities in an easy and efficient way (i.e. at the cost account level, or even higher), rather than a simple replacement of the critical path based scheduling tools. This early warning signal, if analyzed properly, defines the need to eventually drill down into lower WBS levels. In conjunction with the project schedule, it allows to take corrective actions on those activities that are in trouble (especially those tasks that are on the critical path). Lipke et al. (2009) also note that detailed schedule analysis is a burdensome activity and, if performed, often can have disrupting effects on the project team. EVM offers calculation methods yielding reliable results on higher WBS levels, which greatly simplify final duration and completion date forecasting.

As a final remark, the letter to the editor of Harvard Business Review from Cooper (2003) as a response to the article written by Fleming and Koppelman (2003) is cited. In this letter, the author argues that the use of earned value management can be questioned when they are applied in highly complex projects. Due to the cycles of rework, the accuracy of the EVM metrics can be biased, leading to incorrect management decisions. In the next chapter, some advanced topics on EVM are discussed to provide a partial answer to these shortcomings. Most of the work presented there is a brief summary of the research project of Vanhoucke (2010a).

Chapter 13
Advanced Topics

Abstract This chapter gives an overview of the main Earned Value Management
(EVM) research results obtained by a large Monte-Carlo simulation study summarized in the book by Vanhoucke (2010a). The focus is on the prediction of the final
duration of a project in progress using the forecasting methods of Sect. 12.4.1. The
chapter measures the accuracy of these prediction methods and the main drivers
of this accuracy along the various stages in the project life cycle. The chapter
also presents a rather new EVM extension, the so-called p-factor approach, to
measure schedule adherence based on the traditional earned value metrics. Finally,
the chapter presents the main results of integrating the three components of dynamic
scheduling (baseline scheduling, risk analysis and project control) and investigates
whether the integrated approach might lead to a higher efficiency of the project
control phase during its progress.

13.1 Introduction

The literature on the three components of dynamic scheduling is rich and
widespread, and has led to numerous algorithms, techniques and software tools to
better schedule and control a project. Little is known, however, on the contribution
of these tools and techniques to the overall success of the project. While many
research efforts have investigated the dynamic scheduling components in isolation,
the central research question should be "Does dynamic scheduling as an integration
between project scheduling, risk analysis and project control lead to better
projects?". Although it is conjectured that a clever use of the three components
of dynamic scheduling certainly contributes to a better project performance, this
very ambitious question will not be completely answered in this book. However,
research might be able to give partial answers to this question, which, in the long
run, enables project managers to understand the driving factors of project success.
Research has, by nature, a very forward looking attitude, and project success comes
from trying and failing and subsequently, from understanding the failure. In order
to have a long term success in projects, companies should foster the attitude of

M. Vanhoucke, *Project Management with Dynamic Scheduling*,   241
DOI 10.1007/978-3-642-40438-2_13, © Springer-Verlag Berlin Heidelberg 2013

experimentation. Research serves that purpose very well, which is exactly the reason why this more advanced chapter has been incorporated in this book. It is also in the nature of research that many results can be critically interpreted or sometimes rejected by other conflicting results. The need for research to objectivize the various opinions on Earned Value Management and the knowledge that research goes hand in hand with trying and failure have to be seen as expectations in the search for something new, and not something to be seen as waste.[1] This chapter has no intention to offer a final answer to the general project success question nor to claim that it holds the general truth on dynamic scheduling. It, however, hopes that this research is a step into the right direction, which hopefully may inspire many other researchers and practitioners to continue to test and experiment with ideas of dynamic project scheduling, and to share their idea with the project management community. The research summarized in this chapter is inspired by many people, among whom Stephan Vandevoorde (Belgium), Walt Lipke (US) and Kym Henderson (Australia) played a central role. The help and support by many members from the Belgian chapter of the Project Management Institute (PMI) and International Project Management Association (IPMA) is also greatly acknowledged.

The outline of this chapter can be summarized as follows. Section 13.2 present a more advanced concept, known as schedule adherence, which completely relies on the EVM metrics discussed in the previous chapter. Section 13.3 presents the main results of a simulation experiment to investigate the accuracy of various EVM methods to predict the final duration of a project. Section 13.4 integrates these results on the accuracy study with the schedule risk analysis results of Chap. 5 into an integrated project control approach. Moreover, in this section, computational results on the efficiency of alternative project control methods are presented. Section 13.5 gives an overall conclusion and directions for future research.

13.2   Schedule Adherence

Since the introduction of the Earned Schedule (ES) concept (Lipke 2003) as a time related extension of the well-known Earned Value metrics (see Sect. 12.2.4), studies on the time dimension of EVM have been published throughout the popular and academic literature.

Despite the ever growing positive attention to EVM and the commonly accepted agreement on the importance of EVM in a project control environment, both EVM in general and ES more specifically have not been free of criticism. The basic criticism on an EVM system is its assumption of a project setting where activities and precedence relations are known in advance and where estimates (activity durations, resource requirements, unexpected events, etc.) can be given

---

[1] I learned this very positive attitude from Walt Lipke, who always supported any research idea, even if it sometimes led to counterintuitive or wrong results.

within a certain range. However, Loch et al. (2006) mentioned that projects often do not fulfill these assumptions but, on the contrary, are commonly plagued by fundamentally unforeseeable events and/or unknown interactions among various actions and project parts. Consequently, due to the cycles of rework, the accuracy of the EVM metrics can be biased, leading to incorrect management decisions (Cooper 2003).

While the criticism on EVM in general is related to uncertainty characterized by most project environments, the criticism on the ES concept is more related to the questionability of the novelty of the concept and the correctness of the underlying ES formula (Book 2006b; Abba 2008). Despite this criticism, research studies have shown that it offers a valuable alternative to the traditional EVM time forecasting methods (Vanhoucke and Vandevoorde 2007b) and often produces more reliable results.

The p-factor concept is yet another extension on the EVM method and will undoubtedly be part of criticism. Since this new concept has only been introduced as an idea in 2004 and has not yet passed the test of logic, it deserves more attention to test its merits in a dynamic project control environment. Therefore, it needs to be investigated into more detail in order to reveal its strengths and weaknesses. The purpose of this chapter is only to give a start to such a deeper analysis, without claiming to provide a full overview with state-of-the-art methodological details.

13.2.1 The p-Factor Concept

The rationale behind the p-factor approach lies in the observation that performing work not according to the baseline schedule often indicates activity impediments or is likely a cause of rework. Consequently, the premise is that, whenever impediments occur (activities that are performed relatively less efficiently compared to the project progress), resources are shifted from these constrained activities to other activities where they could gain earned value. However, this results in a project execution that deviates from the original baseline schedule and might, consequently, involve a certain degree of risk. Indeed, the latter activities are performed without the necessary inputs, and might result into a certain portion of rework. Based on these observations, the p-factor has been introduced by Lipke (2004) as a measure to provide the connection of project output to EVM. It measures the portion of earned value accrued in congruence with the baseline schedule, i.e. the tasks that ought to be either completed or in progress, as follows:

$$p = \frac{\sum_{i \in N} min(\mathrm{PV}_{i,\mathrm{ES}}, \mathrm{EV}_{i,\mathrm{AT}})}{\sum_{i \in N} \mathrm{PV}_{i,\mathrm{ES}}}$$

with

p   Schedule adherence
                    = 1: perfect schedule adherence
                    < 1: lack of perfect schedule adherence

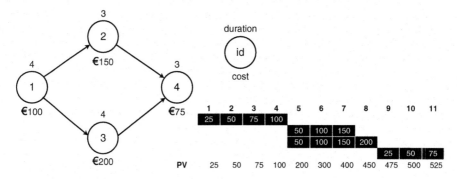

Fig. 13.1 A fictitious four-activity project network

N	Set of activities in the project
$PV_{i,ES}$	Planned value of activity i at time instance ES
$EV_{i,AT}$	Earned value of activity i at the actual time AT

Despite the simplicity of the p-factor formula, it is often subject to confusion. Figure 13.1 shows a fictitious four-activity project with each activity having a predefined duration (above the node) and cost (below the node). An earliest start baseline schedule is shown to the right of this figure, with a planned duration PD = 11 weeks and a budget at completion BAC = €525. The values in the bars of the Gantt chart are cost accrues over time. The figure shows that the planned value accrue is linear, from €0 at the start of the activity to the final activity cost upon completion. In order to illustrate the calculations of the p-factor, a baseline schedule and three possible project executions will be simulated and discussed.

The simulated project progress under the four scenarios is illustrated in Fig. 13.2. Each fictitious project execution represents a different situation, which can be summarized as follows:

1. Activity overlapping: The p-factor concept does not take precedence relations into account, but instead takes a general project view on the schedule adherence. Nevertheless, it should be able to detect the presence of overlaps, which is probably the main reason for lack of information and risk of rework. Figure 13.2a gives an illustration of an overlap between two activities in series, and shows that the p-factor is able to detect this situation.

2. PV/EV accrue deviations: Activities that are completed within their estimated time and budget are not necessarily performed in congruence with their predefined planned value. Since the p-factor is a concept to measure the degree of adherence to the baseline schedule, expressed as a relation between the project progress (Earned Value) and the baseline schedule (Planned Value), it should be able to give an indication of the deviation between PV and EV. In Fig. 13.2b, the EV accrued during the real life project progress is not in line with the PV

a. Activity Overlapping

	1	2	3	4	5	6	7	8	9	10	11	12
	25	50	75	100								
			50	100	150							
						50	100	150	200			
									25	50	75	
EV	25	50	125	200	250	300	350	400	475	500	525	
ES	1	2	4.25	5	5.5	6	6.5	7	9	10	11	
p	1	1	0.7	0.75	0.7	0.83	0.93	1	1	1	1	

b. PV/EV Accrue Deviation

	1	2	3	4	5	6	7	8	9	10	11	12
	15	35	65	100								
					25	75	150					
					100	175	200	200				
									50	60	75	
EV	15	35	65	100	225	350	450	450	500	510	525	
ES	0.6	1.4	2.6	4	5.25	6.5	8	8	10	10.4	11	
p	1	1	1	1	0.83	0.86	1	1	1	1	1	

c. Ahead/Behind Schedule

	1	2	3	4	5	6	7	8	9	10	11	12
	25	50	75	100								
					30	60	90	120	150			
					100	200						
										25	50	75
EV	25	50	75	100	230	360	390	420	450	475	500	525
ES	1	2	3	4	5.3	6.6	6.9	7.4	8	9	10	11
p	1	1	1	1	0.85	0.81	0.86	0.93	1	1	1	1

| **Time** | 1 | 2 | 3 | 4 | 5 | 6 | 7 | 8 | 9 | 10 | 11 | 12 |

Fig. 13.2 A fictitious four-activity project under three progress scenarios

accrue of the baseline schedule, although the project finishes exactly on time. The p-factor measures this lack of schedule adherence.

3. Ahead of schedule and/or delayed project execution: Obviously, deviations from the original baseline schedule during project progress lead to a final project status ending ahead or late. This lack of schedule adherence should be measured and reported by the p-factor concept in order to serve as a dynamic tool to forecast the final project status. Figure 13.2c shows a situation of a delayed project with activities finishing ahead of and behind schedule, resulting in p-factor values lower than 1.

Table 13.1 Illustrative calculations for the p-factor at review period 6 of Fig. 13.2b

Activity	$PV_{i,ES}$	$EV_{i,AT}$	$\min(PV_{i,ES}, EV_{i,AT})$
1	100	100	100
2	125	75	75
3	125	175	125
4	0	0	0
	350		300

Fig. 13.3 Activity impediments and work under risk to measure the p-factor

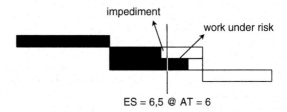

ES = 6,5 @ AT = 6

Table 13.1 illustrates the calculations of the p-factor for the Gantt chart of Fig. 13.2b at review period AT = 6. The earned schedule at AT = 6 is ES = 6.5 and the p-factor is equal to 300/350 = 0.86.

13.2.2 Effective Earned Value

The p-factor assumes that lack of schedule adherence is caused by a combination of the presence of impediments or constraints and work performed under risk. Figure 13.3 shows an intermediate project progress state at the actual time AT = 6 for the project progress of Fig. 13.2b relative to the baseline schedule. This means that the baseline schedule is displayed and the black bars are used to express the activity percentage completed as $PC = \frac{EV}{BAC}$ at the current time instance 6. Consequently, the EV accrued at the current time AT = 6 is given in black and the ES = 6,5. The figure visualizes the p-factor as follows:

- The portion of the work to the left of the ES line is assumed to be performed without risk and indicates the presence of an impediment or project constraint.
- The portion of work to the right of the ES line indicates work that is ahead of the normal project performance and is assumed to have a certain degree of risk.
- The p-factor is equal to the EV (black bars) to the left of ES line divided by the total EV.

Figure 13.3 shows that activity 2 has a lower EV (€75) at time 6 than normally should have been earned at time instance 6.5 (€125), while the opposite is true for activity 3 (EV at time 6 (€175) is higher than PV at time 6.5 (€125)).

It is assumed that this degree of risk is the result of inefficient use of resources that were shifted from the constrained activities to less constrained activities where the resources could gain earned value. However, these shifted resources work without the necessary inputs possibly resulting in a certain portion of rework (i.e. risk). The p-factor is a measure to express the portion of the EV without risk (referred to as EV(p)), while the remaining portion is denoted as EV(r).

A project manager should realize that the remaining EV(r) portion might be subject to risk and possibly results in rework. The *effective earned value* EV(e) is defined as the risk-adapted portion of earned value that is performed within the expected baseline schedule performance, taking into account that only R% of the EV(r) will be accounted as risk-free. Mathematically, these p-factor assumptions can be summarized as follows:

$$EV = p * EV + (1 - p) * EV = EV(p) + EV(r) \rightarrow EV(e) = EV(p) + R\% * EV(r)$$

with

EV	Earned value
EV(p)	Risk-free earned value
EV(r)	Remaining earned value portion performed under risk
EV(e)	Effective earned value
R%	Estimated portion of EV(r) that is usable and requires no rework

More details on the schedule adherence concept are outside the scope of this book and can be found in Lipke (2004) and Vanhoucke (2010a).

13.3   If Time Is Money, Accuracy Pays!

In this section, the scope and the main results of an experimental study in search for drivers of forecast accuracy using Earned Value Management techniques are briefly summarized. The concepts used in this study have been explained in Chaps. 5 and 12 and aim at an integration of Earned Value Management (EVM) and Schedule Risk Analysis (SRA) in order to better control projects.

13.3.1   Research Scope

The scope of the research study is a detailed investigation of project time performance measurement methods and risk analysis techniques in order to validate current and newly developed methods to improve the corrective actions decision making process during project control. More precisely, the target of the research proposal is to measure the project performance sensitivity and the forecast accuracy of the existing and newly developed metrics based on the principles of EVM and SRA. The research question boils down to the determination of when and in which cases SRA and EVM could lead to improved project tracking and corrective actions decision making.

The specific targets and research hypotheses formulated in the research project can be summarized as follows:

- What are the static (before project execution) and dynamic (during project execution) drivers of forecast accuracy? Knowledge about project performance drivers and accurate forecast accuracy measures should allow the project manager to critically analyze EVM performance measures and to accurately predict the final cost and duration of a project. Static and dynamic drivers that have been investigated in detail are:
  - Static drivers:
    - · Project network topology: Characteristics of the project can be easily calculated during the construction of the baseline schedule, and affect the accuracy of the performance measurement during project tracking.
    - · Activity criticality: The degree of activity criticality affects the project tracking process and the performance accuracy.
  - Dynamic drivers:
    - · Schedule adherence: The project schedule and the adherence to that schedule (in terms of precedence logic, EVM measurement system, etc.) should have an effect on the accuracy of project performance measurement.
    - · Time span of control: The time span and the number of review periods during project performance measurement clearly affect the accuracy.
- How does the project time sensitivity affect the accuracy of performance measurement? Information obtained during the scheduling step (baseline plan) as well as sensitivity information and risk analysis obtained through SRA should allow the project manager to improve the project tracking process and the decision making process for corrective actions.
- How does the knowledge on forecast accuracy (two previous research questions) lead to improved corrective actions decision making during project tracking? Since EVM is a methodology to provide an often quick sanity check of the project health on the cost control account level or even higher Work Breakdown Structure (WBS) levels, it cannot be considered as an alternative of the often time-consuming activity-based Critical Path Method (CPM) scheduling approach. The research aims at detecting when and how the EVM tracking approach offers a full alternative to the detailed CPM project tracking, and in which cases a need to drill down to lower WBS levels is necessary to take corrective actions.

In the remaining sections, the methodological approach and the main results are briefly summarized.

13.3.2 Research Methodology

The methodology used can be summarized as a four step procedure as outlined in Fig. 13.4. The approach makes use of the baseline scheduling principles discussed

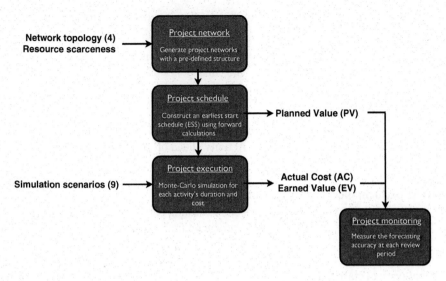

Fig. 13.4 The four step research methodology used for the EVM accuracy study

in Parts I and II of this book, and calculates the performance of the project using techniques that have been presented in Chap. 12.

1. Generate project data: In order to guarantee that the set of project data spans the full range of complexity, network topology measures and resource scarceness measures are used under different settings. Section 8.3 briefly reviewed these network and resource measures. In the study, more than 4,000 fictitious project networks have been generated with the software tool presented in Chap. 15.
2. Construct a project schedule: The construction of a feasible project schedule taking into account precedence relations and renewable resource constraints is one of the main topics of this book and belongs to the project scheduling part of the dynamic scheduling approach. Each project is scheduled with a minimal time scheduling objective, resulting in a planned value curve (PV) necessary to use EVM and a planned project duration PD.
3. Simulate project progress: Project progress results in uncertainty and deviations from the original baseline schedule. Fictitious progress requires a predefined set of scenarios to control the level of project uncertainty and schedule deviations. Each project progress is simulated under nine different scenarios while carefully controlling the nature of the uncertainty. Periodic reviews of the project performance resulted in values for the actual cost (AC) and earned value (EV). Project progress is simulated using Monte-Carlo simulation, and hence, this step can be considered as a Schedule Risk Analysis (Chap. 5).
4. Measure forecast accuracy: During the periodic reviews, all EVM data are available (PV, AC and EV) to measure the time and cost performance of the project, and to forecast the total time (EAC(t)) and cost (EAC) of the project. These predictions are compared with the final real project duration (RD), and deviations are observed as indications of lower forecast accuracy. The current

study calculates the accuracy of the EAC(t) predictions (and not the EAC formulas).

The nine simulation scenarios to simulate fictitious project progress can be explained using Fig. 13.5. Each of the nine boxes makes use of the following abbreviations:

Critical and noncritical activities:
$\qquad$ Activity duration uncertainty (deviation from schedule)
$\qquad -\qquad$: $\qquad$ Activity ahead of schedule
$\qquad 0\qquad$: $\qquad$ Activity on time
$\qquad +\qquad$: $\qquad$ Activity delay
EVM Performance measurement (during progress):
$\qquad \overline{SPI(t)}$: average project early warning performance signal
$\qquad = 1\qquad$: $\qquad$ Average on time signal
$\qquad > 1\qquad$: $\qquad$ Average positive signal (ahead of schedule)
$\qquad < 1\qquad$: $\qquad$ Average negative signal (schedule delay)
Final project state (after finish):
$\qquad$ PD and RD : Planned and Real Duration of the project
$\qquad$ RD = PD $\quad$: $\qquad$ Project on time
$\qquad$ RD >PD $\quad$: $\qquad$ Late project
$\qquad$ RD <PD $\quad$: $\qquad$ Early project

Note that the $\overline{SPI(t)}$ is not the schedule performance index at a current moment in time, as used in the previous chapter, but instead an average of all SPI(t) values measured at regular project tracking intervals. Consequently, this value gives the average performance measured by EVM metrics over all reporting periods in the project life cycle.

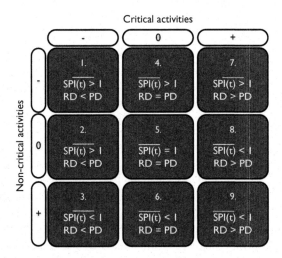

Fig. 13.5 Nine simulation scenarios (step 3 of Fig. 13.4)

The nine simulation scenarios can be classified into three categories, each having a different meaning and purpose, as follows:

True scenarios: Scenarios 1 and 2 report an average project 'ahead of schedule' progress ($\overline{\text{SPI(t)}} > 1$) and the project finishes earlier than planned ($\overline{\text{RD} < \text{PD}}$). Scenarios 8 and 9 report an average 'project delay' progress ($\overline{\text{SPI(t)}} < 1$) and the project finishes later than planned ($\overline{\text{RD} > \text{PD}}$). Scenario 5 reports an 'on-time' progress ($\overline{\text{SPI(t)}} = 1$) and the project finishes exactly on time (RD = PD). Consequently, these five scenarios report on average a true situation (i.e. what you measure is what you get).

Misleading scenarios: Scenario 4 reports an average project 'ahead of schedule' progress ($\overline{\text{SPI(t)}} > 1$) but the project finishes exactly on time (RD = PD). Likewise, scenario 6 reports an average 'project delay' progress ($\overline{\text{SPI(t)}} < 1$) but the project finishes exactly on time (RD = PD). Consequently, these two scenarios report on average a schedule deviation that is not true, and hence, they are called misleading simulation scenarios.

False scenarios: Scenario 3 reports an average 'project delay' progress ($\overline{\text{SPI(t)}} < 1$) but the opposite is true: the project finishes earlier than planned ($\overline{\text{RD} < \text{PD}}$). Scenario 7 reports an average project 'ahead of schedule' progress ($\overline{\text{SPI(t)}} > 1$) but the opposite is true: the project finishes later than planned (RD > PD). Consequently, these two scenarios report a false performance signal, and hence, they are called false simulation scenarios.

13.3.3 Drivers of Forecast Accuracy

In this section, the simulation results are analyzed in search of drivers that influence the accuracy of earned value based predictive methods to forecast a project's final duration. A distinction is made between *static drivers*, which can be calculated before the start of the project (i.e. during the definition and scheduling phases) and *dynamic drivers*, which can be calculated during the project's execution phase. These drivers will be discussed in the next subsections. Details on the research methodology and more extended results can be found elsewhere in literature by Vanhoucke and Vandevoorde (2007a,b, 2008, 2009) and Vanhoucke (2008a,b, 2009, 2010b).

Static Drivers of Forecast Accuracy

The static drivers during the preparation phases of the project (i.e. the definition and scheduling phases) have been displayed in Fig. 13.6, and will be summarized along the following lines of the section.

Definition phase – Influence of network topology: The topological structure of a project network, defined by the number and distribution of the activities and their precedence relations, can be easily measured through the use of often simple

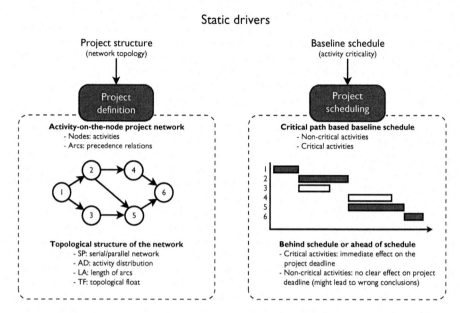

Fig. 13.6 Static drivers of EVM accuracy: project definition and scheduling phase

mathematical calculations of indicators that distinguish between various structures of project networks (see Sect. 8.3.1). These indicators serve as measures of diversity able to detect project networks that differ substantially from each other from a topological structure point of view. The test results have revealed that there is a strong influence of the serial/parallel topological indicator SP on the accuracy of EVM predictive methods. The indicator measures the closeness of a network to a completely serial or completely parallel network and the simulation results clearly show that the more the project network looks like a serial network, the higher the accuracy of the EVM methods to predict the final project duration.

Scheduling phase – Influence of activity criticality: Project scheduling aims at the construction of a baseline schedule where each activity is sequenced subject to the precedence constraints (Part I of this book) and resource constraints (Part II). Traditional scheduling methods result in the presence of a critical path (or alternatively, a critical chain when resources are present). The activity criticality heavily determines the accuracy of earned value based metrics, since changes (delays or accelerations) in critical activities have an immediate effect on the project duration, while changes in noncritical activities might have no effect at all on the final duration of the project. It is exactly for this very reason that Jacob and Kane (2004) argue that the well-known EVM performance measures (SPI, SPI(t), ...) are true indicators for project performance as long as they are used on the activity level and not on the control account level or higher Work Breakdown Structure (WBS) levels. As an example, a delay in a noncritical activity might give a warning signal that the project is in danger, while there is no problem at all when the activity only consumes part of its slack. When the performance measures are calculated on the project level, this will lead to a false warning signal and hence, wrong corrective actions could be taken. However, in the simulation study, these performance measures are calculated on the project level, and not on the level of each individual activity, for very pragmatic reasons. It is recognized that effects (delays) of nonperforming activities can be neutralized by well performing activities (ahead of schedule) at higher WBS levels, which might result in masking potential problems, but it is common belief that this is the only approach that can be easily taken by practitioners (see e.g. the note given in the paper by Lipke et al. (2009) and the conclusions and recommendations at the end of the previous chapter). The earned value metrics are set up as early warning signals to detect in an easy and efficient way (i.e. at the cost account level, or even higher), rather than a simple replacement of the critical path based scheduling tools. This early warning signal, if analyzed properly, defines the need to eventually drill down into lower WBS levels. In conjunction with the project schedule, it allows to take corrective actions for those activities that are in trouble (especially those tasks that are on the critical path). The simulation results have shown that the average activity criticality has a clear influence on the accuracy of the predictive methods as follows: the higher the activity criticality, the better the accuracy of the forecasts. Obviously, a lower activity criticality means a lower probability of being on the critical path, and hence, the more likely a delay (within the activity slack) reported by the SPI and SPI(t) indicators has no effect on the final project deadline.

Dynamic Drivers of Forecast Accuracy

Figure 13.7 gives an overview of the dynamic drivers of EVM forecast accuracy during the life of the project. The adherence of a project to the original baseline schedule (during the execution phase) as well as the choice of the length of the control periods of a project in progress provide dynamic information about the accuracy of the project schedule performance. Details of these two sources of dynamic information parameters are described along the following lines.

Execution phase – Influence of degree of schedule adherence: During the execution of the project, the original activity timetable can be disrupted due to numerous reasons leading to a project execution that is not in congruence with the original baseline schedule. This lack of schedule adherence can be dynamically measured through the use of the p-factor as described in Sect. 13.2.1. While the ES metric measures the current duration performance compared to the baseline schedule and indicates whether the project is ahead or behind schedule, the p-factor measures the performance of the project relative to this ES metric, and hence, measures the degree of schedule adherence given its current (good or bad) performance up-to-date. The simulation experiment has revealed a negative relation between the average p-factor and the forecast accuracy, i.e. lower p-factor values denoting a certain lack of

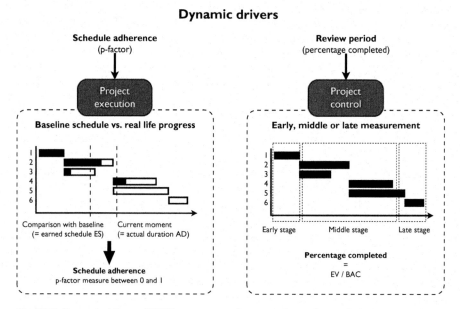

Fig. 13.7 Dynamic drivers of EVM accuracy: project execution and control phase

schedule adherence often result in less accurate forecasts. Hence, the p-factor, which can be dynamically measured during a review of the project (i.e. project tracking) based on the traditional EVM metrics, can be considered as a dynamic warning signal of the duration forecast accuracy.

Control phase – Influence of completion stage: During the control phase, the decision maker (i.e. the project manager) has to determine the length of the review periods as well as the interval in which EVM based predictive metrics might produce reliable results. A crucial assumption of EVM based forecasting is that the prediction of the future is based on information of the performance from the past, and hence, unreliable data from the past might give false predictions to the future. It is therefore of crucial importance to determine the time window in which the EVM metrics produce more or less reliable results. Undoubtedly, the accuracy of forecasts depends on the completion stage of the project. Obviously, the EVM metrics measured at the very beginning of the project are often very unreliable due to the lack of sufficient data to assume that future performance will follow the current performance up-to-date. For these reasons, the accuracy of index-based time forecasts is measured as a function of the completion stage of the project, given by the percentage completed EV/BAC. The average accuracy of these predictions made in the early, middle and late stages of the project execution phase is determined, both for projects ahead of schedule or for projects with a delay. The early stage is defined as the first 30% of the project completion, the middle stage is defined as the interval between 30% and 70% completion and the late stage equals the last 30%

completion of the project. The results from the experiments have shown that the Earned Schedule method outperforms, on average, the other forecasting methods (Planned Value and Earned Duration methods, see Table 12.2) in all stages of the project execution phase. The results also illustrate the unreliable behavior of the SPI indicator (used in the planned value and earned duration methods) at the late stage of the project. Indeed, the late stage forecast accuracy is much better for the ES method compared to the PV and ED methods. The results for the planned value method show that the use of the SPI indicator, which goes to a final value of 100%, regardless of the project performance, leads to very low quality predictions at the late stage of the project. The SPI(t) indicator of the earned schedule method has been developed to overcome this unreliable behavior, leading to an improved forecast accuracy at the end of the project. Obviously, measuring project performance and predicting future performance based on the resulting data leads to the lowest accuracy at the early stages of the project execution phase.

13.4   Project Tracking Efficiency

The main theme of this book, referred to as dynamic scheduling is used to refer to dynamic interplay between its three components: baseline scheduling, schedule risk and project control. The construction of a baseline schedule plays a central role in a dynamic scheduling environment, both for measuring schedule risk and in a project control environment. Schedule Risk Analysis (SRA – Chap. 5) is a technique to measure the sensitivity of project activities and to predict the expected influence of variability in activity durations/costs on the project objective. A schedule risk analysis study is done based on Monte-Carlo simulations that repetitively simulate project progress and compare each project run with the baseline schedule. Earned Value Management (EVM – Chap. 12) is a project tracking and control technique which compares the project performance relative to the baseline schedule. Figure 13.8 shows the three building blocks of dynamic scheduling and

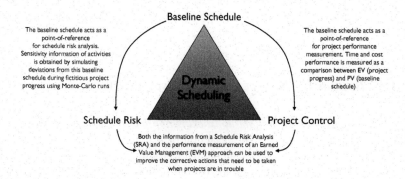

Fig. 13.8   Does dynamic scheduling lead to a higher efficiency in project tracking?

shows the relevance of the baseline schedule as a point of reference for both schedule risk and project control.

The focus of the current section is on the importance and crucial role of the baseline scheduling component for the two other components, and the integration of the schedule risk and project control component in order to support better corrective action decision making when the project is in trouble. While previous results have shown that EVM metrics provide good and accurate forecasts for some projects (see Sect. 13.3.3), it is still an unanswered question whether a higher degree of accuracy leads to a better decision making process during the project execution phase. More precisely, the topic of this section is to discuss the missing link in the dynamic scheduling principle: can schedule risk analysis and earned value management be integrated into a single project tracking approach to better support the decision making process of corrective actions? The next two sections briefly discuss this topic, without going into many technical details.

13.4.1 Top-Down Project Tracking Using EVM

It has been mentioned throughout this chapter that project tracking using earned value management should not be considered as an alternative to the well-known critical path based scheduling and tracking tools. Instead, the EVM methodology offers the project manager a tool to calculate a quick and easy sanity check on the control account level or even higher levels of the work breakdown structure (WBS). In this respect, an earned value management system is set up as an early warning signal system to detect problems and/or opportunities in an easy and efficient way, which is obviously less accurate than the detailed critical path based scheduling analysis of each individual activity. However, this early warning signal, if analyzed properly, defines the need to eventually drill down into lower WBS levels. In conjunction with the project schedule, it allows taking corrective actions on those activities that are in trouble (especially those tasks which are on the critical path). In this section, this *top-down tracking approach* is called a *project based tracking method*. Figure 13.9 displays a fictitious work breakdown structure (WBS) to illustrate the project based project tracking approach of earned value management.

13.4.2 Bottom-Up Project Tracking Using SRA

Figure 13.10 illustrates the *bottom-up tracking approach* of schedule risk analysis, which is the topic of Chap. 5. The detection of activity sensitivity information is crucial to steer a project manager's attention towards a subset of the project activities that have a high expected effect on the overall project performance. These highly

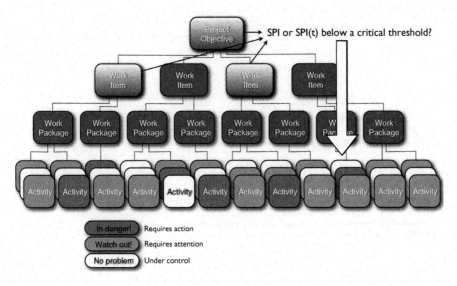

Fig. 13.9   The top-down project based tracking approach of earned value management

sensitive activities are subject to intensive control, while others require less or no attention during project execution. This approach is referred to as an *activity based tracking approach* to denote the bottom-up control and tracking approach to take corrective actions on those activities with a highly expected effect on the overall project objective. This bottom-up project tracking approach has been previously discussed using Fig. 5.7.

13.4.3   Project Tracking Efficiency

Vanhoucke (2010a) has experimentally validated the efficiency of the two alternative project tracking methods of Figs. 13.9 and 13.10. In this study, the efficiency of corrective actions taken on a project in trouble is measured for various projects, ranging from parallel to serial projects. Those corrective actions are triggered by information obtained by a schedule risk analysis (bottom-up) or an EVM warning signal (top-down). Figure 13.11 shows an illustrative graph of this tracking efficiency for both tracking approaches, as follows:

- The x-axis shows the network topology of all projects of the study. The network topologies of the projects are measured by the Serial/Parallel SP indicator of Sect. 8.3.1 and range from completely parallel to completely serial networks.

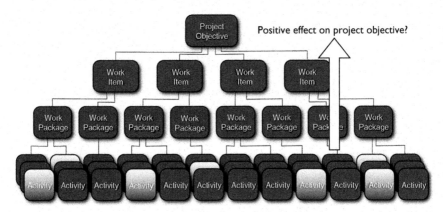

Individual activity control as a trigger for corrective actions
= Obtain with the minimal effort the maximal return!

Fig. 13.10 The bottom-up activity based tracking approach of schedule risk analysis

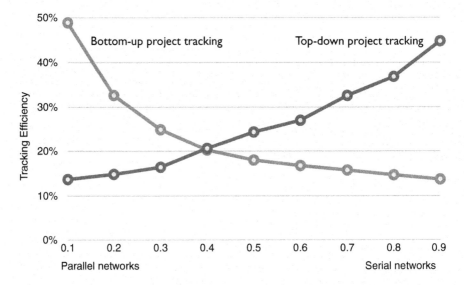

Fig. 13.11 The tracking efficiency of a bottom-up and top-down tracking approach

• The y-axis displays the efficiency of the project control phase. The lower the effort is for a project manager in controlling a project in progress and the higher the positive return is of corrective actions taken by the project manager in case the project is in danger, the higher the tracking efficiency is.

The graph clearly demonstrates that a top-down project based tracking approach using the EVM performance measures leads to a very efficient project tracking approach when the project network contains more serial activities. It should be noted that this top-down approach makes use of the SPI(t) indicator to predict the final duration, and not the SPI indicator, which is known to provide unreliable predictive performance results (see Chap. 12). The bottom-up activity based tracking approach using sensitivity information of activities obtained through a standard schedule risk analysis is particularly useful when projects contain a lot of parallel activities. This bottom-up approach requires often subjective distribution information of individual activities, which implies a certain activity risk estimate, but simplifies the tracking effort to those activities with a high expected effect on the overall project objective (see Chap. 5).

13.5 Conclusions

Project baseline scheduling, risk analysis and project control are crucial steps in the life of a project and are integrated under the dynamic scheduling label discussed throughout the various chapters of this book. The project manager uses the project schedule to help planning, executing and controlling project activities and to track and monitor the progress of the project. A major component of a project schedule is a work breakdown structure (WBS). However, the basic critical path method (CPM) schedules, or its often more sophisticated resource extensions, are nothing more but just the starting point for schedule management. Information about the sensitivity of the various parts of the schedule, quantified in schedule risk numbers, offers an extra opportunity to increase the accuracy of the schedules and might serve as an additional tool to improve project control or tracking. Consequently, project scheduling and controlling tools and techniques should give project managers access to real-time data including activity sensitivity, project completion percentages, actuals and forecasts on time and cost in order to gain a better understanding of the overall project performance and to be able to make faster and more effective corrective decisions. All this requires understandable project performance dashboards that visualize important project metrics that quickly reveal information on time and cost deviations at the project level or the activity level. During control and tracking, the project manager should use all this information and should set thresholds on the project level or on lower WBS levels to receive warning signals during project execution. These thresholds serve as triggers to take, when exceeded, corrective actions.

The purpose of this chapter was to give a brief summary of a large simulation experiment to test the contribution of two dynamic scheduling components – scheduling and risk analysis – on the efficiency of the third component (project control). The main contributions of the research study summarized in this chapter can be given along the following lines

- The research offers a comparative study to both academics and practitioners and provides an overview of and general results on EVM and SRA used during project performance measurement and project tracking.

- The research offers various project tracking and corrective action decision guidelines based on extensive simulation tests on a wide and diverse set of more than 4,000 fictitious projects. It distinguishes between top-down project tracking (EVM performance measurements as triggers at high WBS levels to drill down into lower WBS levels) and bottom-up project tracking (traditional activity based CPM project tracking, extended with project sensitivity information). Both tracking systems are used as trigger systems to warn for the need for corrective actions and their use highly depends on characteristics of the project.
- The research lays its main focus on the translation of general results to case-specific guidelines and rules-of-thumb, directly applicable to individual projects. Consequently, this makes the research a valuable tool for the project management discipline with great potential and a high practical value. In order to support this idea, a new software tool ProTrack has been developed, which contains all simulation results and allows the user to replicate the simulation experiment using their own data. This tool will be briefly discussed in Chap. 15.

Chapter 14
The Mutum-Paraná II Bridge Project (C)

Abstract The case description of this chapter is a last case exercise in a series of three exercises presented in Chaps. 6 and 11. It acts as an integrated exercise to get acquainted with the project control principles and special topics discussed in Part III of this book.

The primary goal of this fictitious case study is to get acquainted with the Earned Value Management approach to control projects. The goal of the student is to analyze the data of three projects in progress and to summarize their performance in the best possible way to the management committee. The data allows the incorporation of the Earned Schedule (ES) based Schedule Performance Index (SPI(t)) as an alternative to the traditional SPI metric that shows an unreliable behavior at the end of the project.

Similar to the first two case studies, the data in the case allows a deeper analysis based on the wishes and needs of the teacher and students, and contains data for the following special topics: the introduction of the schedule adherence concept, the use of schedule risk analysis to set action thresholds, the topological network structure as a driver for project control, etc.

14.1 Introduction

Since 1995, the Brazilian construction company Curitiba Pontes Ltd. has successfully completed large bridge and highway projects in the southern part of America. The company is known for its high level of experience in the construction area, its ability to work under challenging work conditions and tight schedules, and its profound knowledge of the project management discipline, which often resulted in projects completed on budget, on time and safely. Although its activities are spread out over different countries in South America, the main construction activities are located on the Brazilian market, with a strong focus on the bridge constructions located at and around the Paraná river.

M. Vanhoucke, *Project Management with Dynamic Scheduling*,
DOI 10.1007/978-3-642-40438-2_14, © Springer-Verlag Berlin Heidelberg 2013

For more than a decade, José Silva Coelho was a well-established value in the Brazilian bridge construction company Curitiba Pontes Ltd.. Although he was known for his often pragmatic view on project management and control and his often conflicting meetings when presenting performance results, he has obtained excellent results as a project manager of various bridge construction projects during the past decade. The news about the leave of José Silva Coelho by the end of 2012 announced at the quarterly project performance meeting held at September 30, 2012 came as a shock to most members of its project team, but Curitiba Pontes Ltd. has gone through harder times during the last decade than the resignation of one of its most meritorious employees. The management committee finally decided that Carlos Garez has enough experience in the bridge construction sector to take over the role of the project manager of the project. As a young and enthusiastic employee of the company, Carlos accepted the challenge with a great amount of enthusiasm and became responsible for the three projects that were under the guidance of José. It is now end of March 2013, exactly 3 months ago that Carlos Garez took over from José Silva Coelho as a project manager and the time is near to report the quarterly project results of the three projects to the management committee.

14.2   The Project Portfolio

At the time of his resignation decision, José was mainly responsible for three bridge construction projects carried out with his young and enthusiastic permanent project team: the Mutum-Paraná II bridge project, the Iguaçú III bridge project and the Bermejo I bridge project. It is a long tradition for the Brazilian company Curitiba Pontes Ltd. that each bridge construction project gets a number, referring to the number of bridges they have constructed over that river in the past. All projects have roughly the same set of project activities but differ in their activity duration and cost estimates, in their project network logic and hence in their activity timing of execution. The schedules were constructed by José using a commercial software tool based on time and cost information about the individual activities. All projects used the same activity list template, as given in Table 14.4. The network logic, activity durations, resource requirements and corresponding costs depend on the project, and are displayed in Table 14.5.

The Mutum-Paraná II bridge project is the main construction project of the company, since it is part of a bigger highway construction project containing several subprojects. This highway was a promise from the government to the poor people of the interior to link their region to Buenos Aires. Therefore, large investments were made to stimulate the economy. The second longest river in South America after the Amazon, the Paraná River joins with the Paraguay and Uruguay Rivers before emptying into the Ro de la Plata estuary on its way to the Atlantic Ocean. The river begins its 3,032-mile (4,879-km) course in east-central Brazil. The Paraná flows mainly among high plateaus through Paraguay and Argentina.

The Iguaçú III bridge river project is the third bridge constructed by Curitiba Pontes Ltd. over the Iguaçú river. The Iguaçú river is formed by headstreams rising in the Serra do Mar near Curitiba. It winds generally westward through the uplands for about 820 miles (1,320 km) before joining the Paran River at the point where Argentina, Brazil, and Paraguay meet. It forms a small portion of the Brazilian-Argentine border. The width of the river at the point of the bridge is 131 m.

The Bermejo I bridge project is the most recent construction project to connect the two sides of the Bermejo river. The Bermejo River is a river in South America that travels a total of 1,450 km from Bolivia to the Paraguay River in Argentina. The river is born in a mountain range known as Sierra de Santa Victoria around coordinates near Tarija, a few kilometers southeast of Chaguaya in Bolivia, and not far from La Quiaca, Jujuy Province, Argentina. The river is generally called Bermejo in spite of its different names along its way, but it also has its own Native American names, such as Teuco and Ypitá. It is the first time that Curitiba Pontes Ltd. constructs a bridge over the Bermejo river.

Table 14.1 displays the expected project release times (with (*planned release date*) and without (*critical path finish*) resource leveling), the corresponding baseline schedule budget for the project portfolio as well as information on the project network structure. The structure of the project network, consisting of project activities and precedence relations, is measured by the degree of seriality/parallelism (SP), ranging from 0% (completely parallel) to 100% (serial network). Figure 14.1 presents a graphical timeline of the current portfolio under responsibility of José.

Carlos has received all documents from José but has had little time to discuss things in detail. He knew that José was a project manager who ranked experience above project tools and techniques, but was nevertheless impressed by the rich amount of planning and performance measurement data for the three projects.

Table 14.2 shows the quarterly performance results for the three projects. These results were used as reporting tools during the management committee meeting held end of March, June, September and December 2012. The table also contains the results of the analysis made by Carlos and his team member Orlando during the first quarter of March 2013, which will be presented during the next meeting. The next meeting, scheduled at April 03, 2013, is coming soon, and Carlos is eager to show that the results presented on the previous meeting should be put in perspective. Carlos does not understand the improving performance of the Mutum-Paraná II bridge project as shown by the Schedule Performance Index for March, 2013 (an increase from 65% to 92%). Based on what he has heard from the project team, he could only conclude that the figures mask a possible problem,

Table 14.1 Network, time and cost information for the three projects

Project	SP(%)	Baseline Start	Critical path Finish	Planned Release date	Budget(€)
Mutum-Paraná II	29	06/02/2012	06/08/2012	21/01/2013	1,275,200
Iguaçú III	44	02/04/2012	07/01/2013	07/08/2013	1,267,200
Bermejo I	70	02/07/2012	31/07/2013	29/11/2013	1,246,400

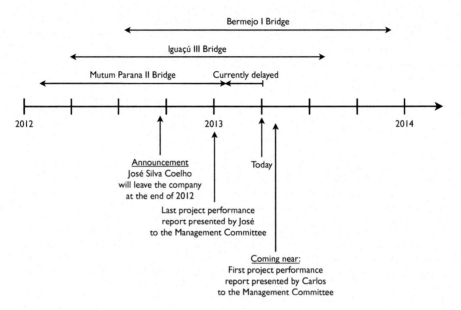

Fig. 14.1 A graphical timeline for the current project portfolio

Table 14.2 Overview of the main results reported to the management committee during the previous meetings

		03/12	06/12	09/12	12/12	03/13
		Approved	Approved	Approved	Approved	On agenda
	SPI	0.53	0.69	0.65	0.65	0.92
Mutum-Paraná II	SPI(t)	–	–	–	–	0.71
	CPI	0.56	0.68	0.68	0.70	0.74
	SPI	n.a.	1.10	1.27	1.04	0.97
Iguaçú III	SPI(t)	–	–	–	–	0.98
	CPI	n.a.	1.25	1.18	99	0.96
	SPI	n.a.	n.a.	0.99	0.86	0.77
Bermejo I	SPI(t)	–	–	–	–	0.85
	CPI	n.a.	n.a.	85	0.83	0.79

or maybe the performance analysis was done in an incorrect way. He therefore decides to analyze all EVM tables in a more profound way, hoping to find out what really went wrong in the quarterly reports presented to the management board. He considers that as a crucial step for the future performance meetings to correctly understand the past.

The project performance results of Table 14.2 are completely based on the efforts taken by Orlando Carvalheiro, one of the project team members, who is experienced in monitoring project progress using Earned Value Management. Orlando, who has collaborated with José for many years, has made all detailed reports that were used

Table 14.3 Monthly EVM metrics for the three projects used as internal performance communication tool

	Mutum-Paraná II			Iguaçú III			Bermejo I		
	PV(€)	AC(€)	EV(€)	PV(€)	AC(€)	EV(€)	PV(€)	AC(€)	EV(€)
02/12	74,400	74,400	41,429	n.a.	n.a.	n.a.	n.a.	n.a.	n.a.
03/12	202,960	198,400	110,478	n.a.	n.a.	n.a.	n.a.	n.a.	n.a.
04/12	301,280	303,280	183,182	61,200	55,320	75,067	n.a.	n.a.	n.a.
05/12	381,200	401,680	265,800	102,800	108,720	140,357	n.a.	n.a.	n.a.
06/12	511,920	517,820	351,477	194,160	170,770	213,875	n.a.	n.a.	n.a.
07/12	617,200	623,420	430,246	233,040	241,700	314,246	41,600	41,600	34,577
08/12	769,520	739,420	516,674	331,440	312,360	403,044	83,690	94,090	78,313
09/12	865,360	819,420	560,077	385,840	412,950	488,731	126,950	148,220	126,400
10/12	982,560	903,170	608,722	470,000	503,730	571,103	179,600	198,150	177,269
11/12	1,183,040	1,039,750	713,745	598,960	635,730	662,138	234,340	251,170	214,952
12/12	1,252,480	1,166,200	813,486	704,560	741,330	734,966	296,340	305,570	253,694
01/13	1,275,200	1,253,240	891,427	801,200	830,850	818,668	366,130	370,420	300,056
02/13	1,275,200	1,391,590	990,400	865,840	888,930	860,004	450,860	436,790	348,519
03/13	1,275,200	1,594,150	1,174,055	940,160	952,180	915,262	561,420	546,290	432,350

as internal communication tools within his own team. Each quarter, a summary was handed to José for the quarterly management committee meeting. Carlos was intrigued by these detailed reports and committed himself to investigate all EVM metrics in detail in order to understand what has happened in the past for the three projects. These detailed reports can be found in Table 14.3.

14.3   The Management Committee Meeting

The main task that Carlos faces in the short run is the preparation of the project performance report for the next management committee meeting scheduled at April 3, 2013. Apart from putting the results from previous meetings in perspective, Carlos is motivated to show a new and improved way of reporting the project portfolio performance. Together with Orlando, he sets up a plan to perform extra analyses for each individual project as well as to give estimates about the progress of each activity. While the main focus should be on the performance of the three projects over the past, he also demands to the various members of his project team to calculate certain characteristics of the project, such as the risk profile of each project activity and the percentage completed for each activity at the current time. Table 14.6 displays the current project status measured at the end of March, 2013 with the three key metrics of earned value management and the percentage completed as estimated by the team members. Table 14.7 shows various time sensitivity measures for all project activities obtained by a classical schedule risk analysis tool performed on the project schedules before resource leveling (i.e. on the critical path based project schedules).

Carlos plans an internal meeting with his team, and honestly congratulates them with the rich amount of information that they gathered during the past quarters. He explains that the use of project performance reporting using EVM goes far beyond the use of only the metrics. He explains that the three basic EVM metrics (planned value (PV), actual cost (AC) and earned value (EV)) can be used to calculate other, often more relevant metrics, and therefore provides additional information above the traditional SPI and CPI metrics used in the reports by José. Moreover, he explains that the task of the team is to throw a critical eye on the metrics and draw project specific conclusions to improve the actions that need to be taken in case problems arise.

Carlos gives an overview of the four main topics worth considering and stresses that these are outlined in order of importance:

- Reporting the correct time and cost performance. While the traditional CPI metric is often a reliable cost performance measure, he explains that the SPI often contains a flaw and can be extended to a more reliable measure. Due to the time criticality of the three projects, he asks Maria Mota Pereira, the account manager of Curitiba Pontes Ltd., to calculate extended SPI metrics, based on the Earned Schedule technique and the data from Table 14.6. Although Maria has never heard about this Earned Schedule technique, she accepts the job with great pleasure and immediately decides the wrap up the EVM metrics and look for this new Earned Schedule (ES) technique on the internet. The SPI(t) indicator, as shown in Table 14.2 for the first quarter of 2013 is one of those ES based metrics that was never used by José and is therefore new to the committee board and most members of Carlos' team.
- Analysis of dynamic information that measures the adherence to the project baseline schedule. At a project management conference, Carlos has learned about a possible analysis of potential threads and project impediments through the use of the so-called p-factor approach, which is a dynamic measure to calculate the schedule adherence based on EVM data. Carlos realizes that this is a completely new way of approaching EVM and is not sure about the benefits of this approach. For this reason, he decides that he will analyze this part himself, knowing that it might lead to unsuccessful results.
- Show potential problems related to the use of EVM management. Carlo briefly explains to the team that the use of performance metrics on the project level might lead to warning signals that are sometimes misleading or even completely wrong. He therefore calls their attention of a careful use and interpretation of performance metrics and highlights the importance of drilling down in the work breakdown structure and investigate potential problem or opportunities in individual project activities as warned by the project performance metric values. Since Maria Mota Pereira has already accepted a similar task, she volunteered to also take up this job.
- Integration of the time sensitivity results obtained by a schedule risk analysis (SRA) with EVM based performance reports in order to detect potential future project monitoring directions. Carlos conjectures that the sensitivity information of Table 14.7 and the network topology information displayed in Table 14.1 can be used to provide some general guidelines. Based on his experience in schedule

risk analysis and his technical background, Carlos decides that this would be a perfect job for Orlando Carvalheiro, the resource manager of the company.

14.4 The Agenda

Immediately after the internal team meeting, Carlos has sent an email to the chairman of the management committee explaining that he wants to throw a critical eye on the performance reports of last year and will present the newly quarterly performance results. To that purpose, he has put three items on the agenda of next meeting:

- Look back analysis: Analysis on the past project performance reports presented at the previous management committee meetings and put things in perspective (based on Tables 14.3 and 14.6)
- Current portfolio performance: Preparation of the performance report for the new quarterly management committee meeting based on an extended view of EVM metrics (based on the percentage completion (PC) estimates of Table 14.6)
- Go beyond the EVM metrics: Lessons learned and actions to be taken – what can we learn from these reports and how can we improve this communication? (based on information from all tables)

Carlos feels a healthy sense of nervousness, not only because of the rapid speed of the management committee deadline coming near, but also because he feels that he can put his stamp upon a completely new approach of project performance measurement, which, unlike the approach taken by José, sheds a completely new light on project monitoring in general and EVM in particular. Still 3 days to go from today, he knows that the successful finalization of all documents for the meeting heavily depends on the speed and quality of the analyses accepted by Orlando and Maria. Meanwhile, he thinks about the main topics he wants to present to the executive committee and decides to recapitulate the main EVM courses he had during his training to become a project manager at Curitiba Pontes Ltd.. While he is preparing his meeting reports, he suddenly starts thinking about the quote he has learned from the Nobel prize winning philosopher Bertrand Russell. "The greatest challenge to any thinker is stating the problem in a way that will allow a solution". "It certainly is", he thinks, while the deadline is coming near . . .

14.5 Appendix

All project files and tables are available in ProTrack or MS Excel format and can be downloaded from www.protrack.be/examples (Tables 14.4–14.7).

Table 14.4 Activity list
template used by Curitiba
Pontes Ltd

ID	Description
1	Preparatory work and move in
Mobilization	
2	Mobilize Pile Rig 1
3	Mobilize Pile Rig 2
4	Mobilize Pile Rig 3
Excavation	
5	Excavate Abutment 1
6	Excavate Abutment 2
7	Excavate Abutment 3
Drive piles	
8	Drive Piles Abutment 1
9	Drive Piles Abutment 2
10	Drive Piles Abutment 3
Demobilization	
11	Demobolize Pile Rig 1
12	Demobolize Pile Rig 2
13	Demobolize Pile Rig 3
14	Forms, Pour and Strip Footing 1
15	Forms, Pour and Strip Footing 2
16	Forms, Pour and Strip Footing 3
Abutment activities	
17	Forms, Pour and Strip Abutment
18	Forms, Pour and Strip Abutment
19	Forms, Pour and Strip Abutment
20	Backfill Abutment 1
21	Backfill Abutment 2
22	Backfill Abutment 3
23	Set Girders and Forms Deck 1–2
24	Set Girders and Forms Deck 2–3
Finishing work	
25	Pour Deck
26	Saw Joints
27	Strip Deck and Rub Concrete
28	Clean Up and Final Inspection

Table 14.5 Activity information and the network logic for the three projects

ID	Mutum-Paraná II			Iguaçú III			Bermejo I		
	Predecessors	Time(w)	Cost(€)	Predecessors	Time(w)	Cost(€)	Predecessors	Time(w)	Cost(€)
1	-	6	148,800	-	10	104,000	-	8	83,200
2	1SS+2w	1	19,600	1SS+2w	1	19,600	1SS+2w	1	19,600
3	1FS+5w	1	23,600	1FS+5w;2FS+1w	1	23,600	1FS+5w;2FS+1w	1	23,600
4	1FS+5w	1	22,000	1FS+5w;3FS+1w	1	22,000	1FS+5w;3FS+1w	1	22,000
5	1FS	1	10,400	1FS	1	10,400	1FS;4FS	1	10,400
6	1FS+8w	1	10,400	1FS+8w	1	10,400	1FS+8w ;5FS	1	10,400
7	1FS+8w	1	10,400	1FS+8w	1	10,400	1FS+8w ;6FS	1	10,400
8	2FS;5FS+3w	3	60,000	2FS;5FS+3w	6	81,600	2FS;5FS+3w	6	81,600
9	3FS;6SS+6w	3	60,000	3FS;6SS+6w	6	81,600	3FS;6SS+6w;17FS;19FS	6	81,600
10	4FS;7SS+3w	1	20,000	4FS;7SS+3w	3	40,800	4FS;7SS+3w	3	40,800
11	8FS	1	21,200	8FS	1	21,200	8FS	1	21,200
12	9FS	4	104,000	9FS	4	104,000	9FS	4	104,000
13	10FS	4	84,800	10FS	4	84,800	10FS	4	84,800
14	8FS	1	24,000	8FS;11FS+1w	1	24,000	8FS;11FS+1w	1	24,000
15	9FS	8	211,200	9FS;12FS+1w	8	211,200	9FS;12FS+1w	8	211,200
16	10FS	1	24,000	10FS;13FS+1w	1	24,000	10FS;13FS+1w	1	24,000
17	11FS;14FS	2	78,400	11FS;14FS	4	73,600	11FS;14FS	4	73,600
18	12FS;15FS	1	44,800	12FS;15FS	2	46,400	12FS;15FS	2	46,400
19	13FS;16FS	2	78,400	13FS;16FS	4	73,600	13FS;16FS	4	73,600
20	17FS	4	25,600	17FS	4	25,600	17FS	4	25,600
21	18FS	2	12,800	18FS	2	12,800	18FS	2	12,800
22	19FS	3	19,200	19FS	3	19,200	19FS	3	19,200
23	17FS;18FS	2	56,000	17FS;18FS	2	46,400	17FS;18FS	2	46,400
24	18FS;19FS	2	56,000	18FS; 19FS	2	46,400	18FS; 19FS	2	46,400
25	23SS+1w;24SS+1w	1	25,600	23SS+1w;24SS+1w	1	25,600	23SS+1w;24SS+1w	1	25,600
26	25FS+1w	2	3,200	25FS+1w	2	3,200	25FS+1w	2	3,200
27	25FS+2w	1	11,200	25FS+2w;26FS	1	11,200	25FS+2w;26FS	1	11,200
28	20FS;21FS;22FS;26FS;27FF+2w	1	9,600	20FS;21FS;22FS;26FS;27FF+2w	1	9,600	20FS;21FS;22FS;26FS;27FF+2w	1	9,600
			1,275,200			1,267,200			1,246,400

Table 14.6 Status report of the three projects at 29/03/2013

ID	Mutum-Paraná II				Iguaçú III				Bermejo I			
	PV(€)	AC(€)	EV(€)	PC(%)	PV(€)	AC(€)	EV(€)	PC(%)	PV(€)	AC(€)	EV(€)	PC(%)
1	148,800	267,220	148,800	100	104,000	78,000	104,000	100	83,200	100,100	83,200	100
2	19,600	34,300	19,600	100	19,600	13,720	19,600	100	19,600	18,620	19,600	100
3	23,600	23,600	23,600	100	23,600	21,830	23,600	100	23,600	29,500	23,600	100
4	22,000	22,000	22,000	100	22,000	14,300	22,000	100	22,000	19,250	22,000	100
5	10,400	11,960	10,400	100	10,400	13,520	10,400	100	10,400	13,520	10,400	100
6	10,400	5,980	10,400	100	10,400	10,400	10,400	100	10,400	5,460	10,400	100
7	10,400	12,220	10,400	100	10,400	6,760	10,400	100	10,400	15,080	10,400	100
8	60,000	111,500	60,000	100	81,600	116,620	81,600	100	81,600	114,580	81,600	100
9	60,000	78,500	60,000	100	81,600	66,980	81,600	100	0	0	0	0
10	20,000	36,500	20,000	100	40,800	37,060	40,800	100	40,800	58,140	40,800	100
11	21,200	21,730	21,200	100	21,200	19,610	21,200	100	21,200	29,150	21,200	100
12	104,000	137,150	104,000	100	104,000	124,150	104,000	100	0	0	0	0
13	84,800	89,570	84,800	100	84,800	53,530	84,800	100	84,800	111,830	84,800	100
14	24,000	33,600	24,000	100	24,000	4,200	6,462	27	24,000	30,600	24,000	100
15	211,200	283,140	211,200	100	211,200	306,240	211,200	100	0	0	0	0
16	24,000	37,200	24,000	100	24,000	12,000	24,000	100	24,000	0	0	0
17	78,400	35,280	78,400	100	7,360	0	0	0	73,600	460	350	0
18	44,800	52,640	44,800	100	46,400	38,860	46,400	100	0	0	0	0
19	78,400	116,620	78,400	100	0	0	0	0	18,860	0	0	0
20	25,600	26,240	19,259	75	0	0	0	0	12,960	0	0	0
21	12,800	16,160	12,800	100	12,800	14,400	12,800	100	0	0	0	0
22	19,200	26,240	17,397	91	0	0	0	0	0	0	0	0
23	56,000	95,900	56,000	100	0	0	0	0	0	0	0	0
24	56,000	18,900	12,600	22	0	0	0	0	0	0	0	0
25	25,600	0	0	0	0	0	0	0	0	0	0	0
26	3,200	0	0	0	0	0	0	0	0	0	0	0
27	11,200	0	0	0	0	0	0	0	0	0	0	0
28	9,600	0	0	0	0	0	0	0	0	0	0	0

Table 14.7 Time sensitivity (in %, based on SRA without resource constraints)

ID	Risk class	Mutum-Paraná II				Iguaçú III				Bermejo I			
		CI	SI	SSI	CRI	CI	SI	SSI	CRI	CI	SI	SSI	CRI
1	Chaos	100	100	81.55	84.95	100	100	85.44	88.31	100	100	75.47	79.59
2	Foreseen uncertainty (+)	0	9.36	0	3.2	0	14.96	0	0.69	0	33.56	0	3.1
3	Foreseen uncertainty (+)	0	39.47	0	4.84	0	39.65	0	6.43	100	100	3.88	8.23
4	Foreseen uncertainty (+)	0	13.72	0	3.8	0	12.24	0	4.4	100	100	4.35	11.82
5	Unforeseen uncertainty	0	25.02	0	3.8	0	16.97	0	6.68	100	100	6.38	1.93
6	Unforeseen uncertainty	95	99.06	8.3	12.71	100	100	5.65	11.68	87	96.38	5.42	15.5
7	Unforeseen uncertainty	5	42.53	0.39	7.67	0	18.65	0	6.32	87	96.37	4.87	4.29
8	Foreseen uncertainty (+)	0	50.5	0	0.89	0	55.33	0	5.75	13	87.51	3.44	0.43
9	Foreseen uncertainty (+)	95	99.6	15.63	7.96	100	100	21.38	15.87	100	100	23.59	20.03
10	Foreseen uncertainty (+)	5	42.54	0.28	3.34	0	40.4	0	5.26	87	98.41	10.52	10.21
11	Variation	0	24.77	0	4.86	0	16.96	0	2.58	13	58.87	0.59	3.17
12	Variation	0	50.19	0	11.17	100	100	15.15	25.1	100	100	16.71	26.7
13	Variation	5	72.21	1.21	8.12	0	47.06	0	6.47	87	98.67	15	22.45
14	Variation	0	24.72	0	9.33	0	16.93	0	8.21	13	59.05	0.58	6.17
15	Variation	95	99.82	46.69	53.36	100	100	31.77	40.51	100	100	35.05	43.99
16	Variation	0	18.11	0	4.92	0	18.57	0	4.97	87	96.35	3.88	3.55
17	Variation	0	40.21	0	9.41	0	44.92	0	5.04	13	82.69	2.37	9.66
18	Variation	95	99.01	5.99	13.6	100	100	8.14	14.65	100	100	8.98	17.03
19	Variation	5	57.77	0.63	8.14	0	47.14	0	6.44	87	98.69	15.81	22.01
20	Unforeseen uncertainty	0	44.28	0	9.11	0	33.49	0	8.06	0	13.86	0	4.13
21	Unforeseen uncertainty	0	32.67	0	18.45	0	28.11	0	19.44	0	28.13	0	16.04
22	Unforeseen uncertainty	0	39.52	0	12.57	0	25.95	0	16.25	0	10.64	0	13.16
23	Unforeseen uncertainty	95	99.41	16.88	7.1	100	100	11.48	10.53	100	100	12.67	11.69
24	Unforeseen uncertainty	100	100	15.72	16.03	100	100	10.16	16.85	100	100	11.21	17.86
25	Variation	100	100	5.51	26.26	100	100	3.56	24.84	100	100	3.93	28.71
26	Variation	0	65.72	0	11.61	100	100	8.87	18.57	100	100	9.78	16.92
27	Variation	100	100	6.89	21.2	100	100	4.45	17.02	100	100	4.91	18.96
28	Foreseen uncertainty (−)	100	100	5.89	8.92	100	100	3.81	6.78	100	100	4.2	1.64

Part IV
Scheduling with Software

Chapter 15
Dynamic Scheduling with ProTrack

15.1 Introduction

ProTrack (acronym for *Pro*ject *Track*ing) is a project scheduling and tracking software tool developed by OR-AS[1] to offer a straightforward yet effective alternative to the numerous project scheduling and tracking software tools. The software has been built based on the results of the research studies discussed in Vanhoucke (2010a) and the many discussions with practitioners using software tools for dynamic scheduling. The project scheduling, risk analysis and project control approach is based on the current best practices from literature. ProTrack has been developed based on many research projects on the three dimensions of dynamic scheduling. Moreover, ProTrack also contains three additional engines based on state-of-the-art research in dynamic scheduling: a project generation engine, a simulation engine and a time forecasting engine. Each of these engines will be discussed in the current chapter.

Figure 15.1 shows the three dimensions of dynamic scheduling in ProTrack and is taken from the ProTrack website www.protrack.be. This chapter briefly highlights the main characteristics of ProTrack that are novel compared to traditional project management software tools and presents an overview of the features discussed throughout the various chapters in this book. More detailed information about the specific features of ProTrack, as well as tutorials to set up a dynamic schedule can be freely downloaded from the ProTrack website.

ProTrack has been released at the end of 2008 under four different versions as a critical path scheduler using earned value management to control the project progress. The second major version (ProTrack 2.0) has been released on February 2010 incorporating the option of scheduling renewable resources using basic functionalities of Chap. 7 in each of the four versions. The third major version

---

[1]OR-AS is a company founded in 2007 in order to bring principles and methodologies from the *O*perations *R*esearch discipline to a practical environment through software *A*pplications and/or consultancy *S*olutions. For more information, visit www.or-as.be.

M. Vanhoucke, *Project Management with Dynamic Scheduling*,
DOI 10.1007/978-3-642-40438-2_15, © Springer-Verlag Berlin Heidelberg 2013

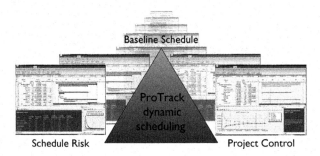

Fig. 15.1 Dynamic scheduling in ProTrack

ProTrack 3.0 has been released in the summer of 2011. In this third release, it has been decided to further develop only the smart version (the most extended ProTrack version) at a much cheaper price. The incorporation of the so-called ProTrack's assistant is one of the main functionalities that has been added to this third release. The main functionalities of ProTrack 3.0 are briefly described in this chapter. However, some of the new features that will be added to ProTrack 4.0 are also briefly mentioned. For an overview of the four versions of ProTrack 2.0, the reader is referred to Vanhoucke (2010a). As previously mentioned, all functionalities of these four versions have now been integrated in the single ProTrack 3.0 version. For an updated list of the current ProTrack functionalities, check www.or-as.be/protrack. ProTrack's main functionalities are summarized along the following lines:

- **Baseline scheduling:** ProTrack contains the standard baseline scheduling functionalities as discussed throughout this book. It allows the construction of the critical path using forward and backward calculations (see Chap. 2) as well as the incorporation of renewable resources to construct a resource feasible baseline schedule using priority rule based scheduling techniques discussed in Chap. 7.
- **Schedule risk analysis:** ProTrack integrates the option to perform a risk analysis on the baseline schedule using a unique *simulation engine*. More specifically, it allows multiple advanced simulation runs to scan the sensitivity of all project activities, as discussed in the schedule risk analysis Chap. 5.
- **Project control:** Controlling projects using earned value management, including the option to measure the earned schedule and schedule adherence, are basic functionalities of ProTrack 3.0. Most topics discussed in Chaps. 12 and 13 are standard options in ProTrack 3.0.
- **And more:** ProTrack is unique in its kind by incorporating many extra functionalities that make it an ideal learning tool. The automatic generation of project network data using the *project generation engine*, discussed in Sect. 15.5, is an example to facilitate the use of ProTrack for new users. Moreover, the so-called *time forecasting engine* allows the user to go back in time to learn how EVM works for a particular project. More precisely, it allows the generation of fictitious tracking periods from the start till the finish of a project, which automatically generates earned value based tracking information. In doing so, the user can

get easily acquainted with the EVM metrics for a project and can also perform multiple simulation runs to measure how accurate EVM time and cost forecasts are for the project under study. Finally, the project scheduling game discussed in Chap. 3 has also been integrated in ProTrack 3.0.

The outline of this chapter is as follows. In the first three sections, the integration of the dimensions of dynamic scheduling in ProTrack are briefly discussed. Section 15.2 reviews the main project scheduling options available in ProTrack. Section 15.3 reviews how schedule risk analysis can be done while Sect. 15.4 highlights the main earned value management project tracking possibilities of ProTrack. Section 15.5 presents some additional functionalities of ProTrack: the automatic generation of project data, the standard and advanced EVM features and the ability to perform time and cost forecast accuracy calculations. Section 15.6 briefly reviews the features of the project scheduling game of Chap. 3 and Sect. 15.8 draws overall conclusions with links to additional sources of information. The aim of this chapter is not to give a complete overview of the characteristics of ProTrack, but instead to provide a brief overview of how the dynamic scheduling dimensions have been incorporated in the software tool.

15.2   Baseline Scheduling

Throughout the various chapters of this book, it has been continuously mentioned that the construction of a project baseline schedule is often a time-consuming and cumbersome task that nevertheless plays a central role in a schedule risk analysis and in the project control phase. The general starting point of view of this book is that the usability of a project schedule is to act as a point of reference in the project life cycle, and hence, a project schedule should especially be considered as nothing more than a predictive model that can be used for resource efficiency calculations, time and cost risk analyses, project tracking and performance measurement, and so on. Hence, care must be taken to construct a resource feasible and realistic schedule that meets all requirements of the project manager and the members of his/her team.

ProTrack 3.0 contains many of the basic baseline scheduling options discussed in Chaps. 2, 7, 8 and 12 and can therefore be considered as a project scheduling tool similar to many alternative tools available on the commercial market. However, ProTrack 3.0 also makes the connection between baseline scheduling, schedule risk and project control to incorporate all dynamic scheduling dimensions into a single software tool.

15.3   Schedule Risk Analysis

The Schedule Risk Analysis technique discussed in Chap. 5 connects the risk information of project activities to the baseline schedule and provides sensitivity information of individual project activities as a way to assess the potential impact of uncertainty on the final project duration. ProTrack's schedule risk analysis makes use of two simulation engines that are hidden behind the simulation screen of the software tool. Both engines serve different needs that can be briefly summarized along the following lines:

- The standard simulation engine allows the user to start a quick and easy simulation without a thorough study on the risk profiles of the various project activities. This standard engine does not require data about estimated probability distributions for the activity durations, but instead makes use of the nine predefined simulation scenarios shown in Fig. 13.5.
- The advanced simulation engine requires a more detailed risk quantification for each project activity using activity duration distributions based on triangular distributions. This advanced engine can be considered as the most advanced schedule risk analysis option in ProTrack, based on the topics discussed in Chap. 5.

ProTrack is able to generate sensitivity measures and reports for the duration and cost of each activity as well as for the resources linked to these activities using the sensitivity measures of Sect. 5.3. Note that the use of these two simulation engines is not restricted to a schedule risk analysis. The two engines can also be integrated with the time forecasting engine to perform a project performance and forecast accuracy study as briefly discussed in Chap. 13. Such an accuracy study, based on real data of fictitious project data will help the user to easily understand the project control dimension of dynamic scheduling in general and earned value management in particular. More information can be found in the book written by Vanhoucke (2010a).

15.4   Project Control

Project control is the process performed to observe project execution in order to identify potential problems and/or opportunities in a timely manner such that corrective actions can be taken when necessary. The key benefit is that the current project status is observed on a regular basis, which enables the calculation of the project performance variance that is equal to the gap between actual performance and the baseline schedule. Since the current project performance is measured by variances from the project management plan, the baseline schedule plays a central and unambiguous role during the project tracking process. ProTrack employs a strict definition of a unique baseline schedule for each tracking period, such that it is always clear during the complete project execution what the active baseline schedule is. ProTrack allows the user to define multiple tracking periods in order to get a clear view of the progress of the project over time. Each tracking period is linked to a unique status date and a corresponding baseline schedule, and measures the current progress up to the status date of the project compared to the active baseline schedule. Note that the user needs to select a single baseline schedule for each tracking period. Consequently, this strict baseline schedule definition guarantees a clear and unambiguous interpretation of the current performance (i.e. the current performance compared to the active baseline schedule at the status date) and guarantees that only one baseline schedule is active at the same time.

These and more advanced project control features discussed in Chaps. 12 and 13 are available in ProTrack 3.0.

15.5 ProTrack's Advanced Features

This section briefly reviews some advanced features that are incorporated in Pro-Track 3.0. These advanced features are the subject to continuous updates, changes and extensions, and will probably be even more advanced at the time of publication of this book. For an overview of the most recent functionality extensions, the reader can visit ProTrack's website.

15.5.1 Automatic Project Generation

The generation of fictitious project data is an easy and powerful tool to let the user start immediately with ProTrack to gain experience with all its features even before entering real project data. In order to generate a fictitious project that reflects the characteristics of real project data, the user can make use of two project generation options, one measuring the network topology and one related to the use of renewable and nonrenewable (or consumable) resources.

Network Topology

The basic project data required for ProTrack's baseline scheduling can be generated automatically using the following data field:

- Number of activities: Number of tasks in the project network.
- Precedence relations: The number of links between activities is measured by the Serial/Parallel (SP) indicator of Sect. 8.3.1, which indicates how close the project network lies to a completely parallel (no links) or completely serial (maximum number of links) project.
- Time and cost estimates: The time and cost estimates for each activity will be generated randomly from a user-defined interval. In case the project makes use of renewable and/or nonrenewable resources, the activity cost can be split up into the various resource costs (see Sect. 7.6.1).
- Activity constraints information (cf. Sect. 2.2.4):

– Percentage of tasks with constraints (0–100%), randomly added to the project activities.
– Time window for scheduling: Activity constraints imply a certain date in the project life. The minimal project time window is equal to the critical path (minimum value). This time window can be extended to maximum the double of the critical path (maximum value), and the constraints will be randomly assigned in this time window interval.
– Feasibility of constraints (yes/no): Activity constraint can lead to scheduling conflicts and infeasibilities. Putting the feasible option on avoids these constraints conflicts.

In Chap. 8, it has been shown that the structure of a project network can be measured using various network topology measures. ProTrack allows network topology calculations using the four topology measures of Sect. 8.3.1: the Serial/Parallel indicator SP, the Activity Distribution indicator AD, the Length of Arcs indicator LA and the Topological Float indicator TF.

Automatic Resource Generation

Next to the automatic generation of a project network with a user-defined network structure, all resource related project data can also be automatically generated, allowing the user to set up a fictitious resource-constrained project schedule with a minimum amount of manual interventions. The resource related information needed to automatically generate the resource-constrained schedules can be summarized along the following lines:

1. Generate a user-defined number of renewable and nonrenewable resources. The resource availability of all renewable resources will be set automatically on 100%.
2. Generate values for the resource costs (cost per use and cost per unit) from user-defined ranges.
3. Generate resource demand for the project activities based on some resource scarceness measures of Sect. 8.3.2 using the following parameters:

   • Resource Use: Average number of activities that make use of the resource (expressed as a percentage between 0% and 100% of the activity set of the project).
   • Resource demand values:

     – Average Demand, measured by the Resource Constrainedness (RC). The RC measures the average use of the renewable resource by all project activities relative to its availability, ranging from 0% (no use) to 100% (resource demand is equal to its availability for all activities). Since the renewable resource availability is automatically set to 100% during resource generations, the renewable resource demand of activities is restricted to maximum 100%.

- Maximum Demand: Maximum number of units requested by the activity for the nonrenewable resources. Since there is no availability of the nonrenewable resource, this number is not restricted to a maximum value.
- User-defined probability values to specify that the nonrenewable resource demand of project activities have a fixed or variable demand, as discussed in Sect. 7.6.

15.5.2 Standard and Advanced EVM Features

ProTrack incorporates all basic and advanced features of project tracking and earned value management discussed in Chaps. 12 and 13. One of the primary tasks during project tracking is periodically updating the baseline schedule to reflect the actual progress of the work done and to present a realistic forecast of the remaining work. The tracking Gantt chart gives a prediction of the future schedule based on the inputs of actual and remaining durations/costs. However, it is important to realize that the schedule prediction of the tracking Gantt chart discussed here might differ from the schedule predictions using Earned Value Management (see the EAC and EAC(t) formulas of Sect. 12.4). Both contain a schedule prediction but differ as follows:

- Tracking Gantt chart prediction: The schedule prediction displayed in the tracking Gantt chart displays the remaining project schedule, given the actual start dates of the started activities and their actual and remaining durations. The remaining duration of the activities that have not been started yet is equal to their baseline duration.
- Earned Value Analysis prediction: The schedule predictions using the EVM metrics of Sect. 12.4 completely rely on the percentage completed (PC) estimates and their corresponding earned value metrics. Obviously, the PC estimate might completely differ from the actual and remaining duration estimates.

Many of the ProTrack EVM features have been implemented in most standard software tools, but others are completely new and rely on the results of a large Earned Value simulation study discussed in Chap. 13. The main EVM features are briefly summarized along the following lines:

- Earned Value Management: Automatic calculation of the standard EVM key metrics and extensions to earned schedule project tracking and performance measurement.
- Schedule adherence: Automatic calculation of the p-factor to dynamically measure schedule adherence. ProTrack provides two alternative views on the project's Gantt chart when showing the p-factor calculations. One shows the tracking Gantt chart, showing real progress of the project and another shows the earned value accrue of the project relative to the baseline schedule (similar to Fig. 13.3).

- Time/Cost forecasting: EVM time and cost forecasting based on the predictive methods of Sect. 12.4.
- Forecast accuracy: ProTrack is an ideal EVM learning tool and contains simulation engines to simulate fictitious project progress to measure the accuracy of time and cost forecasts (see Sect. 15.5.3).
- Gantt chart tracking: A choice between retained logic and overridden logic (all intermediate levels inclusive) to predict the remaining work shown in a tracking Gantt chart. This Gantt chart can replace the current baseline schedule (i.e. rebaselining) when necessary. Details are outside the scope of this chapter.
- Reporting: A wide range of flexible reports customized with performance measurement metrics, progress updates and resource and cash flow estimates can be easily generated.

15.5.3   Forecasting Accuracy Calculations

ProTrack allows to redo all accuracy studies briefly discussed in Sect. 13.3 using the EVM predictions for the total cost and duration of a project (EAC and EAC(t)) discussed in Chap. 12 and ProTrack's standard simulation engine. In order to evaluate the EAC and EAC(t) forecasting measures and to determine the forecast accuracy of each technique, two straightforward measures are calculated. The measures calculate the average deviations between the total project costs/durations predicted during project execution (the EAC and EAC(t) values at each reporting period) and the final real project cost (RC) and duration (RD) observed after the finish of the project. Obviously, the lower their value, the more accurate the average duration prediction. The two measures are the Mean Percentage Error (MPE) and the Mean Absolute Percentage Error (MAPE). While the MAPE evaluates the forecast accuracy as average absolute deviations between all predictions and the real project time and cost value, the MPE can be calculated in a similar way, but, unlike the MAPE, positive and/or negative values are possible to measure over- and/or underestimations of the final project cost and duration, respectively. In order to calculate these values, the following abbreviations have been defined:

T	Total number of reporting periods over the complete project horizon
RD	Real Duration of the project (known at the project finish)
RC	Real Cost of the project (known at the project finish)
EAC^{t_1}	Cost estimate at reporting period t_1 ($t_1 = 1, 2, \ldots, T$)
$EAC(t)^{t_1}$	Duration estimate at reporting period t_1 ($t_1 = 1, 2, \ldots, T$)

The formulas are displayed in Table 15.1 and a detailed discussion can be found at Vanhoucke (2010a).

Table 15.1 Forecasting accuracy measures in ProTrack

	Time	Cost
MPE	$\frac{1}{T}\sum_{t_1=1}^{T} \frac{EAC(t)^{t_1}-RD}{RD} * 100$	$\frac{1}{T}\sum_{t_1=1}^{T} \frac{EAC^{t_1}-RC}{RC} * 100$
MAPE	$\frac{1}{T}\sum_{t_1=1}^{T} \frac{|EAC(t)^{t_1}-RD|}{RD} * 100$	$\frac{1}{T}\sum_{t_1=1}^{T} \frac{|EAC^{t_1}-RC|}{RC} * 100$

15.5.4 Project Control Charts

Project control systems in general and Earned Value Management in particular are systems to indicate the direction of change in preliminary planning variables compared with actual performance. The systems are set up such that, in case the current project performance deviates from the planned performance, a warning is indicated by the system in order to take corrective actions. However, little or no guidance is given by the current EVM systems how deviations should be defined and when warning signals should be used to trigger corrective actions.

ProTrack 4.0 tries to partially solve this problem by using a warning signal process that automatically makes a distinction between normal and abnormal project performance. In doing so, the system is able to guide the project manager in the corrective action decision making process in order to facilitate his/her project control efforts. This automatic control system is briefly discussed along the following lines.

Setting Performance Tolerance Limits

Measuring the performance of a project in progress using EVM provides periodic performance measures for the time and cost as proposed in Chap. 12. However, these performance measures have little or no value if they are not used in a corrective action decision making process. Indeed, these measures should be used within a system that triggers corrective actions when critical values are exceeded in order to exploit project opportunities or to solve problems and therefore, should be able to discriminate between random cause and assignable cause variation.

The use of tolerance limits in project control is based on the Statistical Process Control applications used in manufacturing in which a state of control is identified with a process generating independent and identically distributed normal random variables. Control charts such as the Shewhart chart and its extensions serve as on-line procedures to monitor process stability, to detect assignable variation or to forecast process movements in industrial processes. A process is said to be in-control when only common cause variation is present. This type of variation is characterized as coming from phenomena constantly active in a process, which can be predicted probabilistically. A process is said to be out-of-control if a second type of variation is present known as assignable cause variation. Assignable cause variation arises when a new, previously unanticipated phenomenon is present in the system and should cause a signal.

In project control, the baseline schedule is assumed to define the expected project progress, and small deviations from this baseline schedule should be considered as part of the normal variation while significant deviations should allow the project manager to find reasons for assignable cause variation. The difference between the normal and assignable cause variation should be defined by tolerance limits on the performance measures that act as thresholds to trigger the need for corrective actions. These tolerance limits can be set based on three techniques, as explained along the following lines:

- Rule-of-thumb control limits: The periodic time (SV, SPI, SV(t) and SPI(t)) and cost (CV and CPI) performance measures available in EVM are mostly used as warning signals to trigger corrective actions when the periodic values are no longer tolerable and exceed certain thresholds. These thresholds are often set based on practical experience, rules-of-thumb and anecdotal evidence of the project manager, and therefore lack any methodological or project specific ground. They often are very subjective and depend on the personal experience of the project manager. At best, they could be set based on data from earlier finished projects.
- Univariate control limits: While the previous control limits are often subjective and do not rely on project specific characteristics, the univariate control charts focus on the construction of project specific tolerances that rely on activity and project network characteristics. In this approach, the normal project progress situation needs to be defined by the project manager in order to construct control charts that distinguish between in-control and out-of-control situations. Therefore, it is assumed that the project baseline schedule is a forecast of what might happen in the future during project progress and determines the in-control situation, subject to some acceptable variation on the activity durations. Both positive and negative deviations within a certain range are assumed to be inherent to any project and are considered as normal while abnormal deviations exceeding certain thresholds should trigger further investigations. Constructing these tolerances to define normal variation can be easily done using the Monte-Carlo simulation approach presented in Chap. 5. These simulation runs will provide a huge amount of data on performance measures obtained by artificial project progress runs, and enable the software to calculate upper and lower tolerance limits. These tolerances are calculated as three-sigma intervals on the original performance measures (X-chart) or on the difference between the performance measures of two consecutive reporting periods (XR-charts). More detailed information can be found in Colin and Vanhoucke (2013a).
- Multivariate project control limits: While the advantage of univariate control charts is that they determine tolerances on the time and cost performance measures based on project specific data, the disadvantage is that the project manager still has no clue which of the charts to use. When considering four measures for time performance (SV, SV(t), SPI and SPI(t)) and two measures

for cost performance (CV and CPI) which can be used to construct X or XR charts, the manager has the choice between 12 control charts. Due to this data overload, the project manager could lose sight over the control metrics and might not always make the right selection of the appropriate metric to be used in order to measure the performance of a project at a particular moment in time. This leads to the situation where a manager resorts to controlling only a few variables, missing out on potentially crucial information. Moreover, since the various performance measures can be correlated, they probably show some degree of redundancy, and therefore add little to no value. A solution to the data overload and redundancy problem lies in the use of multivariate control charts since they integrate all relevant control charts into two alternative control charts. The reduction of the number of variables (performance measures) can be done by using a principal component analysis on all the periodic values of the six performance measures, resulting in the so-called T^2 and SPE control charts. These alternative multivariate control charts can also be used for setting tolerance limits as is the case for the univariate control charts. More detailed information can be found in Colin and Vanhoucke (2013b).

Assessing the Power of Control Charts

Validating the usefulness and power of statistical control charts is like walking on a bridge between two conflicting criteria. On the one hand, control charts should be able to detect significant deviations from the baseline schedule in order to timely provide early warning signals for project problems or opportunities. On the other hand, they should not report unreliable signals when no real underlying deviations occur to avoid overreactions by the project manager. This trade-off is well-known in statistical hypothesis testing as the type I and II errors, which are briefly discussed in the paragraphs below.

The type I error is defined as the possibility of encountering *false positives* and occurs when the performance metric reports an out-of-control situation (thresholds exceeded) when no real deviation occurs. In that case, the project manager is encouraged to take action, or at least will be responsible to investigate which activity is causing the warning signal. However, the search for activity deviations is in this case a waste of time since all activities contain only common cause variation, and hence, no actions are necessary. The time investment of the project manager for the search to deviations can thus be qualified as *overreactions*. The type I error is the frequentist approximation of the *probability of performing such overreactions.*

The type II error is defined as the possibility of encountering *false negatives* and occurs when real activity deviations are not detected by the control charts. In this situation, the project manager has the risk that he/she will not detect the real project problems and/or opportunities. Consequently, no timely corrective actions will be taken, which will possibly have a negative impact on the later project progress. The probability of encountering such false negatives is known as the type II error and determines the *detection performance* of the charts (defined as 1-type II error).

Based on a simulation study measuring the type I and II errors of the previously mentioned control charts, studies have found that the univariate control charts perform much better than the control charts made by the project manager based on rules-of-thumb and practical experience. The multivariate control charts further improve the power of detecting out-of-control situations and can nowadays be considered as the best possible tolerance setting technique.

15.6   PSG: ProTrack as a Teaching Tool

Teaching the impact of the presence of time/cost trade-offs in a reactive scheduling environment using the project scheduling game of Chap. 3 is a basic feature of ProTrack 3.0. Teachers who want to use the game for their project management courses or consultancy services can create their own data and share these data with other ProTrack users, if appropriate.

15.6.1   Simulating Time/Cost Trade-Offs

This section gives a brief overview of some PSG features implemented in ProTrack, without giving any details. More information can be obtained from the PSG tutorial, which can be downloaded from the ProTrack website.

Simulations versus decision making The user must clearly understand the difference between a project simulation and a decision moment. A simulation is a quick and automatic rescheduling test to see the effect of crashing actions taken by the user. From the moment another time/cost combination is taken for an activity, ProTrack automatically reschedules the complete project. Obviously, the software contains an option to go back to the previous project schedule to undo all the actions taken. Intermediate promising schedules can be saved and restored at all times. A decision must be taken when the user is convinced about the quality of the crashing actions taken. It involves the automatic simulation of fictitious project progress under uncertainty and leads to an increase in the actual time pointer. Obviously, there is no option to go back in time and undo the decision of the user.

Access to the game ProTrack owners have full access to the data of the PSG. This includes access to the uncertainty level, project network, time/cost combinations, time limit and number of decision periods. PSG users (e.g. students) only have limited access since they are not allowed to change the underlying project data.

15.6.2   Submitting Project Data

The project scheduling game contains a default project network (see Fig. 3.5), which allows the users to immediately start up the simulation game without additional setup time. However, the most interesting teaching session will be given to an audience that is familiar with the project and its underlying project network features. To that purpose, the PSG functionality of ProTrack can be extended with other projects that satisfy the needs of the user and that reflects the characteristics of the project environment of the software user.

ProTrack PSG users are stimulated to submit their own data via the www. protrack.be/psg support page or via the personal support page of ProTrack owners. The reasons why ProTrack users should submit their own developed project data for the PSG simulation can be twofold:

- Share the example projects with other PSG users: When submitting a project, the users can choose to share their data with other ProTrack users. In doing so, a database of interesting project networks applicable for PSG simulation runs can be created with projects from different sectors. Moreover, it has been said in Sect. 3.4.5 that the game might act as a research tool, and hence, submitting data will certainly contribute to that goal.
- Complete time/cost profile: Obviously, it is interesting to have an idea about the best possible time/cost profile for the projects developed by users. A best known time/cost profile, similar to Fig. 3.9, allows the user to validate the solution obtained by a PSG run. When data is submitted to the website in a correct ProTrack-PSG format, a solution will be posted on the support page of the software user. The data submitted will be entered in a software tool in order to find the best possible time/cost profile for the project. The optimal time/cost profile will be found by the algorithm of Demeulemeester et al. (1998) or, in case the optimal solution cannot be found due to the size of the project, a heuristic solution will be found by the algorithm of Vanhoucke and Debels (2007).

15.7   P2 Engine: ProTrack as a Research Tool

15.7.1   Advancing the State-of-the-Art Knowledge

While ProTrack is an ideal tool for managing a project, including all features discussed in the previous sections, it is often too restrictive to researchers who want to analyze a huge amount of project data to test a novel idea or to develop extensions of the existing algorithms, concepts and techniques. It is for this very reason that OR-AS has developed P2 Engine (www.p2engine.com) that is used by master students and PhD students at Ghent University (Belgium) as well as for business purposes to develop integrated PM software systems.

P2 Engine is a command line utility tool based on the LUA scripting language (www.lua.org) to generate gigabytes of project data. It generates project baseline scheduling data and risk analysis metrics as well as dynamic project progress data that can be used for testing and validating novel research ideas. The algorithms of P2 Engine can be classified into three classes that fit perfectly into the dynamic scheduling theme of this book, as follows:

- Baseline Scheduling: Schedule projects using critical path and resource allocation algorithms
- Risk Analysis: Analyze project risk using basic or advanced Monte-Carlo simulation runs
- Project Control: Generate project performance data and analyze Earned Value Management control data

By giving the P2 Engine user access to a wide variety of intelligent project optimization algorithms incorporated in ProTrack, he/she can solve difficult and critical dynamic project scheduling problems. P2 Engine can easily produce an enormous database of optimization results for a wide range of project management problems faster than ever before in order to advance the state-of-the-art knowledge available today. It runs fast and easy on any stand-alone computer, and the size of the hard disk will probably be the only constraint a researcher will face. However, since researchers tend to be very demanding when it comes to the amount of data they want to process and the complexity of algorithms they use, Ghent University accommodates the most demanding research by providing a super-computing infrastructure to researchers, in order to generate literally gigabytes of data per day. This has led to academic papers on project scheduling, risk analysis and project control as summarized on the www.projectmanagement.ugent.be website. P2 Engine is free to any academic researcher who wants to contribute to the development of state-of-the-art tools and techniques, the creation of new insights in dynamic project scheduling and the invention of future research avenues in order to make project management even better than today. Requesting a free academic license can be done at the P2 Engine website.

15.7.2   Scanning a Project

Through a well-balanced combination between research experience and practical relevance, P2 Engine can be easily used to measure, analyze and validate the characteristics of a project from a dynamic scheduling point of view and to benchmark its strengths and weaknesses in order to improve the integrated project control approach for a company. This so-called project scan is relevant for project managers working in both the private and public sector, and applies to large and small projects with critical performance, time and budget targets.

The central idea of a project scan is to understand the underlying characteristics and to map them with the best practices and research knowledge in order to better control projects and to improve the necessary corrective actions to bring projects in danger back on track. It is based on the methodology published in "Measuring Time" (Vanhoucke, 2010a) and benchmarks a project along the four following dimensions:

- Network scan. The characteristics of a project WBS in terms of network topology and time and cost distributions is a crucial factor in the understanding and selection of the best project control method.
- Resource scan. The efficiency of resource allocations depends on the availability and tightness of the resources and has an impact on the schedule risk analyses and project control methods.
- Sensitivity scan. A Schedule Risk Analysis (SRA) using basic and/or advanced Monte-Carlo simulation runs is crucial to validate the efficiency of a bottom-up control approach for a project.
- Control scan. A project control scan using simulated time/cost accuracy predictions is a prerequisite for understanding the efficiency of a top-down control approach using Earned Value Management/Earned Schedule (EVM/ES) performance systems.

15.8 Conclusions

Project tracking and control constitute the heart of any scheduling tool and play a central role in ProTrack. They all combine Gantt chart schedule forecasts and Earned Value Management performance measurements to control the progress of a project and to make accurate predictions about the future. ProTrack makes use of basic and more advanced state-of-the-art EVM approaches to measure the time and cost performance of a project in a reliable way.

Ideally, a project tracking approach should use all relevant information that project managers have obtained during the construction of the project network and should rely on data from the baseline scheduling step as well as information from the schedule risk analysis phase. This dynamic scheduling approach is the main topic throughout all previous chapters of this book, and is set up as a central theme in ProTrack. More specific information about ProTrack's specific characteristics, the continuous updates and many detailed features can be found in the free ProTrack tutorials which can be downloaded from www.protrack.be.

Part V
Conclusions

Chapter 16
Conclusions

This book gave an extensive overview of the literature and best practices on dynamic project scheduling. The focus on scheduling within the field of project management has its roots in the mathematical field of Operations Research that mathematically determines start and finish times of project activities subject to precedence and resource constraints while optimizing a certain project scheduling objective. The initial research done in the late 1950s mainly focused on network based techniques such as CPM (Critical Path Method) and PERT (Program Evaluation and Review Technique), which are still widely recognized as important project management tools and techniques. The introduction of a personal computer and the never-ending increasing CPU power has led to a substantial increase of research that has been carried out covering various areas of project scheduling (e.g. time scheduling, resource scheduling, cost scheduling). Today the project scheduling research continues to grow in the variety of its theoretical and practical models, in its magnitude and in its application. This book aimed to give an overview of this scheduling history until today and provides some general rules of thumb and best practices interesting for both scheduling researchers and project management practitioners.

A simple project mapping approach is used throughout the book to classify the three dimensions of dynamic scheduling: baseline scheduling, schedule risk analysis and project control. The *baseline scheduling* step involves the construction of a timetable indicating the start and finish time of each project activity, with or without the presence of limited project resources. The *risk analysis* step is an additional phase necessary to reveal the sensitive parts of the baseline schedule in order to be able to detect the potential influence of uncertainty in the various activity estimates on the project objective. These two dimensions can be considered as preparatory steps to support the *project control* phase during project progress in order to guide the corrective action process when the project runs into trouble. The integration of these three dimensions is called dynamic scheduling, which can be, due to the complex relation between these three dimensions, best monitored through the use of dedicated project scheduling software tools.

M. Vanhoucke, *Project Management with Dynamic Scheduling*,
DOI 10.1007/978-3-642-40438-2_16, © Springer-Verlag Berlin Heidelberg 2013

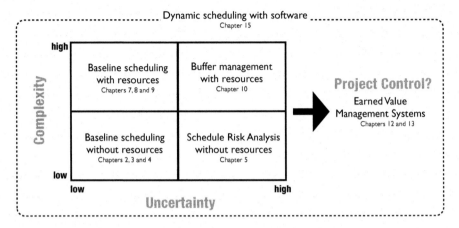

Fig. 16.1 A project mapping approach to reveal the three dimensions of dynamic scheduling

Figure 16.1 gives a general overview of the three dimensions of dynamic scheduling based on the project mapping approach presented in Fig. 1.4, with a reference to the specific chapters of this book. A more detailed summary of the three dimensions will be given along the following subsections.

16.1   Baseline Scheduling

The art of constructing a baseline schedule given the project data is discussed in detail in this book. This scheduling step is discussed from a *complexity* point of view where the presence of renewable resources with limited availability is the main driver of this scheduling complexity.

The art of baseline scheduling involves knowledge of some basic scheduling principles, summarized in the network logic approach initiated by the early PERT/CPM scheduling techniques. Since these scheduling techniques assume that activities can be performed without the constraint of limited resource availability, they are labeled as easy scheduling techniques (i.e. low complexity in Fig. 16.1) that are still widely used as sub-techniques in more complex scheduling environments. The introduction of renewable resources under limited availability over time leads to an increase in the scheduling complexity (high complexity in Fig. 16.1). The main reason lies in the presence of resource conflicts when using the traditional critical path based scheduling approach, which needs to be resolved by shifting certain activities forwards or backwards in time. These activity shifts have an influence on the use of resources as well as on the value of the scheduling objective. Consequently, the need for using scheduling software tools increases along the complexity dimension, due to the inherent complexity increase, as shown

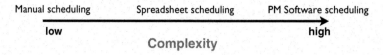

Fig. 16.2 An increasing need for scheduling software tools as the scheduling complexity increases

in Fig. 16.2. It has been shown throughout various chapters of the book that the complexity dimension is triggered by the scarceness of resources for the project.

The main conclusions of the baseline scheduling principles and techniques of Chaps. 2, 3 and 4 of Part I (without resources) and Chaps. 7, 8 and 9 of Part II (with resources) can be summarized along the following lines:

- The basic scheduling principles of PERT/CPM can be considered as general scheduling approaches that are used throughout all chapters of this book. More precisely, the principle of the "focus on the critical path" as the weakest part in a project schedule is retained throughout all further scheduling extensions (such as the "focus on the critical chain" principle when projects are subject to a limited resource availability). This principle is nothing more than a translation of the generally accepted "theory of constraints" to a project management environment and is used as a way to detect the most crucial components of a project that might affect its objective.
- The awareness and definition of an appropriate scheduling objective is a crucial step that needs to be taken before the construction of the baseline schedule. Although the choice of a scheduling objective is often project case specific and is not always incorporated in commercial software tools, it forces the project manager to think about potential efficiency gains, which can be obtained by manual adaptations on the baseline schedule proposed by these tools. Moreover, the knowledge of scheduling objectives can often be translated in simple but interesting rules of thumb to the project scheduler, which might act as triggers to extend the scheduling capabilities of the current software tools.
- The scheduling quality can be measured by the deviation between the solution found by a software tool and the theoretical best possible solution. Since the latter is hard or even impossible to find within reasonable time limits, the quality assessment can be quickly approximated by lower or upper bound calculations that quickly give an idea about the room for improvement.
- Although software only serves as a supportive tool to construct resource feasible schedules, a thorough knowledge about its features, its underlying assumptions and its numerous possible extensions is necessary to be able to construct a resource feasible schedule that satisfies the needs of the project manager. Therefore, any schedule proposed by software tools needs to be evaluated in the light of the choices the user has made about the underlying project assumptions such as the scheduling objective, the use of activity options (splitting, fixed duration mode, . . .) and many more.

16.2 Schedule Risk Analysis

The efficiency that can be obtained by a clever use of scheduling principles and software tools during the baseline scheduling phase needs to be put in the right perspective. Since a baseline schedule is a deterministic prediction of possible start and finish times, uncertainty during project progress can cause schedule disruptions, which might result in a need to adapt the initial baseline schedule to a new, modified reality. Therefore, a careful balance between the complexity dimension of baseline scheduling and the awareness of project uncertainty involved during its progress is necessary to feed the project control phase to take timely corrective actions during project progress when the project is in danger. The *uncertainty* dimension of dynamic scheduling is discussed in this book by measuring the potential effect of variation in the activity estimates on the overall project objective (known as schedule risk analysis) and by protecting the most sensitive parts through the use of time and resource buffers (known as Critical Chain/Buffer Management). The need for doing risk analysis and adding safety buffers in order to shift from a reactive scheduling approach to a more proactive approach increases along the uncertainty dimension, as shown in Fig. 16.3. While the complexity dimension of baseline scheduling can be measured by the resource scarceness of the project, the measurement of potential risk is often more subjective and based on data analysis from previous finished similar projects on experience by the project manager.

The main conclusions of the risk analysis dimension in dynamic scheduling discussed in Chap. 5 of Part I (without resources) and Chap. 10 of Part II (with resources) can be summarized along the following lines:

- A certain awareness of risk during project scheduling is indispensable in a dynamic scheduling environment. Since uncertainty is a matter of degree in projects, a high-quality and accurate baseline schedule is a necessity in the analysis of project risk, and plays a central role in both a resource-unconstrained Schedule Risk Analysis (SRA) and a resource-constrained Critical Chain/Buffer Management (CC/BM) approach.
- Information about the possible impact of variation in the project activity estimates on the total project duration and cost can be obtained by a simple yet effective schedule risk analysis. The information captured in the activity sensitivity measures allows the project manager to distinguish between highly sensitive and insensitive project activities in order to steer the focus of the project

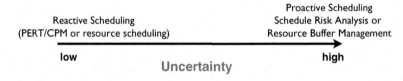

Fig. 16.3 An increasing need for risk analysis as the project uncertainty increases

tracking and control phase to those activities that are likely to have the most beneficial effect on the project outcome. In doing so, the project manager can monitor the intensity of the project control phase by focusing on only a subset of the project, without losing grip on the project performance measurement system. This project control approach is referred to as bottom-up project tracking.

- The Critical Chain/Buffer Management approach integrates complexity of resources and awareness of uncertainty through the use of project, feeding and resource buffers in order to establish a shift from a complex reactive resource-constrained project scheduling method to a more proactive approach. The approach is a translation of the *theory of constraints* to a dynamic scheduling environment and stresses the need to focus on the bottlenecks of a system in order to improve its overall objective.

- Although the CC/BM approach suffers from oversimplification at certain methodological points, the general idea has its merits and the buffering approach has relevance in a practical dynamic scheduling environment. Undoubtedly, there is a strong need for more research that further expands the CC/BM approach to a correct and sound methodological buffering mechanism. Moreover, a call for practical case studies is made in order to continue with translating these and newly developed CC/BM extensions into a practical environment.

16.3 Project Control

In this book, it is conjectured that the ultimate goal of baseline scheduling and schedule risk analysis is to gather information of the project to support the project control phase during the project's progress. This integration of these three dimensions is known as dynamic scheduling and is the central theme of the book. It is different from static scheduling in the sense that it recognizes that the first two dimensions are only supportive steps to gain information that can be later used during the project control step in order to steer the corrective actions in case of problems to bring the project back on track.

The technique used to monitor time and cost of a project in progress is known as Earned Value Management (EVM). It is a generally accepted methodology used to measure and communicate the real physical progress of a project and to integrate the three critical elements of project management (scope, time and cost management). It takes into account the work completed, the time taken and the costs incurred to complete the project and it helps to evaluate and control project risk by measuring project progress in monetary terms.

The basic principles and the use in practice have been comprehensively described in many sources in literature, albeit mainly from a cost point of view. However, a recent EVM extension, known as the Earned Schedule method, has shown that the time dimension can be better measured through the use of an alternative index. Indeed, it has been shown that the traditional EVM metrics fail in predicting the final duration of a project since its schedule performance index (SPI) provides unreliable results near the end of the project. The alternative Earned Schedule method overcomes this problem and is able to give a correct time prediction along the whole life of the project. This new focus on the time dimension of project control using the Earned Schedule method has been critically reviewed through the use of an extensive simulation study, as summarized in Chap. 13.

The main conclusions of the project control dimension in dynamic scheduling discussed in Chaps. 12 and 13 of Part III of this book can be summarized along the following lines:

- The construction of a realistic baseline schedule using a sound methodology is a key component when using EVM during a project's progress. Since time and cost performances are always measured relative to the baseline schedule, a realistic baseline schedule plays a central role in the accuracy of the project control phase. Moreover, an easy extension of the traditional EVM and novel Earned Schedule (ES) concepts, known as the schedule adherence concept (the p-factor), measures the project's performance relative to the current time performance (the ES metric) rather than to the original baseline schedule.

- It is recommended to use the EVM metrics on the project level, or at least on high Work Breakdown Structure (WBS) levels and not on the individual activity level. Since EVM is a methodology to provide an often quick sanity check of the project health on the cost control account level or even higher WBS levels, it cannot be considered as an alternative of the often time-consuming activity-based Critical Path Method (CPM) or Critical Chain scheduling approaches. Despite this, the EVM tracking approach often offers a full alternative to the detailed project tracking of each individual activity, triggering the need to drill down to lower WBS levels if necessary to take corrective actions.

- Project tracking and control can be divided into two extreme approaches. A top-down project tracking approach is used to refer to performance measurement systems (EVM) that serve as triggers at high WBS levels to drill down into lower WBS levels, while a bottom-up project tracking relies on traditional activity based CPM project tracking, extended with project sensitivity information. It has been shown that EVM project tracking provides reliable results in case the project network contains many critical activities. Consequently, in these cases, there is no need for detailed activity based CPM project tracking, but instead, rough project based EVM performance measures can serve as reliable triggers to drill down to lower WBS levels (down to the activity level) to look for possible problems to take corrective actions. CPM project tracking combined with SRA provides reliable results in case the project has many parallel activities. Moreover, the sensitivity information obtained through risk analysis enables the project manager to reduce the effort of CPM project tracking to those activities with a high expected effect on the project performance. Hence, a clear focus on only sensitive activities in order to reduce the tracking effort still leads to reliable results.

- The accuracy of time and cost forecasting methods using EVM based performance measures is key to the success of the project. A large experimental study has been set up to search for the main drivers that affect the forecast accuracy of the EVM time and cost forecasting methods. The project topological structure and the project criticality are the main static drivers of project performance accuracy. The time span between review periods as well as the schedule adherence are the main dynamic drivers of project performance accuracy.

16.4 Summary

The central theme of this book highlights the critical and necessary components of dynamic scheduling in order to steer the project control phase to an overall project success. The main conclusion is that dynamic scheduling leads to a careful balance between optimizing the baseline schedule to obtain efficiency of resources and awareness of uncertainty that can dramatically change the initial expectations as stipulated in the baseline schedule. In the various research projects and consultancy tasks done during the research period before writing this book, it has been shown that project managers often need to fall back on the initial estimates of their dynamic project schedule. The two most important lessons learned during these projects can be briefly summarized along the following lines:

- Baseline scheduling and risk analysis go hand in hand and are crucial preparatory components to provide information for the project control phase. One of the central lessons in training sessions to project managers is that scheduling without any form of risk management makes no sense since it then boils down to an academic and deterministic optimization exercise without much realistic value.
- A project schedule is a dynamic instrument that needs to be adapted when necessary. Project managers need to deal with a continuous stream of unexpected events and need to take corrective actions to bring projects back on track or to update the initial estimates and expectations to a more realistic scenario. In that respect, a dynamic project schedule is the ideal tool to provide information and to support the corrective actions, and hence, the project baseline schedule acts as a point of reference to support these actions, rather than a forecast of the future that needs to be followed at all times.

It should be noted that dynamic scheduling is only part of the project management discipline that might positively contribute to the overall success of a project. The central theme of the book is on the preparation phase and project control phase, with a strong focus on quantitative tools and techniques for planning and performance measurement. Consequently, it is implicitly assumed that other important drivers of project success are under control or at least taken into account during the project life cycle. Topics such as project scope management, communication management, quality management and human resource management are key factors that affect the success of a project and are related to the success or failure of the dynamic scheduling process. These topics have not been covered in this book and readers who wish to relate the dynamic scheduling principles to the other project management topics need to go beyond the information covered in this book.

16.5 Future Developments

The topics discussed in this book are only subparts of the general field of project management and need to be put in the right perspective. Although it is conjectured that a careful use of dynamic scheduling principles might positively contribute to a better project control and possibly to the project's success, a never-ending stream of research remains necessary to extend these principles to more practical oriented environments. The future research contributions that can be considered as logical follow-up studies of the dynamic scheduling topics discussed in this book can be classified in the two following categories:

- Search for the main project control drivers of project success.
- Dynamic and stochastic multi-project scheduling.

These two topics will be briefly outlined along the following lines.

The central theme of this book lies in the integration of the complexity of resource-constrained project scheduling and the awareness of uncertainty through risk analysis to support the project control phase. It is therefore implicitly assumed that a project control phase that is based on a sound methodology using scheduling and risk information would positively contribute to the overall success of a project. An obvious next step could be to investigate this project control phase into more detail in order to reveal the driving factors of project success. The focus of future research should lie in the integration of the project (unconstrained or resource-constrained) scheduling phase with the project control phase (using EVM) to gain knowledge on project performance measurement and the forecasting during the project's progress in order to improve and support the proactive and reactive actions that are necessary for the project's success. As a summary, there is a need to give profound and critical answers to the following questions:

- What is the role and importance of an accurate baseline schedule during project progress and performance measurement?
- What is the expected accuracy of different project measurement systems given characteristics of a particular project?
- What are the dynamic project progress parameters that influence a project's performance measurement accuracy?
- What is the optimal allocation of management reserve and when do you take corrective actions?

It is conjectured that the schedule adherence concepts, as briefly discussed in Chap. 13 through the use of the p-factor as well as the stability of project performance plays a central role in the quality of the project control phase and the probability of project success. Figure 16.4 briefly outlines the potential research

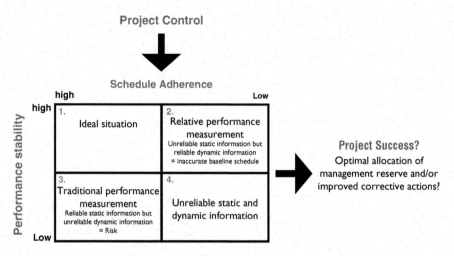

Fig. 16.4 Two important project control drivers that might affect the project success

project control drivers that affect the success of the project. This performance stability/schedule adherence matrix can be seen as a detailed view on the third dimension (i.e. project control) of Fig. 16.1.

The figure distinguishes between four basic project performance situations where each can have a different effect on the project success:

- Quadrant 1: Normal assumed situation: highly accurate baseline schedules with relatively stable project performance.
- Quadrant 2: Influence of inaccurate baseline schedules (i.e. low schedule adherence) on the EVM reliability under relatively stable project performance.
- Quadrant 3: Influence of unstable project performance (high variation) on the EVM reliability using a highly accurate baseline schedule.
- Quadrant 4: Reliability of the EVM metrics in highly unstable project progress environments under very inaccurate baseline schedules (projects performed under chaos).

A second obvious extension of dynamic scheduling of single projects is the stochastic and dynamic scheduling of multiple projects through software tools. The dynamic entrance of projects in a current project portfolio under uncertainty is a reality faced by any company in charge of managing multiple projects at the same time. The challenge is on the integration of dynamic scheduling principles borrowed from single project planning into a dynamic and stochastic resource optimization system of project portfolios under uncertainty.

List of Figures

List of Tables

References

Abba W (2008) The trouble with earned schedule. The Measurable News Fall:29–30

Agrawal M, Elmaghraby S, Herroelen W (1996) DAGEN: a generator of testsets for project activity nets. Eur J Oper Res 90:376–382

Akkan C, Drexl A, Kimms A (2005) Network decomposition-based benchmark results for the discrete time-cost tradeoff problem. Eur J Oper Res 165:339–358

Alvarez-Valdes R, Tamarit J (1989) Heuristic algorithms for resource-constrained project scheduling: a review and empirical analysis. In: Slowinski R, Weglarz J (eds) Advances in project scheduling. Elsevier, Amsterdam

Amor J, Teplitz C (1998) An efficient approximation procedure for project composite learning curves. Proj Manag J 29:28–42

Amor J (2002) Scheduling programs with repetitive projects using composite learning curve approximations. Proj Manage J 33:16–29

Amor J, Teplitz C (1993) Improving CPM's accuracy using learning curves. Proj Manage J 24:15–19

Anbari F (2003) Earned value project management method and extensions. Proj Manag J 34(4):12–23

Archibald RD (1976) Managing high-technology programs and projects. Wiley, New York

Ash R, Smith-Daniels DE (1999) The effects of learning, forgetting, and relearning on decision rule performance in multiproject scheduling. Decis Sci 30:47–82

Badiru A (1995) Incorporating learning curve effects into critical resource diagramming. Proj Manage J 2:38–45

Bartusch M, Möhring R, Radermacher F (1988) Scheduling project networks with resource constraints and time windows. Ann Oper Res 16(1):199–240

Bein W, Kamburowski J, Stallmann M (1992) Optimal reduction of two-terminal directed acyclic graphs. SIAM J Comput 21:1112–1129

Billstein N, Radermacher F (1977) Time-cost optimization. Method Oper Res 27:274–294

Blazewicz J, Lenstra J, Rinnooy Kan A (1983) Scheduling subject to resource constraints: classification and complexity. Discret Appl Math 5:11–24

Book S (2006a) Correction note: "earned schedule" and its possible unreliability as an indicator. The Measurable News Fall:22–24

Book S (2006b) "Earned schedule" and its possible unreliability as an indicator. The Measurable News Spring:24–30

Brucker P, Drexl A, Möhring R, Neumann K, Pesch E (1999) Resource-constrained project scheduling: notation, classification, models, and methods. Eur J Oper Res 112:3–41

Cho J, Yum B (1997) An uncertainty importance measure of activities in PERT networks. Int J Prod Res 35:2737–2758

M. Vanhoucke, *Project Management with Dynamic Scheduling*,
DOI 10.1007/978-3-642-40438-2, © Springer-Verlag Berlin Heidelberg 2013

Christensen D (1993) The estimate at completion problem: a review of three studies. Proj Manag J 24:37–42

Colin J, Vanhoucke M (2013a) A multivariate approach to statistical project control using earned value management. Working Paper, Ghent University (submitted)

Colin J, Vanhoucke M (2013b) Setting tolerance limits for statistical project control using earned value management. Working Paper, Ghent University (submitted)

Cooper D (1976) Heuristics for scheduling resource-constrained projects: an experimental investigation. Manag Sci 22:1186–1194

Cooper K (2003) Your project's real price tag? Letters to the editor. Harv Bus Rev 81:122–122

Crowston W (1970) Network reduction and solution. Oper Res Q 21:435–450

Crowston W, Thompson G (1967) Decision CPM: a method for simultaneous planning, scheduling and control of projects. Oper Res 15:407–426

Dar-El E (1973) MALB - A heuristic technique for balancing large single-model assembly lines. IIE Trans 5:343–356

Davies E (1974) An experimental investigation of resource allocation in multiactivity projects. Oper Res Q 24:587–591

Davis E (1975) Project network summary measures constrained-resource scheduling. AIIE Trans 7:132–142

Dayanand N, Padman R (1997) On modelling payments in projects. J Oper Res Soc 48:906–918

Dayanand N, Padman R (2001a) Project contracts and payment schedules: the client's problem. Manag Sci 47:1654–1667

Dayanand N, Padman R (2001b) A two stage search heuristic for scheduling payments in projects. Ann Oper Res 102:197–220

De Boer R (1998) Resource-constrained multi-project management - A hierarchical decision support system. PhD thesis, Institute for Business Engineering and Technology Application, The Netherlands

De P, Dunne E, Ghosh J, Wells C (1995) The discrete time-cost tradeoff problem revisited. Eur J Oper Res 81:225–238

De P, Dunne E, Ghosh J, Wells C (1997) Complexity of the discrete time/cost trade-off problem for project networks. Oper Res 45:302–306

Delisle C, Olson D (2004) Would the real project management language please stand up? Int J Proj Manag 22:327–337

Demeulemeester E (1995) Minimizing resource availability costs in time-limited project networks. Manag Sci 41:1590–1598

Demeulemeester E, Herroelen W (1996) An efficient optimal solution for the preemptive resource-constrained project scheduling problem. Eur J Oper Res 90:334–348

Demeulemeester E, Herroelen W (2002) Project scheduling: a research handbook. Kluwer Academic Publishers, Boston

Demeulemeester E, Dodin B, Herroelen W (1993) A random activity network generator. Oper Res 41:972–980

Demeulemeester E, De Reyck B, Foubert B, Herroelen W, Vanhoucke M (1998) New computational results on the discrete time/cost trade-off problem in project networks. J Oper Res Soc 49:1153–1163

Demeulemeester E, Vanhoucke M, Herroelen W (2003) Rangen: a random network generator for activity-on-the-node networks. J Sched 6:17–38

De Reyck B (1998) Scheduling projects with generalized precedence relations: exact and heuristic procedures. PhD thesis, Katholieke Universiteit Leuven

Drexl A, Nissen R, Patterson J, Salewski F (2000) ProGen/πx - an instance generator for resource-constrained project scheduling problems with partially renewable resources and further extensions. Eur J Oper Res 125:59–72

El-Rayes K, Moselhi O (1998) Resource-driven scheduling of repetitive activities. Constr Manage Econ 16:433–446

Elmaghraby S (1977) Activity networks: project planning and control by network models. Wiley, New York

Elmaghraby S (1995) Activity nets: a guided tour through some recent developments. Eur J Oper Res 82:383–408

Elmaghraby S (2000) On criticality and sensitivity in activity networks. Eur J Oper Res 127: 220–238

Elmaghraby S, Herroelen W (1980) On the measurement of complexity in activity networks. Eur J Oper Res 5:223–234

Elmaghraby S, Kamburowsky R (1992) The analysis of activity networks under generalized precedence relations. Manag Sci 38:1245–1263

Elmaghraby S, Fathi Y, Taner M (1999) On the sensitivity of project variability to activity mean duration. Int J Prod Econ 62:219–232

Etgar R, Shtub A (1999) Scheduling project activities to maximize the net present value - the case of linear time-dependent cash flows. Int J Prod Res 37:329–339

Fleming Q, Koppelman J (2003) What's your project's real price tag? Harv Bus Rev 81:20–21

Fleming Q, Koppelman J (2005) Earned value project management, 3rd edn. Project Management Institute, Newtown Square

French S (1982) Sequencing and scheduling: an introduction to the mathematics of the Job-shop. Ellis Horwood/Wiley

Goldratt E (1997) Critical chain. North River Press, Great Barrington

Goldratt E, Cox J (1984) The goal. North River Press, Croton-on-Hudson

Gong D (1997) Optimization of float use in risk analysis-based network scheduling. Int J Proj Manag 15:187–192

Goto E, Joko T, Fujisawa K, Katoh N, Furusaka S (2000) Maximizing net present value for generalized resource constrained project scheduling problem. Working paper, Nomura Research Institute, Japan

Gutierrez G, Paul A (2000) Analysis of the effects of uncertainty, risk-pooling, and subcontracting mechanisms on project performance. Oper Res 48:927–938

Harris R, Ioannou P (1998) Scheduling projects with repeating activities. J Constr Eng Manag 124:269–278

Hartmann S, Briskorn D (2010) A survey of variants and extensions of the resource-constrained project scheduling problem. Eur J Oper Res 207:1–15

Heimerl C, Kolisch R (2010) Scheduling and staffing multiple projects with a multi-skilled workforce. OR Spectr 32:343–368

Herroelen W, De Reyck B (1999) Phase transitions in project scheduling. J Oper Res Soc 50: 148–156

Herroelen W, Leus R (2001) On the merits and pitfalls of critical chain scheduling. J Oper Manag 19:559–577

Herroelen W, Van Dommelen P, Demeulemeester E (1997) Project network models with discounted cash flows a guided tour through recent developments. Eur J Oper Res 100:97–121

Herroelen W, De Reyck B, Demeulemeester E (1998) Resource-constrained project scheduling: a survey of recent developments. Comput Oper Res 25:279–302

Herroelen W, Demeulemeester E, De Reyck B (1999) A classification scheme for project scheduling problem. In: Weglarz J (ed) Project scheduling - Recent models, algorithms and applications. Kluwer Academic Publishers, Dortrecht, pp 1–26

Herroelen W, Leus R, Demeulemeester E (2002) Critical chain project scheduling: do not oversimplify. Proj Manag J 33:48–60

Hindelang T, Muth J (1979) A dynamic programming algorithm for decision CPM networks. Oper Res 27:225–241

Hulett D (1996) Schedule risk analysis simplified. Project Management Network July:23–30

Icmeli O, Erenguc S, Zappe C (1993) Project scheduling problems: a survey. Int J Oper Prod Manag 13:80–91

Jacob D (2003) Forecasting project schedule completion with earned value metrics. The Measurable News March:1, 7–9

Jacob D (2006) Is "earned schedule" an unreliable indicator? The Measurable News Fall:15–21

Jacob D, Kane M (2004) Forecasting schedule completion using earned value metrics? Revisited. The Measurable News Summer:1, 11–17

Kaimann R (1974) Coefficient of network complexity. Manag Sci 21:172–177

Kaimann R (1975) Coefficient of network complexity: erratum. Manag Sci 21:1211–1212

Kang L, Park IC, Lee BH (2001) Optimal schedule planning for multiple, repetitive construction process. J Constr Eng Manag 127:382–390

Kao E, Queyranne M (1982) On dynamic programming methods for assembly line balancing. Oper Res 30:375–390

Kazaz B, Sepil C (1996) Project scheduling with discounted cash flows and progress payments. J Oper Res Soc 47:1262–1272

Klein R (2000) Scheduling of resource-constrained projects. Kluwer Academic, Boston

Kolisch R, Hartmann S (2006) Experimental investigation of heuristics for resource-constrained project scheduling: an update. Eur J Oper Res 174:23–37

Kolisch R, Sprecher A, Drexl A (1995) Characterization and generation of a general class of resource-constrained project scheduling problems. Manag Sci 41:1693–1703

Kuchta D (2001) Use of fuzzy numbers in project risk (criticality) assessment. Int J Proj Manag 19:305–310

Kelley J, Walker M (1959) Critical path planning and scheduling: an introduction. Mauchly Associates, Ambler

Kelley J (1961) Critical path planning and scheduling: mathematical basis. Oper Res 9:296–320

Lipke W (2003) Schedule is different. The Measurable News Summer:31–34

Lipke W (2004) Connecting earned value to the schedule. The Measurable News Winter:1, 6–16

Lipke W (2006) Applying earned schedule to critical path analysis and more. The Measurable News Fall:26–30

Lipke W, Zwikael O, Henderson K, Anbari F (2009) Prediction of project outcome: the application of statistical methods to earned value management and earned schedule performance indexes. Int J Proj Manage 27:400–407

Loch C, De Meyer A, Pich M (2006) Managing the unknown: a new approach to managing high uncertainty and risk in project. Wiley, New Jersey

MacCrimmon K, Ryavec C (1967) An analytical study of the PERT assumptions. In: Archibald, R.D. and Villoria, R.L. (eds) Network-based management systems (PERT/CMP). Wiley, New York, pp 24–26

Mastor A (1970) An experimental and comparative evaluation of production line balancing techniques. Manag Sci 16:728–746

Mika M (2006) Modelling setup times in project scheduling. In: Perspectives in modern project scheduling, vol 92, International series in operations research & management science. Springer, New York, pp 131–163

Moder J, Phillips C, Davis E (1983) Project management with CPM PERT and precedence diagramming. Nostrand Reinhold, New York

Möhring R (1984) Minimizing costs of resource requirements in project networks subject to a fixed completion time. Oper Res 32:89–120

Moselhi O, El-Rayes K (1993) Scheduling of repetitive projects with cost optimization. J Constr Eng Manage 119:681–697

Nembhard D, Uzumeri M (2000) An individual-based description of learning within an organization. IEEE Trans Eng Manag 47(3):370–378

Özdamar L, Ulusoy G (1995) A survey on the resource-constrained project scheduling problem. IIE Trans 27:574–586

Pascoe T (1966) Allocation of resources - CPM. Revue Française de Recherche Opérationnelle 38:31–38

Patterson J (1976) Project scheduling: the effects of problem structure on heuristic scheduling. Nav Res Logist 23:95–123

Patterson J (1979) An implicit enumeration algorithm for the time/cost trade-off problem in project network analysis. Found Control Eng 6:107–117

Pinnell S, Busch J (1993) How do you measure the quality of your project management? PM Network December:35–36

Piper C (2005) Cpsim2: the critical path simulator (windows version). Richard Ivey School of Business, London

PMBOK (2004) A guide to the project management body of knowledge, 3rd edn. Project Management Institute, Inc., Newtown Square

Port O, Schiller Z, King R, Woodruff D, Phillips S, Carey J (1990) A smarter way to manufacture. Business Week April 30:110–115

Robinson D (1975) A dynamic programming solution to cost/time trade-off for CPM. Manag Sci 22:158–166

Schwindt C (1995) A new problem generator for different resource-constrained project scheduling problems with minimal and maximal time lags. WIOR-Report-449, Institut für Wirtschaftstheorie und Operations Research, University of Karlsruhe

Sepil C, Ortac N (1997) Performance of the heuristic procedures for constrained projects with progress payments. J Oper Res Soc 48:1123–1130

Shtub, A. (1991). Shtub A (1991) Scheduling of programs with repetitive projects. Proj Manage J 22:49–53

Shtub A, Bard J, Globerson S (1994) Project management: engineering, technology and implementation. Prentice-Hall Inc, Englewood Cliffs

Shtub A, LeBlanc L, Cai Z (1996) Scheduling programs with repetitive projects: a comparison of a simulated annealing, a genetic and a pair-wise swap algorithm. Eur J Oper Res 88:124–138

Skutella M (1998) Approximation algorithms for the discrete time-cost tradeoff problem. Math Oper Res 23:909–929

Tavares L (1999) Advanced models for project management. Kluwer Academic Publishers, Dordrecht

Tavares L, Ferreira J, Coelho J (1999) The risk of delay of a project in terms of the morphology of its network. Eur J Oper Res 119:510–537

Thesen A (1977) Measures of the restrictiveness of project networks. Networks 7:193–208

Ulusoy G, Cebelli S (2000) An equitable approach to the payment scheduling problem in project management. Eur J Oper Res 127:262–278

Uyttewaal E (2005) Dynamic scheduling with Microsoft Office Project 2003: the book by and for professionals. Co-published with International Institute for Learning Inc, Boca Raton

Vandevoorde S, Vanhoucke M (2006) A comparison of different project duration forecasting methods using earned value metrics. Int J Proj Manag 24:289–302

Vanhoucke M (2005) New computational results for the discrete time/cost trade-off problem with time-switch constraints. Eur J Oper Res 165:359–374

Vanhoucke M (2006a) An efficient hybrid search algorithm for various optimization problems. Lect Notes Comput Sci 3906:272–283

Vanhoucke M (2006b) Work continuity constraints in project scheduling. J Constr Eng Manag 132:14–25

Vanhoucke M (2007) Work continuity optimization for the Westerscheldetunnel project in the Netherlands. Tijdschrift voor Economie en Management 52:435–449

Vanhoucke M (2008a) Measuring time using novel earned value management metrics. In: Proceedings of the 22nd IPMA World Congress (Rome), vol 1, pp 99–103

Vanhoucke M (2008b) Project tracking and control: can we measure the time? Projects and Profits, August:35–40

Vanhoucke M (2008c) Setup times and fast tracking in resource-constrained project scheduling. Comput Ind Eng 54:1062–1070

Vanhoucke M (2009) Static and dynamic determinants of earned value based time forecast accuracy. In: Kidd T (ed) Handbook of research on technology project management, planning, and operations. Information Science Reference, Hershey, pp 361–374

Vanhoucke M (2010a) Measuring time - Improving project performance using earned value management, vol 136, International series in operations research and management science. Springer, New York

Vanhoucke M (2010b) Using activity sensitivity and network topology information to monitor project time performance. Omega Int J Manag Sci 38:359–370

Vanhoucke M (2011) On the dynamic use of project performance and schedule risk information during project tracking. Omega Int J Manag Sci 39:416–426

Vanhoucke M, Debels D (2007) The discrete time/cost trade-off problem: extensions and heuristic procedures. J Sched 10:311–326

Vanhoucke M, Debels D (2008) The impact of various activity assumptions on the lead time and resource utilization of resource-constrained projects. Comput Ind Eng 54:140–154

Vanhoucke M, Vandevoorde S (2007a) Measuring the accuracy of earned value/earned schedule forecasting predictors. The Measurable News, Winter:26–30

Vanhoucke M, Vandevoorde S (2007b) A simulation and evaluation of earned value metrics to forecast the project duration. J Oper Res Soc 58:1361–1374

Vanhoucke M, Vandevoorde S (2008) Earned value forecast accuracy and activity criticality. The Measurable News Summer:13–16

Vanhoucke M, Vandevoorde S (2009) Forecasting a project's duration under various topological structures. The Measurable News Spring:26–30

Vanhoucke M, Demeulemeester E, Herroelen W (2001a) Maximizing the net present value of a project with linear time-dependent cash flows. Int J Prod Res 39:3159–3181

Vanhoucke M, Demeulemeester E, Herroelen W (2001b) On maximizing the net present value of a project under renewable resource constraints. Manag Sci 47:1113–1121

Vanhoucke M, Demeulemeester E, Herroelen W (2002) Discrete time/cost trade-offs in project scheduling with time-switch constraints. J Oper Res Soc 53:741–751

Vanhoucke M, Demeulemeester E, Herroelen W (2003) Progress payments in project scheduling problems. Eur J Oper Res 148:604–620

Vanhoucke M, Coelho J, Debels D, Maenhout B, Tavares L (2008) An evaluation of the adequacy of project network generators with systematically sampled networks. Eur J Oper Res 187:511–524

Vanhoucke M, Vereecke A, Gemmel P (2005) The project scheduling game (PSG): simulating time/cost trade-offs in projects. Proj Manag J 51:51–59

Van Peteghem V, Vanhoucke M (2010a) A genetic algorithm for the preemptive and non-preemtive multi-mode resource-constrained project scheduling problem. Eur J Oper Res 201:409–418

Van Peteghem V, Vanhoucke M (2010b) Introducing learning effects in resource-constrained project scheduling. Technical report, Ghent University, Ghent, Belgium

Walker M, Sawyer J (1959) Project planning and scheduling. Technical Report Report 6959, E.I. duPont de Nemours and Co., Wilmington

Wauters M, Vanhoucke M (2013) A study on complexity and uncertainty perception and solution strategies for the time/cost trade-off problem. Working Paper, Ghent University (submitted)

Wiest J, Levy F (1977) A management guide to PERT/CPM: with GERT/PDM/DCPM and other networks. Prentice-Hall, Inc, Englewood Cliffs

Williams T (1992) Criticality in stochastic networks. J Oper Res Soc 43:353–357

Wright T (1936) Factors affecting the cost of airplanes. J Aeronaut Sci 3:122–128

Yelle L (1979) The learning curves: historical review and comprehensive survey. Decis Sci 10(2):302–328

Printed by Printforce, United Kingdom